"If you feel imperfect and need some grace or if you deal with imperfect people, imperfect circumstances in this imperfect world and desire to be a grace giver, Nancy Kay Grace extends the grace of God to us all."

— PAM FARREL, author of 40 books including *7 Simple Skills For Every Woman* and *Becoming a Brave New Woman*.

"*The Grace Impact* is a first-grab option for times when life's harshness assaults your soul. Full of stories, analogies and word-pictures to help you dissect your pain, each daily dose provides hope and help for a wounded heart."

— MARNIE SWEDBERG, International Leadership Mentor

"In thirty well-written chapters, Nancy Kay Grace shows us how to receive, live and walk in the favor and kindness of the Father… Nancy demonstrates this reality through her touching stories and wonderful biblical insights. Let God's grace captivate you through this powerful book."

— KURT W. BUBNA, pastor and author, *Epic Grace: Chronicles of a Recovering Idiot* and *Mr. & Mrs.: How to Thrive in a Perfectly Imperfect Marriage*

"Nancy brings grace to life for the reader. This book, working alongside the Holy Spirit, will make grace more than just something you talk about."

Searching for Sanity: 52 1

The Grace Impact

a devotional

Grow in grace
Nancy Kay Grace
2 Cor 9:8

NANCY KAY GRACE

CROSSRIVER

BREWSTER, KANSAS USA

To my husband Rick — who has shown me
much of God's grace in our marriage and ministry,

To my son, Erick and daughter, LeeAnne —
who've shared many family adventures in grace,

To my Savior — Who gave the
ultimate life-changing grace.

THE GRACE IMPACT

Table of Contents

Exasperation or Grace

The giggles of two small children from behind the closed door hushed into whispers. Moments later, the squeals and giggles resumed. I leapt from the sofa to investigate the activity in the next room.

As I opened the door, the laughter stopped and coughing began. Billowing clouds of fine white powder hung in the air, making it hard to breathe. The partners in crime stood like statues, covered from head to toe in baby powder. Blue eyes framed with white eyelashes looked up at me, blinking. Little arms stretched toward me for hugs. The two playmates had shaken a brand new canister of baby powder until it was empty. I was fuming at the huge mess they had created, and now they wanted hugs. However, I was grateful they could breathe in spite of the opaque air. The pair received a scolding with instructions not to do it again.

As the powder settled, it lay thick on the window blinds and deep in the crevices of the woodwork. Cleaning it took several days — vacuuming the floor multiple times, wiping down the blinds, and washing the curtains. The powder was stirred up every time I cleaned in the room. Finally the mess was gone, and we could breathe easier.

A few days later, I again heard familiar giggles. Rushing into the nearby room, I caught them in the act of doing the same thing. Powdered blue eyes stared at me.

By the grace of God, this time I was more exasperated than angry with them. I extended my arms for hugs before giving a gentle correction. Love was given to the guilty ones, forgiveness extended when a penalty was deserved.

This is how the Holy God interacts with us — unconditional love through His grace.

The Expanse of Grace

Grace is defined as "favor or kindness shown without regard to the worth or merit of the one who receives it and in spite of what that person deserves. Grace is one of the key attributes of God. The Lord God is 'merciful and gracious, long-suffering, and abounding in goodness and truth.' (Ex. 34:6) Therefore, grace is almost always associated with mercy, love, compassion, and patience."[1]

Grace is present throughout the Bible. In the opening pages, God created humankind in His own image and gave us free will. But Adam and Eve chose something outside of God's will. Even when sin occurred, God responded with grace. Although He banished them from the garden, God's grace was extended to them allowing them life instead of the deserved penalty of death.

Grace is revealed throughout both the Old and New Testaments. God reached into the world with grace, bringing redemption to the failures of people and transformation to those who were weak. In the Old Testament, the Hebrew word rendered as *favor* can also be translated as *grace*; these words can be used interchangeably.[2] Noah found grace in the eyes of God and was saved from destruction. Job persevered through misery by God's grace. Moses made excuses, but God overrode them and used him to set the Israelites free. Hannah cried out to God in faith, believed the promise spoken to her by Eli, waited in hope, and was granted favor from God in the fulfillment of the birth of her son, Samuel. Mary found favor with God, believed the word spoken by the angel, and carried The Promise to life. That Promise, Jesus Christ, lived a life of grace, forgiving and loving with extraordinary power. The power of grace was fully displayed in His resurrection, but it didn't stop there. God went on to share this grace with the disciples who had abandoned Christ. Empowered by the Holy Spirit, the disciples went on to spread their story and experiences with God. Lives were transformed over the millennia.

God's grace reaches us even today. His forgiving love is available to anyone who will accept it. God accepts us as we are, with all our imperfections and sin. He loves us too much to leave us in our broken, sinful condition.

The truth of unconditional acceptance is explained in Ephesians 2:4-5, 8-9.

> But because of his great love for us, God, who is rich in mercy, made us alive with Christ even when we were dead in transgressions. ...For it is by grace you have been saved, through faith — and this is not from yourselves, it is the gift of God — not by works, so that no one can boast.

We can do nothing to earn grace. We can only accept the gift. Our eyes need to be opened to see the grace around us. Then, God calls us to extend His grace to this hurting world.

Captivated by Grace

I have been captivated by grace for many years, not only because of my name — in Hebrew, the language of the Old Testament, the name "Nancy" means "grace" — but also because grace has transformed me, strengthened me, and sustained me through difficult times. It is a crown jewel with many facets given by the Lord for our relationship with Him. Too often we get wrapped up in trying harder, comparing ourselves to others, and straining toward unreachable perfection. Only the grace of Jesus Christ can help us relax and grow into who God designed each of us to be.

This book began through my own exploration of grace when I started a monthly e-mail devotional, *GraceNotes*, showing how God's grace is active in today's world. I have expanded the monthly e-mails into a blog on my website (www. NancyKayGrace.com), Facebook (Nancy Kay Grace/Grace-Notes), and Twitter posts (@nancykaygrace).

The Grace Impact is a compilation of some of those devotionals. This book can be used as a devotional or as a Bible study. It is divided into four sections exploring elements of 2 Corinthians 9:8, "God *is* able to make all grace abound toward you, that you, always having all sufficiency in all *things* at all times, may have an abundance for every good work." (NKJV) The Amplified Bible further explains and expands the meaning.

> And God is able to make all grace (every favor and earthly blessing) come to you in abundance, so that you may always *and* under all circumstances *and* whatever the need be self-sufficient [possessing enough to require no aid or support and furnished in abundance for every good work and charitable donation.]

In section one, we will examine the grace found in God's character and why He is able to make grace abound. Section two is about the sufficiency of God's grace, giving us what we need to live the Christian life. In section three we'll explore the sustaining power of grace in all things at all times. Section four encourages us to have an abundance of grace for every good work, sharing the blessing of grace with others. Each daily reading begins with a Bible verse and has an observation about grace. The section at the end of each day, "Deepening the Grace Impact," includes questions for meditation, additional Bible verses to study, and a prayer. In 2 Peter 3:18 the apostle Peter wrote, "But grow in the grace and knowledge of our Lord and Savior Jesus Christ." This section is designed to help you dig deeper into understanding grace and its impact on you. I pray you will be encouraged in practical ways to live in His grace.

Amazing Grace

Many have written about grace — this marvelous gift from God. Most notably is John Newton, a harsh slave trader who was transformed by God's grace. Two decades after his dramatic conversion he wrote a poem entitled "Faith's Review and Expectation," based on a statement when King David reflected on the Lord's goodness in his life: "Who am I, LORD God, and what is my family, that you have brought me this far?" (1 Chronicles 17:16) This passage is reflected in the phrase of the song "Amazing Grace:" "Through many dangers, toils, and snares, I have already come, 'tis grace that brought me safe thus far, and grace will bring me home."

The poem "Faith's Review and Expectation" became the beloved hymn "Amazing Grace."[3] Looking at faith, grace, and the expectation of hope in the Lord is the essence of this book. My prayer is that God will meet you in these pages, increasing your awareness of His grace. Like Newton, perhaps you will have your own faith review and expectation. Read the words to this great hymn and reflect on the immensity of God's grace, and may God's grace abound to you!

Amazing grace, how sweet the sound that saved a wretch like me,

I once was lost but now am found, was blind but now I see.

'Twas grace that taught my heart to fear and grace my fears relieved.

How precious did that grace appear the hour I first believed.

Through many dangers, toils, and snares, I have already come,

'Tis grace that brought me safe thus far, and grace will bring me home.

The Lord has promised good to me, His word my hope secures;

He will my shield and portion be, as long as life endures.

Yes, when this flesh and heart shall fail, and mortal life shall cease,

I shall possess, within the veil a life of joy and peace.

The earth shall soon dissolve like snow, the sun forbear to shine;

But God who call'd me here below, will be forever mine.[4]

Deepening the Grace Impact

QUESTIONS: What do you know about the grace of God from your own experience? How do you understand the grace of God as it applies to your life?

SCRIPTURES FOR MEDITATION: John 1:14,17; Romans 3:24; Ephesians 2:4-5, 8-9

PRAYER: Lord, open my eyes to see, my mind to learn, and my heart to share more of Your grace. Amen.

"God is Able to Make All Grace Abound Toward You..."

The grace impact originates with God revealing His character to us. In section one, we will begin to grow in understanding the complexity of God's grace. He is able and chooses to make grace overflow, revealing His character to us. Like a light shining on a multifaceted diamond, grace radiates through God's magnificent nature. He is even called the "God of all grace" in 1 Peter 5:10. He is the source and creator of grace. We don't deserve it, but God pours grace out on us that we may know Him. He does not remain aloof, but through grace, reveals Himself to you and me. God yearns for relationship with us.

We'll look at a few of God's qualities that reflect this marvelous grace that impacts us: how grace draws us to God's holiness, how grace nurtures us through God's care, how grace gives us hope in God's promises, how grace reveals God's faithfulness, and how grace lets us savor God's love. Because of God's great love, we behold the wonder of His grace as He became like us through the birth of Jesus. Section one concludes as we see the power of God's redeeming grace through the resurrection.

God alone is able to set into motion what I call the "grace impact" — His ability to work in and through any situation, revealing His love and forgiveness to us, thereby drawing us to Himself, ultimately through the life, death, and resurrection of Jesus Christ. The initial impact of God's grace to each of us comes by accepting salvation through Jesus Christ. It continues in us and through us as our lives are transformed by yielding more to the Lord. As we grow in faith, we share God's grace with others. Like a drop of water released on a smooth lake, the ripples of the grace impact continue to reach outward to many.

Grace Draws Us to God's Holiness

Holy, holy, holy is the LORD Almighty;
the whole earth is full of his glory. — Isaiah 6:3

P itch black engulfed us; nervousness settled over me. Unable to see my hand directly in front of my nose, I gripped my young daughter's arm, assuring her of my presence.

Our family participated in a cave tour while on vacation in the Black Hills of South Dakota. A college-age guide led us through narrow passages to the bottom of a large cavern. Her flashlight and a few dim light fixtures lit our way. Once in the lowest opening, our guide explained the geologic formations. She then clicked off the flashlight and flipped the light switch.

A collective gasp echoed through the room. Anxious, we huddled in absolute darkness as she explained how our eyes would adjust in a few moments. However, when a thoughtless tourist in the group flashed his camera, it blinded all of us. My eyes ached from the intense light. I squinted, seeing nothing except bright spots.

The above experience illustrates our reaction when we encounter light in the midst of blackness. When we begin to understand God's holiness, we shield our eyes spiritually from the brightness. Such holiness is so pure it is blinding in the darkness around us. God is described as the one "who alone is immortal and who lives in unapproachable light, whom no one has seen or can see."(1 Tim. 6:16a)

The word *holy* comes from a root word meaning "to separate." God is separated from — or exalted above — all things.[1] His qualities of purity and holiness set Him apart from everything He has created. His holiness is almost incomprehensible to our limited, inadequate minds. God is perfect and pure — deserving our reverence and adoration. When we learn more about God's nature as revealed in His Word, we can begin to recognize His holiness.

The prophet Isaiah witnessed God's holiness in the midst of despair. He lived during the time of King Uzziah who reigned fifty-two years as a godly and powerful king. His death was a national tragedy in the ancient world, causing fear and uncertainty for the future of the nation. It was at this point of discouragement that Isaiah saw a vision of the Lord described in Isaiah 6:1-5.

> In the year King Uzziah died, I saw the Lord, high and exalted, seated on a throne; and the train of his robe filled the temple. Above him were seraphim, each with six wings: With two wings they covered their faces, with two they covered their feet, and with two they were flying. And they were calling to one another: "Holy, holy, holy is the LORD Almighty; the whole earth is full of his glory." At the sound of their voices the doorposts and thresholds shook and the temple was filled with smoke. "Woe to me!" I cried. "I am ruined! For I am a man of unclean lips, and I live among a people of unclean lips, and my eyes have seen the King, the LORD Almighty.

When faced with the astounding holiness of God, Isaiah

saw his own ungodliness and unworthiness. He realized his despair and sin, but God didn't leave him in his hopelessness. Isaiah 6:6-7 continues:

> Then one of the seraphim flew to me with a live coal in his hand, which he had taken with tongs from the altar. With it he touched my mouth and said, "See, this has touched your lips; your guilt is taken away and your sin atoned for."

God initiated an act of grace by reaching out to Isaiah with forgiveness so he could stand in God's holy presence. The impact of God's grace on Isaiah changed his life. He went from fearful and discouraged to bold and courageous as he responded with a willingness to serve the holy God of the universe.

Likewise, we decide how we will respond to God's holiness. We have sinned and are unworthy of being in God's presence. In spite of our unworthiness, God beckons us to consider His holiness as Isaiah did and be moved — by a crisis if need be — to see how much we need Him.

God does not remain unapproachable, but desires personal reconnection with each one of us. He initiates the relationship by extending grace. At the crossroad where God's grace and our lives intersect we have a choice to turn away from God or to embrace Him. That is where the grace impact begins for us. By accepting His grace, we receive total forgiveness, complete acceptance, and unconditional love from God. At this point, the Holy Spirit initiates transformation in the yielded heart. Pastor Charles Swindoll defines grace as:

> Unmerited favor. Grace is what God does for mankind, which we do not deserve, which we cannot earn, and

which we will never be able to repay. Awash in our sinfulness, helpless to change on our own, polluted to the core with no possibility of cleaning ourselves up, we cry out for grace. It is our only hope.[2]

Grace allows us, as imperfect sinners, to have a connection with God. Only by God's initiative of extending grace to us, can we enter such a relationship. This invitation of grace is further explained in Isaiah 57:15.

> For this is what the high and exalted One says — he who lives forever, whose name is holy: "I live in a high and holy place, but also with the one who is contrite and lowly in spirit, to revive the spirit of the lowly and to revive the heart of the contrite.

Here is a magnificent mystery: the holy, exalted God of the universe chooses to restore our relationship with Him. He does not cast us away from His presence because of anything we have done or not done, but desires to connect with us in spite of our undeserving condition.

I first responded to God as a scrawny, teenage girl struggling with low self-esteem. I felt distant from my family and from God. To me, the mirror reflected loneliness and emptiness. I believed I had little worth. Though I tried to be happy and carefree, inside I felt the sting of self-condemnation. Driven by perfectionism to excel, I also lived in the shadow of comparing myself to others. A web of tension kept me wrapped in insecurity, self-pity, and desiring acceptance. A turbulent home life created by a lack of communication and an alcoholic father brought further distress. I found peace in music; playing the piano brought solace to my heart.

One weekend a visiting choir came to my church, and it changed my life forever. I first experienced the grace impact through hearing a verse from the Bible. In the midst of their song, the words of 2 Corinthians 5:17 were spoken as an antiphonal chant with a catchy rhythm. "Therefore, if anyone is in Christ, the new creation has come: The old has gone, the new is here!"

Those words penetrated my mind and went straight to my heart. My soul stirred with an awareness of God's presence reaching out to me. When I found the passage in the Bible, the words jumped into my empty heart. I received His acceptance, forgiveness, and love. I traded my sin-stained self-image for one that reflected the image of the loving God. The holy, exalted God of the universe extended grace to me, and I gratefully took hold of it.

The holiness of God requires a decision from us. We can be fearful and turn away from Him, as if turning away from a bright light exposing us in our darkness; or we can draw closer to Him through His grace. God's holiness leads us to look inward to see where we sin, or fall short of God's standard.

We cannot reach God by ourselves. God made a way to span the chasm created by sin that separates us from Him. He sent His son Jesus Christ to pay the penalty for our sin through the sacrifice of His life on the cross. Through His resurrection Jesus became the bridge that connects us to God. By acknowledging our position of sin and imperfection, we can receive God's forgiveness through His grace, and then we see a glimpse of His holiness. We are transformed by His grace, right where we are, when we are in His presence.

God's grace draws us to Him, and has redeemed us from sin. We are empowered by the Lord to face the challenges of our lives with new strength and hope because of the grace impact.

Deepening the Grace Impact

QUESTIONS: What comes to mind when you think of the holiness of God? How have you been changed by God's grace?

SCRIPTURES FOR MEDITATION: Exodus 15:11; I Samuel 2:2; Isaiah 57:15

PRAYER: Lord God, I praise You for being holy and pure. I praise You that Your holiness does not remain far off, but reaches me in my everyday life. I thank You for drawing me to Your holiness by Your grace, for creating a crossroad of grace in my life. Thank You for the impact of Your grace that reaches to me. Help me, by Your grace, to live for You. Amen.

Grace Protects through His Attentive Care

I lift my up eyes to the mountains — where does my help come from? My help comes from the LORD, the Maker of heaven and earth. — Psalm 121:1-2

Anticipation grew as the Israelite family prepared for the long journey. The father gathered the lambs, goats, and donkeys while the mother bundled food and a few simple belongings for the family. The children buzzed with excitement about the adventure.

They would soon join neighboring families also making the journey to Jerusalem for the religious feasts and festivals. This pilgrimage could take many days as they crossed through rocky hillsides, set up camp by wells, and slept under the stars. Danger was a constant threat. Without warning, thieves could rob their meager belongings or wild animals could attack.

From all over the region, long streams of Israelites hiked the rock-hewn roads three times a year en route to Jerusalem. The dutiful Jewish families trekked with their lambs for sacrifice and donkeys laden with tents. The trip was tedious, slow, and dangerous but was made out of love and obedience in order to worship the Lord. They trusted in the grace of God for their protection.

While on the journey, they would daily recite the Psalms of Ascent, Psalms 120 through 134. Psalm 121 would have been said or sung by the Israelites as they traveled through the rocky Judean plains on their way to Jerusalem, a city on a hill. They looked forward to arriving at their destination, believing in God's watchful care through the dangers of the trip. This particular psalm offers us the same steadfast hope in the One who protects us with love. Let's examine the promises of this psalm.

> I lift up my eyes to the mountains — where does my help come from? My help comes from the LORD, the Maker of heaven and earth. (Ps. 121:1-2)

These verses teach us where to focus our eyes as we make our own pilgrimage through life. Instead of only looking at the problems around us, we are reminded to look to the Lord for His presence, comfort, and strength. The psalmist's statement "my help comes from the LORD" is one of steadfast faith and confident assurance.

> He will not let your foot slip — he who watches over you will not slumber; indeed, he who watches over Israel will neither slumber nor sleep. (Ps. 121:3-4)

This promises safety and security. As the Israelites traveled, they knew the journey was dangerous; they needed protection. The term translated "to keep watch" or "preserve" is used six times in Psalm 121. While the thought of God's watchfulness may seem intimidating, it is also comforting to know that no matter what we are going through, the Lord knows about it. God is not watching as a harsh sentinel or critical judge, neither is He a sleeping guard. The Lord is the attentive, loving Creator. Even when He seems quiet, God's grace is ever present.

The LORD watches over you — the LORD is your shade
at your right hand; the sun will not harm you by day, nor
the moon by night. (Ps. 121:5-6)

This promise reminded the Israelites of the grace of God's
presence on the journey. It is a promise for us, too. Even in the
heat of trials or the loneliness of night, the Lord is there watching over you with tender love. He is *Immanuel*, the God who is
with us. The Creator watches over the creation because of His
love for us.

After the birth of my first grandchild, I drove six hours to
help the new parents. I arrived late in the night after the baby
was already asleep. I couldn't wait until morning to see him; I
had to take a peek. Quietly I opened the door to his room, tip-
toed close to the bassinet, and bent over to see his golden-brown
hair glistening in the moonlight. His tiny body, swaddled in a
soft blanket, rested in deep sleep. He exhaled a sigh. I smiled
with love as I watched my grandson gently breathe in sweet
sleep. This wasn't a hasty glance, but a long, loving look at the
miracle of life. This is a glimpse of how God watches over us.

The LORD will keep you from all harm — he will watch
over your life; the LORD will watch over your coming
and going both now and forevermore. (Ps. 121:7-8)

Psalm 121 concludes with a promise of protection for daily
living. The dangers were great, but by keeping their focus on
the Lord, the Israelites trusted Him for protection on the journey. In the midst of all the distractions and uncertainties of
life, we especially need to center our hearts daily on the Lord.
Steadfast faith and dependence on His grace brings peace of
mind. The Lord knows where our steps will lead us. All these

promises begin when we look to the Lord, the Maker of heaven and earth. Then we can know the attentive care and the grace impact for help, guidance, and protection.

Deepening the Grace Impact

QUESTIONS: When have you looked to the Lord for His protection during a difficult time on your faith journey? What does it feel like to rest in His care? Can you identify a time when the Lord's protection guided you out of a difficult circumstance, but you were unaware of His care at the time?

SCRIPTURES FOR MEDITATION: Psalm 121; 1 Peter 5:7; Psalm 145:8

PRAYER: Heavenly Father, I praise You for being so watchful and involved in my life. Thank You for Your protection, often unseen, on my life's journey. Thank You that by Your grace I am secure in Your attentive care. Amen.

Grace Hopes with God's Promises

The LORD is trustworthy in all he promises and faithful in all he does. — Psalm 145:13b

A mom concludes her talk about telling the truth with her nine-year-old daughter and holds up her little finger. The seriousness in her voice commands direct eye contact and the attention of the child. The girl responds by entwining her pinky with her mom's. "Pinky promise," they state together. An oath has been made and will be taken seriously. Trust is established.

When a promise is made, we anticipate it will be fulfilled. If it isn't, the promise is empty, leaving us disappointed and hurt. Broken promises are like glass shards in our hands, painful and sharp, leaving scars in their wake. We can live in the aftermath of broken trust for years.

The promises in the Bible are solid words of hope for the believer, like anchors to which a rock climber clings for life. Abraham received the covenant promise from God and grasped it until its fulfillment. David humbly accepted God's word that one of his descendants would be on the throne forever. Mary believed the angel and gave birth to The Promise, Jesus Christ. The power of God's grace enables the fruition of His divine promises. In other words, grace flows through God's character to secure His promises. Because we have seen the declarations of God consistently completed in the past, we can firmly believe in them for today and the future. God is faithful to bring about the culmination of His promises.

We can confidently depend on God's promises because each one is rooted in God's character. Past promises that prove true are evidences of the grace impact at work around us giving hope, guidance, and strength. An explanation of the purpose of the promises is offered in 2 Peter 1:3-4.

> His divine power has given us everything we need for a godly life through our knowledge of him who called us by his own glory and goodness. Through these he has given us his very great and precious promises, so that through them you may participate in the divine nature, having escaped the corruption in the world caused by evil desires.

It is mind boggling to imagine sharing in the holy nature of God, but that is what grace allows us to do. It does not mean we become god-like, but rather we can have a relationship with God through the promise of Jesus Christ. The very great and precious promises flow from God's nature of revealing Himself to us, undergirded by His grace. We escape the corruption of the world through salvation but also through the hope of God's promises.

When circumstances are confusing and I don't know what to do, I know the Bible will offer strength and wisdom. Sometimes I turn to it readily, other times, I read it as a last resort. God's promises give me hope, change my perspective, and direct my prayers when I choose to read the Bible. It's easy to slip into the default mode of worry and fret instead of being still before God and letting His Word speak to me.

Several years ago my husband and I believed that the Lord had led us to relocate to a different state for him to serve as senior pastor in a multi-staff church. The job started with high expectations but soon crumbled into broken promises and chaos. As time passed, staff tensions increased — people vied for leadership positions and control. The ever-changing economy also threatened to eliminate personnel, even the need for my husband's position. We lived in uncertainty for months, not knowing how things would resolve. Although we prayed and trusted God, the situation had not gone as we'd hoped or expected. I felt scared and uncertain for our future. I had a choice — to look at the crisis with fear or remember God's declarations for assurance.

Opening my Bible, I turned to Psalm 37, a passage that had brought hope to me in the past. I read "Take delight in the LORD, and he will give you the desires of your heart." (Ps. 37:4) The words of this verse helped me refocus on the Lord. As I began meditating on Bible verses, they drew me closer to the Lord and bolstered my hope. The passage continued, "Commit your way to the LORD; trust in him and he will do this: He will make your righteous reward shine like the dawn, your vindication like the noonday sun." (Ps. 37:5) This reminded me that God sees the big picture, not just the day-to-day struggles of life. Reading these words brought peace to my restless heart. His promises can indeed be trusted. Eventually, our situation resolved, our ministry continued, and I learned to trust God more.

In *My Utmost for His Highest*, Oswald Chambers wrote of the strength of God's promises, with an important caveat of wisdom.

The promises of God are of no value to us until, through obedience, we come to understand the nature of God. We may read some things in the Bible every day for a year and they mean nothing to us. Then, because we have been obedient to God in some small detail, we suddenly see what God means and His nature is instantly opened up to us. "All the promises of God in Him are Yes, and in Him Amen." (2 Corinthians 1:20) Our "Yes" must be born of obedience; when by obedience we ratify a promise of God by saying, "Amen," or, "So be it." That promise becomes ours.[1]

Obedience comes through diligently seeking God and letting Him transform our hearts and minds. The promises of God await our compliance so the "Amen" can be spoken.

The Bible is full of promises. Here are some to encourage and bring us hope.

• When we are vulnerable, we have the assurance of God's protection — "I am your shield." (Gen. 15:1)
• God offers guidance when we don't know what to do — "He guides the humble in what is right and teaches them his way." (Ps. 25:9)
• When we need empowerment to carry on, God pledges inner power — "I will strengthen you." (Is. 41:10)
• God assures provision — "I will strengthen you and help you." (Is. 41:10)
• When we are weary, He vows His rest — "Come to me, all you who are weary and burdened, and I will give you rest." (Matt. 11:28)
• When we are lonely, we have the promise of God's presence — "Never will I will leave you; never will I forsake you." (Heb. 13:5b)

Realigning our attitude with God's promises can bring order to a chaotic heart. Through focusing on God's unchanging nature and believing His word, our trust in Him grows. We gain inner stability when uncertainty shakes our world. Because of the grace impact, our hope is restored through God's promises.

Deepening the Grace Impact

SCRIPTURES FOR MEDITATION: Reread the listed promises and accompanying verses above.

QUESTIONS: Which one touches your heart right now? Which promise do you need to embrace for a specific situation in your life?

PRAYER: Pray that verse by personalizing it. For example, here is Hebrews 13:5 as a prayer.

Lord, I thank You for Your presence that You will not leave me. Even in [situation] You are with me. I thank You for being faithful to Your word. Thank You for the hope in Your great and precious promises. Amen.

Grace Abides in God's Faithfulness

Because of the LORD's great love we are not consumed, for his compassions never fail. They are new every morning; great is your faithfulness. — Lamentations 3:22-23

Seasons and growth follow an orderly manner, like trees in spring with new buds, in summer with full leaf, in autumn with changing colors and in winter with barren branches. The progression is regular and expected. But when predictable seasons seem out of order, confusion is created in the life cycle. The growth of the tree can be affected by the disruption. A warm week in winter causes premature budding. A late spring frost delays or kills new growth. A drought causes summer leaves to brown and wither, while excessive rain turns them yellow.

Several years ago, a severe ice storm struck our area after some mild winter weather. Thankfully the forecasters prepared us for the worst. Thick tree limbs, coated in a half-inch of ice, snapped under the weight. Power outages lasted five days. Life was frozen in time. Every tree in the hills of northwest Arkansas was affected by the storm.

It took months to clean up the debris. Piles of branches, sometimes over six feet tall, lined the streets of our city like walls. As spring came, new leaves sprouted on the broken limbs. Lower branches, now exposed to sunlight, grew for the first time in years.

The ice destruction in our area is still evident years later. Recovery of the damaged trees continues with the growth of each passing season.

When our life's seasons overlap, we can struggle with the emotional, feeling overwrought from intermingling of intense sadness and the exhilaration of joy. The result can be tiresome and even paralyzing. I lived in that strain during a time when our family dynamics were changing and expanding in various ways. It began when my mother was critically ill and entered hospice. I lived seven hundred miles from her and felt heavyhearted by her deteriorating health. I had to come to grips with the fact that she was at the end of her life. At the same time, my adult children each announced their engagements, which brought joy. It was the end of my season as a daughter while at the same time beginning a new season of motherhood — launching my children into marriage and becoming a mother-in-law. Grief continued to press into our lives as my husband's parents also passed away during this period of months. The grace of God sustained me through the intertwining periods of grief and joy, saying goodbye to my mother, mother-in-law, and father-in-law and welcoming a daughter-in-law and son-in-law within seven months. God brought new strength and life after a devastating emotional storm.

The grace of God's faithfulness stabilizes us when the seasons of life overlap. The Lord is still in control. He is faithful to His character, unchanging and true. God's grace abides in the midst of uncertainty. He is steadfast to keep His word and His promises. He is a steady light that shines in all seasons. Eventually life settles down into a pattern, but a lot of change and struggle takes place first.

Thomas Chisholm wrote the lyrics to "Great Is Thy Faithfulness." He did not write this hymn as a result of a specific experience in his life, but rather, as a result of seeing the day-by-day personal faithfulness of God throughout his life. At age seventy-five he wrote, "My income has never been large at any time due to impaired health in the earlier years which has followed me on until now. But I must not fail to record here the unfailing faithfulness of a covenant-keeping God and that He has given me many wonderful displays of His providing care which have filled me with astonishing gratefulness."[1]

The prophet Jeremiah wrote about God's faithfulness as he was carried into captivity. He trusted God beyond the bleak circumstances, and we are encouraged to do the same. Look closely for the fingerprints of God's faithfulness throughout the seasons of your life. God's grace is steadfast no matter what season you are now in.

Deepening the Grace Impact

QUESTIONS: What overlapping seasons have you experienced? When have you seen God's grace supporting you through a time when both sadness and joy were in your life? How has God been faithful during these times?

SCRIPTURES FOR MEDITATION: Deuteronomy 32:4; Psalm 33:4; 1 Thessalonians 5:24

PRAYER: Lord, I praise You for being faithful in all the seasons of my life. Thank You for being constant and unwavering even when this life changes so fast. Open my eyes to see Your grace and faithfulness every day. Amen.

Grace Savors God's Love

*The LORD appeared to us in the past, saying: I
have loved you with an everlasting love; I have
drawn you with unfailing kindness.* — Jeremiah 31:3

Blossoming trees awaken in the spring. Bright sunshine warms after a chilly rain. Laughter shared with friends. Each of these gifts needs to be savored and enjoyed, but all too often we overlook these everyday blessings to rush to the next event on our calendars.

Disruptions of our fast-paced life can force us to slow down and notice the simple joys. A phone call from a doctor's office can disrupt a quiet day and change your life, as it did mine.

"I have some good news and some bad news." The doctor's calm voice sounded serious. He had my attention. I sat at the kitchen table and picked up a pen to write what he would tell me.

"The bad news is that it's cancer, but the good news is that we got it all and it's very treatable."

He explained the diagnosis, but my mind froze on his first statement. *Cancer?* I choked back tears. *Tongue cancer?* Because of the stitches and swelling in my tongue, I struggled to form words as my mind flooded with questions.

After hanging up, I thought about how I had gotten to this point. It had begun with a sore on my tongue that would not heal. Eventually the dentist sent me to an oral surgeon who removed the affected tissue on my tongue. He thought it looked like an ulcer. I didn't fit the profile of one at risk for oral cancer, and the doctor almost didn't send it off for a biopsy. While all the tissue was removed, I had to face the fact that I had cancer.

That evening I plopped onto my bed in despair. Desperately I called out to God in my spirit with tears streaming down my face. Weary and restless, I moved to my piano where I played hymns and prayed through my fingers. In those moments of worship, a gentle but powerful exchange occurred in my heart as I released my anxiety. God gave me a special assurance — a deeper peace than I had ever known. The Lord accepted my "what if" questions and replaced them with the precious affirmation of His love. The grace of God's love would sustain me in this health crisis. I had found an inner sanctuary that became my refuge.

In the following weeks, I had to retrain my tongue to say some words, for a while my name was "Nanthy Gwathe." I pulled back from my church activities to sort out the confusion of this unexpected diagnosis. My speaking ministry was put on hold. Jesus became my safe hiding place throughout the recovery. Intentional time spent reading Scripture, praying, and journaling brought steady healing to my soul. I gained perspective; God would use this trial for His good. God's love was shown in the kindness of family and encouragement from friends. In my uncertainty and despair the God of the universe did not remain far off, but gave me His peace and assurance in the shelter of His love. I again realized I didn't have to do anything to be loved; I could only accept God's love. Resting in the refuge of God brought a deeper awareness of His love for me.

Thankfully I did not need chemo or radiation. My only treatment has been frequent doctor visits and removal of any suspicious tissue that reappears. Thus far, I've had five biopsies on my tongue. Three came back benign; two were cancerous.

Each time God's grace and presence were near.

I have become more aware of the need to slow down and treasure the everyday blessings like a cardinal's song, a butterfly on a flower, or the hug of a child. The cancer experience has also strengthened my resolve to use my faltering tongue to proclaim the good news and hope of Jesus Christ.

God's love pours over us in abundance, and He does the same for you. "See what great love the Father has lavished on us, that we should be called children of God! And that is what we are!" (1 John 3:1)

Take a moment to press the pause button on your hectic schedule before a disruption forces you to slow down. Savor God's love. Reflect on the depth of God's love for YOU. Even when you are having the worst day possible, God's love still remains steady and sure. Brennan Manning points to the importance of grasping God's love.

> Do you really accept the message that God is head over heels in love with you? This question is at the core of our ability to mature and grow spiritually. If in our hearts we really don't believe that God loves us as we are, if we are still tainted by the lie that we can do something to make God love us more, we are rejecting the message of the cross.[1]

God sent His son, Jesus, out of love for us, to bring us back into relationship with Him. He loves each of us with an everlasting love. Nothing can separate us from His love. Even in hard times His love carries us.

It seems impossible to grasp the depth and breadth of God's love for us. The words of the hymn "O the Deep, Deep Love of Jesus" express the magnitude of this love. As you contemplate the lyrics, ask God to enlarge your understanding of His love.

"O the deep, deep love of Jesus —
Vast, unmeasured, boundless free!
Rolling as a mighty ocean
In its fullness over me.
Underneath me, all around me,
Is the current of Thy love.
Leading onward, leading homeward,
To my glorious rest above." [2]

Grace allows us to relish the small moments of life — the taste of your favorite dessert or the beauty of a sunset after a storm. Savor the grace impact when you take time to allow your thoughts to linger on God's awesome love. Bask in the truth of knowing you are loved more than you ever thought possible.

Deepening the Grace Impact

QUESTIONS: Is there a specific time you have recently experienced God's love? Why do we so easily forget His deep love for us? What can you do to cultivate an awareness of God's love for you?

SCRIPTURES FOR MEDITATION: John 3:16; Romans 8:35-39; Ephesians 3:14-20; 1 John 4:8

PRAYER: Lord, I want to savor Your love in every area of my life. Help me understand of the depth of Your love for me. I pray that through Your grace, I will rest in the refuge of Your love. Thank You that nothing can separate me from Your amazing love. Amen.

The Wonder of Grace: God Becomes One of Us

But when the set time had fully come, God sent his Son, born of a woman, born under the law, to redeem those under the law. — Galatians 4:4-5a

Flickering candles on the mantle, sounds of joyful Christmas music, twinkling lights on the tree, and the aroma of cookies baking in the oven create a calm atmosphere in the home during December.

Though we yearn for this serenity, all too often, the reality we face is the opposite. The more common scenario is a harried schedule of school and church activities, decorating the outside and inside of the house, sending dozens of cards, the frantic buying and wrapping gifts, spending more money than anticipated, and generally feeling overwhelmed with the expectations and details of Christmas. We run out of time and energy wondering how we will get everything done.

The busyness of the weeks leading up to Christmas often threatens to diminish our awe and wonder of the first Christmas in Bethlehem. God's greatest gift was given to us at Christmas, sent in an unlikely form, a small, helpless baby named Jesus. God went to great lengths to enter our history and to identify with us through His Incarnation.

God revealed His grace to hurting, hopeless people through this child of redemption. The holy, all-knowing God of the universe sought a relationship with us —the pinnacle of His creation — and became one of us.

God masterminded the plan for our redemption, bringing world events and the fulfillment of prophecies together in what Paul described as "when the set time had fully come."

Jesus' birth was wrapped in history. Rome had conquered much of the known world, and enforced what is known as the *Pax Romana*, or Roman peace. It was marked by unprecedented peace, economic prosperity, and safe travel. The excellent roads of the Roman Empire were built for the purpose of moving its army and trade commodities with ease, but God also used these roads for Mary and Joseph to travel to Bethlehem to register for the census.

Another unique feature of this era was that a common trade language was used. *Koiné,* or common Greek, was as close to a universal language as the world had known since the tower of Babel. (Gen. 11) God used the everyday dialect so people could tell the good news of the birth of Jesus and pass on the story of faith throughout the ancient world.

The second phenomenon Jesus came wrapped in was prophecy. More than three hundred Old Testament prophecies were fulfilled at the birth of Jesus. Here is just one example to show the continuity between the Old and New Testaments. The prophecy of Isaiah 7:14 reads: "Therefore the Lord himself will give you a sign: The virgin will conceive and give birth to a son, and will call him Immanuel." It is shown in its fulfillment in Matthew 1:22-23, "All this took place to fulfill what the Lord had said through the prophet: 'The virgin will conceive and give birth to a son, and they will call him Immanuel,' (which means 'God with us')."

What Isaiah prophesied in the eighth century BC, Matthew declares as fulfilled in the birth of Jesus of Nazareth. Many more prophecies were spoken in the Old Testament and fulfilled in the life of Jesus.

Finally, Jesus also came wrapped in our humanity. When we hold a newborn baby, we are touched by the gentleness of new life. The downy head, tiny fingers, and delicate skin all stir tender love within us. We marvel as the infant stretches out after being curled up for nine months. Even a heart hardened by the storms of life softens when holding a newborn. God came as a baby, to soften our calloused hearts to receive a new and transformed life that would be offered to us in the now incarnate Jesus.

The helpless, dependent infant bore the name "God with us." Throughout all stages of our lives, Jesus is still Immanuel, God with us. He is with us when we are lonely or scared. He is with us when we celebrate joys. He is with us in the valley of the shadow of death.

God knew the world needed the touch of His grace. He orchestrated history, prophecy, and the sharing of our humanity to bring us the gift of redemption. The revelation of God appearing as a baby is written in Galatians 4:4-5a.

"But when the set time had fully come" — God's perfect timing
"God sent his Son" — Jesus is divine
"born of a woman" — Jesus was human
"born under the law" — Jesus was born into our world, with our restrictions
"to redeem those under the law" — His own purpose

People looked for a Messiah to come with power. Instead, God entered the world as a baby that would bring redemption for all.

Through the grace of the Incarnation, God revealed Himself in a way that relates to us — living on the earth and breathing our air.

This child of grace brings the gift of eternal life. Though undeserved, all we need to do is accept this gift of redemption by faith. No work is required on our behalf to earn this saving relationship with God. "For it is by grace you have been saved, through faith — and this is not from yourselves, it is the gift of God — not by works, so that no one can boast." (Eph. 2:8-9)

When we receive the touch of God's grace, our lives are transformed by the power of the Holy Spirit. Too often we lose sight of this transformation during Christmas because of the demands of the season. We strive to get everything done by December 25 and often end up exhausted. In the midst of the craziness of Christmas preparations, we can allow God to renew our hearts. This is illustrated in the children's story *A Charlie Brown Christmas.*

In the Christmas pageant preparations, Charlie Brown is given the task of choosing the tree. He selects the scrawniest one and is chastised by his friend Lucy for such a poor choice. Charlie Brown identified with the lowly tree. In the end, grace is shown when the children decorate and transform it into a beautiful Christmas tree.

God sees us in a similar manner. We come to Him plain and unlovable, but we are made beautiful by His grace. In the midst of our busyness, God comes to us right where we are. Through the grace impact, God appeared as a baby who would become our Savior. The wonder of Christmas leads us to worship God.

Deepening the Grace Impact

QUESTIONS: How do you see Christ's birth as God's gift of grace? How do you pause in the chaos of life to ponder God becoming one of us?

SCRIPTURES FOR MEDITATION: John 1:14; Romans 1:1-6; 1 John 4:14

PRAYER: Heavenly Father, thank You for the wonder of grace at the birth of Jesus. Only You could have masterminded world events so Jesus would be born at the appointed time. Thank You that because of Your Son's birth, the wonder of grace is available to each person. Thank You for becoming one of us, setting redemption's plan in motion through Your grace. Amen.

The Power of Grace: God Redeems

Praise be to the God and Father of our Lord Jesus Christ! In his great mercy he has given us new birth into a living hope through the resurrection of Jesus Christ from the dead. — 1 Peter 1:3

My husband, Rick, and I were in Russia during the Easter season to teach and encourage a young church. During a worship service, I shared with the children about the last week of Jesus' life using resurrection eggs. These are plastic eggs that contain miniature symbols like silver coins, a crown of thorns, a cup, nails, a cross, etc. to explain the Easter story to children.

A dark-haired little girl fidgeted with the last plastic egg, turning the top to open it. The other children found small items in their eggs. Hers was lightweight and didn't rattle. When it finally opened, a confused look crossed her face. The egg was empty.

"He disappeared....He's gone," she whispered.

"Jesus didn't disappear in a magic trick," I explained through the interpreter. "He left the tomb, alive again by the power and grace of God. Because of the resurrection we have hope." Her eyes widened as awe swept across into a bright smile as she listened to the Easter story for the first time.

By continually hearing the account of Christ's resurrection for many years, it is easy to hear it as a repetitive story and lose the wonder of the redeeming character of God amidst the bunnies, eggs, and jellybeans. The power of resurrection grace is foundational to Christian belief. All other religious leaders died, were buried, and remain in their graves. Jesus Christ is the only one who rose from the grave.

Without His resurrection there is no Christianity. There would be no hope for redemption, no comfort when facing death, and no possibility of eternal relationship with God. With the resurrection we have everything — forgiveness and redemption from sin, hope in the valley of death, and a relationship with God that goes beyond this life.

Christ's resurrection proves God's love for us. God did not abandon us in our sin. He resolved the problem of sin through His love. Jesus died as a sacrifice for our sin because of God's amazing love for us. The apostle John stated it this way. "For God so loved the world that he gave his one and only Son, that whoever believes in him shall not perish but have eternal life." (John 3:16) God's love for us was His motivation for our redemption.

Jesus' resurrection completed God's plan for our redemption.

The most impressive change is a hardened heart transformed with love and a new perspective based on the resurrection of Jesus.

Old Testament law demanded the priests to offer a continual sacrifice for the redemption and forgiveness of the people's sins. However, the sin barrier that separated God from humanity was removed permanently through the sacrifice of Jesus' death and His resurrection. We can now approach God without a sacrifice. In 2 Corinthians 5:18-19 we read, "All this is from God, who reconciled us to himself through Christ and gave us the ministry of reconciliation: that God was reconciling the world to himself in Christ, not counting people's sins against them."

The resurrection declares us not guilty before God; sin has been atoned for. Jesus became our sin penalty. "This is love: not that we loved God, but that he loved us and sent his Son as an atoning sacrifice for our sins." (1 John 4:10) The slate of sin keeping us separated from God is wiped clean.

When I was in elementary school, it was a privilege to help the teacher clean the chalkboards at the end of the week. Even though the spelling words were erased daily, they could still be read through the math problems on the grey slate. On Fridays the boards were washed down with a sponge and water, and the chalkboards were again glossy and free of the white dust.

This is how redemption works. The forgiving blood of Jesus erases the stain of sin on our hearts. Enduring the pain of the crucifixion, Jesus pleaded forgiveness for all of us. In agony He said, "Father, forgive them, for they do not know what they are doing." (Luke 23:34) It is each person's decision to accept His forgiveness through humble repentance. We are made clean and our hearts are purged of sin when we accept God's forgiveness. The gospel is about life transformation. The most impressive change is a hardened heart transformed with love and a new perspective based on the resurrection of Jesus.

Another impact of the resurrection is that it brings great peace and triumph over the despair that death brings. I stood by my mother's bedside during her hospice care and reflected on how God had sustained me during the difficult months she battled heart and lung diseases. She had lived a life of quiet faith, and was now in her last days. Heavy sadness draped over my heart.

When Mom slipped into eternity, hot tears stung my face as grief pierced my soul. I felt the anguish of loss; death is harsh. Yet in the midst of my sorrow, I felt God's peace with me. I know I will see her again in heaven. The hope of the Lord carried me through the days leading up to the funeral. This was evidence to me of God's grace. When we are in the valley of the shadow of death, the Lord holds out a ray of hope for us to look toward. Christians do not have to fear the end of this life. We can look forward to a future in heaven because of the resurrection. Death was conquered through the perfect sacrifice of Jesus. Before His journey to the cross, Jesus spoke these words of hope. "I am the resurrection and the life. The one who believes in me will live, even though they die; and whoever lives by believing in me will never die." (John 11:25-26a)

This hope is why the apostle Paul wrote, "But thanks be to God! He gives us the victory through our Lord Jesus Christ." (1 Cor. 15:57)

The grace impact shook the world with Jesus' resurrection. Redemption from sin, forgiveness, restored relationship with God, hope in the midst of the despair, and triumph over death continue to influence lives. All because of God's power to save us, and His love that redeems.

Chocolate and jellybeans at Easter are fun, but they don't last. The plastic eggs will be put away for another year. In contrast, the power of the resurrection lives. The grace impact draws us to look at the empty tomb with wonder and praise.

Deepening the Grace Impact

QUESTIONS: Is Jesus' resurrection important to you? How would life be different if there was no resurrection? How will you live in light of the resurrection?

SCRIPTURES FOR MEDITATION: 1 Corinthians 15:3-6; Hebrews 7:27; Ephesians 1:18-23

PRAYER: Lord Jesus, thank You for Your resurrection. You proved Your love for us through power and grace, defeating sin and death. The power of resurrection is hard to grasp, but I praise You for redemption's plan that brings me You. I praise You for the hope that is found in You. Amen.

"That you, always having all sufficiency…"

Once we accept the forgiving grace of Jesus Christ, God continues to transform us to more of His likeness. While we look to God and realize He is all-sufficient, we also look within ourselves and see that we are insufficient, limited in our resources for handling the challenges of life. God has given us the promise that His grace is more than enough. Second Corinthians 12:9 states "my grace is sufficient for you, for my power is made perfect in your weakness." He meets us in our frailty and still works in us.

We can approach Him and grow in understanding His ways. God's grace is always plentiful for every day and situation — when we are discouraged, exhausted or fearful. God is with us in the details of life, even when we think He doesn't see us. God provides what we need to make it through another day, when we humbly come to Him.

The grace impact stirs our hearts toward gratitude and thankfulness as we are more aware of all God has done for us. God's grace recharges us when we are weak and gives us direction when we seek Him. His grace is enough, helping us press in to the Lord, press out the fears and press on during the trials of life.

Approaching God's Holiness

Who may ascend the mountain of the LORD? Who may stand in his holy place? The one who has clean hands and a pure heart, who does not trust in an idol or swear by a false god. — Psalm 24:3-4

It's late afternoon, the kids are outside playing in the sandbox, and they are starving.

"Time to eat!" They respond to mom's call, bolt into the house, sit down, and start to fill their plates while mom is still putting a few dishes on the table. She notices they have not washed their hands and sends them to go scrub before dinner. Leaving the table, they gripe and poke at each other and return with even grumpier attitudes because they got into a fight while at the sink.

Rewind. Take two.

"Time to eat!" Mom calls from the kitchen. The kids have been playing outside in the sandbox and are starving. They bolt into the house but this time remember to go wash their hands before sitting down at the table to wait for everyone. The meal begins, and pleasant dinner conversation follows.

Two scenes, the same people with ultimately the same outcome, but the attitude is different. In approaching God, we are similar to the kids. We can rush into His presence forgetting the need for inner cleansing, or we can pause to prepare our hearts. It's better for us to come near to our heavenly Father with the attitude of knowing we have dirty hands — sin in our heart — and seek His cleansing before rushing into His holy presence. While the Lord accepts us as we are, we need to continually seek His forgiveness and cleansing from sin.

In Psalm 24, David shows us who can approach the Holy God of the universe. The one who has clean hands and a pure heart is offered grace to stand in His presence.

During biblical times, priests participated in ceremonial cleansing in preparation to enter God's presence. Their hands had to be made clean, representing external cleansing, before they could offer the ritual sacrifices. For us, the work of our hands refers to the actions we take with our hands, for good or for bad. Approaching God with clean hands means taking responsibility for sinful conduct through confession. It is restated in James 4:8, "Come near to God and he will come near to you. Wash your hands, you sinners, and purify your hearts, you double-minded."

Confession means "saying the same thing" — that is, affirming one's agreement with a particular spiritual reality.[1] It is agreeing with God about what He has already said about sin in your life, not trying to hide our offense. Confession dismantles the barrier between your heart and God, allowing grace to flow from God to you. Regret for past sin is followed by repentance — a desire to change.

Repentance means making a 180-degree turn in the way you think and act. The Greek word for "repentance" denotes a change of mind — a rejection of past sinful ways. But it also connotes remorse for sin, accompanied by a desire to turn away from one's sin and toward God for salvation. Repentance is not just a one-time experience, as the recognition of daily sins and shortcomings provides the occasions for renewed acts of repentance.[2] The combination of confession and repentance leads to a clean heart.

The psalmist also explains the need to have a pure heart, referring to inward character and motives of the heart. I have traveled in several countries where the water is not clean and am always cautioned to drink bottled water. Drinking impure water leads to sickness. Water is safest when it is pure and filtered.

To purify your thoughts and heart, apply Philippians 4:8 as a filter, "whatever is true, whatever is noble, whatever is right, whatever is pure, whatever is lovely, whatever is admirable — if anything is excellent or praiseworthy — think about such things." Reframing your thoughts will guide you to see what is true, noble, right, etc. about a situation or person.

> *Clean hands and a pure heart are essential in approaching the holiness of God.*

This verse challenges me to refocus self-centered thoughts back onto God's desires, to resist the lure of being drawn into a spiritually toxic situation that could lead to anger or bitterness. These soul pollutants are what Paul wrote about in Colossians 3:8-10. "But now you must also rid yourselves of all such things as these: anger, rage, malice, slander, and filthy language from your lips. Do not lie to each other, since you have taken off your old self with its practices and have put on the new self, which is being renewed in knowledge in the image of its Creator." Through the help of the Holy Spirit, we can put off the old self and put on the new self. This leads to the process of purifying the heart. A pure heart is shown in moral character and is in right standing with God because sin has been confessed. Jesus said in the Sermon on the Mount, "Blessed are the pure in heart, for they will see God." (Matt. 5:8)

Clean hands and a pure heart are essential in approaching the holiness of God. Through God's grace, He accepts us as we are and grants inward and outward cleansing when we ask. Our intentional confession of sin and repentance puts us in a position to approach God with a clear conscience. Because of the grace impact, God allows us to respond to Him so we can come into His presence with clean hands and a pure heart.

Deepening the Grace Impact

QUESTIONS: How do you prepare to have clean hands and a pure heart when approaching God? What is difficult about it? What is the easiest part for you?

SCRIPTURES FOR MEDITATION: Psalm 51:10; Philippians 4:8; 1 John 1:9

PRAYER: Lord, I look to You to cleanse my heart, my soul, and my mind. Remove anything that is impure or distracts me from You so I can be in Your holy presence. Thank You for forgiving me. Amen.

Grace and Gratitude

Give thanks to the LORD, for he is good.
His love endures forever. — Psalm 136:1

Rick's car pulls into the driveway; the engine turns off. Upon hearing his footsteps, our young children rush to the door. "Daddy's home! Daddy!" Opening the door, two blond-haired kiddos race to him, jumping into his arms with giggles.

Daddy was their hero, especially since he often had a surprise for each of them when returning from a trip. They searched his pockets until their small hands found the Matchbox® car or the My Little Pony.® Each discovery brought more squeals and excitement. It didn't take them long to realize when Daddy came home, they got a treat. Week after week this joyful homecoming scene played out before me.

Rick was away from home one night every week for several years as he completed his seminary degree. After two days of being with me, the kids were eager to see Daddy arrive home, but within a few months the scene changed a little. Instead of joyful hugs when he opened the door, Rick heard the question, "What did you bring me?" Dismayed, he still requested a hug before they could search for the treasures.

Many of us approach God in this manner, looking for a blessing of grace from the hand of the Father before pausing to give thanks for who He is and for all He has done. It must sadden God to know we only want His gifts while ignoring the Giver.

God, His grace, and our gratitude are closely intertwined. The "God of all grace" is one of the names given to God in Scripture. (1 Pet. 5:10) The blessings in daily life such as family, sustenance, or even our next breath, are gifts given to us out of grace. The greatest expression of this grace is salvation through Jesus Christ, freely given though we are not deserving of it.

Grace and gratitude are related words. In New Testament Greek, the word for grace is *charis*. It is interesting that the Greek word for gratitude is also charis. Grace is God reaching to those who do not deserve His mercy. The response from those receiving that mercy is gratitude. We respond to God's charis (grace) with charis (gratitude) of our own.[1]

It is important to note a key nuance in the how the word is used. The first, *charis* — grace — is initiated by the Giver, whereas the other meaning of *charis* — gratitude — is the response of the receiver. Grace flows from God to us; our response of gratitude should flow back to Him.

No matter what season in life you are experiencing, whether it's a time of great blessing when things are going right or a time of distress when problems overwhelm you, look to the God of all grace with a heart of gratitude. Receive both the small and large blessings of life with thankfulness. Approach the heavenly Father with gratitude for the grace He pours into your life.

The psalmist wrote, "Enter his gates with thanksgiving and his courts with praise; give thanks to him and praise his name. For the LORD is good and his love endures forever; his faithfulness continues through all generations." (Ps. 100:4-5)

Grateful praise begins with acknowledging who God is and what He has done. We can be thankful for the impact of God's redeeming grace. Take a moment today to express your gratitude to God for all He has done.

Deepening the Grace Impact

QUESTIONS: What are some examples of God's grace in your life? What can you do to cultivate an ongoing gratitude for God's grace?

SCRIPTURES FOR MEDITATION: John 1:16; Romans 3:22-24; Ephesians 2:8-9; 1 Peter 5:10

PRAYER: Lord, thank You for Your amazing grace and all its blessings. Thank You for the blessings I don't deserve. Let my heart see Your grace and grow in gratitude. Help me be more thankful every day. Amen.

The Divine Power Source

Therefore we do not lose heart. Though outwardly we are wasting away, yet inwardly we are being renewed day by day. — 2 Corinthians 4:16

Technology has invaded many aspects of life and creates an ongoing need to learn how to use smart phones, digital cameras, and Global Positioning Systems (GPS). One thing all these devices have in common, besides the on-off switch, is that their battery power runs out if not replenished. I have to remember to charge them, and when I travel, take the power adaptor with me. Simple enough, but remembering this detail has created interesting scenarios.

When Rick and I traveled to Ireland, I was eager to take pictures of the sights. We spotted a pod of dolphins playing offshore in the Irish Sea. I positioned the digital camera only to find it wouldn't work. The battery was dead. I remembered the last question Rick asked before we left for the airport. "Do you have the camera?" Yes, I had the camera. But as I stood in Ireland feeling helpless, I realized the question should have been "Do you have the camera *and* the charger?" Camera? Yes. Charger? No.

Once during an overnight trip, I called home at the end of the day. The cell phone was on its last bar of power, and the call was dropped because I had neglected to pack the power adaptor. Fortunately, a friend let me borrow a charger.

For safety while driving, I added a hands-free device for my cell phone. I tucked the device in my ear before heading out, but instead of accepting a call, I received aggravation. You guessed it; the telltale beeps informed me it had run out of power.

I learned a simple truth: While portable, electronic devices add convenience to our lives, they also need to be charged. Otherwise they just take up space, bringing frustration and disappointment. I am learning how to incorporate technology into my life and remember to pack the chargers because I don't want to be caught anymore without a power source.

The same can be said for walking with the Lord. Time spent with the spiritual power source replenishes the spirit. If I don't take the time to refresh my soul with worship, my heart with prayer, and my mind with Bible reading, I get easily disheartened and my patience wears thin. However, my time with the Lord recharges me, and I am more equipped with His peace and confidence to handle the everyday pressures of life. The Lord gives sufficient daily grace, but we must be plugged in to the power source to receive it. Our faith needs to be re-energized regularly. The grace given to us yesterday cannot sustain us today.

In 2 Corinthians 4:16 we read this encouragement: "Therefore we do not lose heart. Though outwardly we are wasting away, yet inwardly we are being renewed day by day." God's grace renews us, revitalizing us so we can handle life's demands.

Connecting with the grace and presence of God is like being connected to a *Divine Power Source*. God's mercies are never on the final charging bar, nor will He drop the connection. We can experience the empowerment of the grace impact daily.

Deepening the Grace Impact

QUESTIONS: What do you do to recharge your walk with the Lord? How can you improve your connection with the Divine Power Source?

SCRIPTURES FOR MEDITATION: 2 Corinthians 4:16; Isaiah 40:31; Romans 12:2

PRAYER: Lord, thank You that I can come to You everyday to receive Your power. Recharge my spiritual battery with Your grace and hope. Thank You for being the Divine Power Charger. Amen.

Recalculating Direction

*Guide me in your truth and teach me, for
you are God my Savior and my hope is
in you all day long.* — **Psalm 25:5**

Sitting on the sofa watching after-Thanksgiving football, I couldn't help but notice all the TV commercials
for portable Global Positioning Systems.
I was hooked by an ad and stated, "I need one!"

My adult son asked skeptically, "Why would you need that?"

"You've never traveled with Mom. She NEEDS it," responded
my daughter. "That's why I call our outings Adventures with Mom."

As the conversation ended, I didn't know whether to feel
chastised or embarrassed for making a few wrong turns.

That Christmas I was thrilled to open a package and receive a GPS for my car. No more getting lost for me. This
little device directs me wherever I need to go. I program it
and follow the voice to the destination, listening to audio directions instead of looking at a map.

The unfamiliar voice gives commands for when and where
to turn. Generally it is pleasant and helpful. But when I turn
a different way than instructed, the intonation becomes stern
and says, *"RECALCULATING."* The nerve! Does it have to be
so blatant and correct me in front of everyone? At least it's not

the sound of a familiar voice from the person next to me saying "You turned the wrong way." Maybe *recalculating* sounds nicer coming from the device after all.

I feel confident knowing I have access to any directions I need. I can arrive without difficulty, just ask anyone who has traveled with me…wait a minute. They might tell you otherwise. Sometimes it sends me on unexpected roads. Like the time it guided me on a hilly county road instead of the interstate highway. After passing cows and fields, I eventually came upon a farmer on the road and asked for directions. He was more helpful than the GPS, and I finally arrived at my destination. Perhaps the gadget instills false confidence.

Although my fancy device takes me where I want to go most of the time, it can lead me astray, but guidance from the Bible never points off track. It steers us in the right direction, even when we are lost in a maze of choices. The Bible convicts our hearts if we are going awry. This is another impact of grace. The psalmist David wrote a prayer we can offer up to God still today.

> Show me your ways, LORD,
> teach me your paths.
> Guide me in your truth and teach me,
> for you are God my Savior,
> and my hope is in you all day long. — Psalm 25:4-5

The Word of God is essential to staying on course; it is a compass that points true north when we've lost our bearings. This ancient book is still relevant, offering direction and hope. Its message speaks to the conscience and heart. Recalculating is necessary when we are out of God's will. At those times, we can lean into the wisdom of God's Word and find redirection from Him. Because God loves us, He is trustworthy to lead us.

Being in the Word of God and a relationship with Jesus Christ is the best GPS we can have. He is with you wherever you go. (Matt. 28:20) A similar promise is in Deuteronomy 31:8, "The LORD himself goes before you and will be with you; he will never leave you nor forsake you. Do not be afraid; do not be discouraged." The Bible aligns us with God's will. "Trust in the LORD with all your heart and lean not on your own understanding; in all your ways submit to him, and he will make your paths straight." (Prov. 3:5-6) Allowing God's Word to direct our daily decisions is another aspect of the grace impact. Recalculating your direction won't be as difficult when you trust in the Lord and His Word as the compass for your decisions.

Deepening the Grace Impact

QUESTION: In what areas of your life do need guidance from the Lord? How will you allow God's Word to direct your decision?

SCRIPTURES FOR MEDITATION: Psalm 37:23-24; Proverbs 3:5-6; Jeremiah 6:16

PRAYER: Lord, I look to You for guidance. Thank You for Your grace that guides me. Show me Your ways in whatever I do. Help me to recalculate my path so I am in alignment with Your Word. May You lead me each day to grow in Your ways. My hope is in You. Amen.

DAY TWELVE

Seeing Grace in God's Ways

As for God, his way is perfect; the LORD'S word is flawless; he shields all who take refuge in him. — Psalm 18:30

Nervous about going into a country where I didn't speak the language, I prayed about what I needed to pack. Rick and I were preparing to travel to far eastern Russia for a short-term mission trip to train the leaders of a new church and teach adults and children about the love of God. In addition to my Bible, I took some Russian Bible study materials, music, and ministry tools to use with the children. I didn't know how or if any of these items would be used. Although we felt God's call to go, I was apprehensive about just the two of us going into a country where we weren't familiar with the government or everyday customs.

I wondered how I might share a gift of music, or if a piano would be available. I had hoped to play the piano during the Easter worship service. Though the day turned out differently than I had anticipated, I saw grace work through God's ways.

We arrived safely in Russia, but missing one of my bags. Three days later on Sunday morning, our translator called saying my luggage had arrived, but my excitement quickly turned to disappointment. Instead of getting my luggage later in the afternoon,

I had to go to the airport right away to claim my bag. Because of my lost luggage, I would miss celebrating Easter with our sister congregation — something I had anticipated for months. Exasperated, I went with our translator, hoping to return for part of the worship service. However, with all the delays of traffic and then going from office to office at the airport to claim my bag, I realized I would miss the entire service. I felt emotionally weary.

We headed back through busy traffic to the rented hall arriving just as the service concluded. Rick was uplifted and joyful from the cross-cultural worship experience. Though I was relieved to be back with him, I felt disheartened from the unexpected activity of my morning. Tears spilled from my frazzled disappointment. Possibly the only opportunity to share music or children's ministry was preempted by a suitcase.

After a short break, the afternoon teaching session began. I was still trying to compose my disheveled emotions when the musicians took their places. They had sung a special song during the worship service and wanted to sing it for me.

The praise band began. The singer's angelic voice filled the room. As I listened, more tears streamed down my face — she sang the exact same song I had prepared to play for them. The moment was a special gift from God. The morning's disappointment melted away as God orchestrated the events of the afternoon.

I remembered God's declaration of sovereignty: "As the heavens are higher than the earth, so are my ways higher than your ways and my thoughts than your thoughts." (Isa. 55:9) God's ways caused what started as a day of frustration to end as a day of celebration. God worked through someone I had gone to serve and blessed me with a deeper insight into the expanse of His grace across the world.

Afterward it was hard to explain to the singer why I was so tearful during the lovely song. But from one musician's heart to another, we both knew God spoke to each of us, crossing language and cultural barriers.

A few days later, we shared music together at the musician's home. I sight-read her music while she sang in Russian. This precious time was another evidence of God's fingerprints of grace.

During our time in Russia, God used everything I brought for ministry in surprising ways. The Bible study books were given to the grateful women. The teaching aids, which were left there for future use, helped the children learn the story of Jesus. As for the music, it continues to minister…to me.

In Russia I never played the song I had prepared, "Via Dolorosa." Every Easter since then, I play that special song, meditating on the words. It speaks to my heart each time as I reflect on how God's ways are perfect through the grace impact.

Deepening the Grace Impact

QUESTION: How have you seen God use unlikely things in unexpected ways? When have you seen God's grace transform a difficult situation into a blessing?

SCRIPTURES FOR MEDITATION: Psalm 18:30; Deuteronomy 32:4; Romans 8:28

PRAYER: Heavenly Father, Help me see Your grace as You lead me. You see the beginning, the middle, and the end, while I just see the moment. Your ways are best for me. I rest in that thought. Open my eyes to see Your grace at work. Thank You. Amen.

Pressing In to Grace, by Faith

Let us then approach God's throne of grace with confidence, so that we may receive mercy and find grace to help us in time of need. — Hebrews 4:16

The day started out well. During my devotional time I studied verses on faith that lifted my confidence and strengthened my spirit. I was on my A-game — accomplishing much throughout the morning. No problems, just progress.

In the afternoon I had a dental appointment to fix a tooth. Because I've had a lot of dental work and get nervous when the needle gets near my mouth, I cope by keeping my eyes closed when I am in the chair. I made the mistake of opening my eyes just as he was going to numb my jaw. Bad move. I didn't want to open my mouth, lest I would bite him. After a deep breath, I was okay to proceed. Though the tooth was repaired successfully, I was into my B-game — managing, but not doing my best.

With a numb mouth I didn't want to talk to anyone, but I needed groceries. My quick stop at Walmart turned into a lengthy shopping experience because of the after-school crowd. My head pounded from a headache, and I hoped I didn't drool at the checkout. At home I unloaded everything, sat down, and put my feet up for a few minutes. I should have stayed in the comfort of my recliner, but instead decided I'd feel better playing in the dirt through flower therapy.

Off I went to buy bedding plants. Two stores later, feeling hot and sweaty, I still hadn't found what I wanted. I picked out some begonias anyway.

On my way home, hunger struck. I hadn't eaten since breakfast. Chewing was still uncomfortable with my numb jaw, even five hours after the procedure. Tired and hungry, I slipped into my C-game — doing what I had to do to survive the moment.

The urge for a milkshake led me to the parking lot of an ice cream shop. I found a space in the front near the outdoor seating. A large family of adults and young children filled the picnic table. The grandparents looked my way as I left the car.

I got my milkshake and a sundae for my hubby. Mission accomplished! A faint smile crossed my lips. Now I could head home — or so I thought. Getting in my car, I noticed the entire group staring at me. The grandmother got up and approached our cars. She walked to her vehicle and rubbed a tiny spot of paint where my car door touched her SUV.

"That wasn't there before."

I apologized. She persisted. She then flagged her husband to come over, asking him if he thought the spot could be buffed out. She rubbed it again, stared at me and rubbed some more. They both glared at me like I was a criminal. My jaw tingled as the Novocaine wore off. I wanted to take my milkshake and go home. The lady walked back to where the grandchildren hung on the chain link fence watching the scene.

Her husband was now my judge.

"What do you want me to do?" I felt drained.

He peered at me with silence.

"Do you want cash or my insurance information?" I had to offer something.

"No, nothing." He stared at me and then to the tiny spot.

He could have demanded payment, but didn't. Though a small gesture, he extended grace to me, forgiving my carelessness.

"I'm sorry. I'll be more careful." I felt wilted. "God bless."

I drove home feeling discouraged. My comfort food, a soupy milkshake, wasn't satisfying.

That evening my choice was clear — I could continue to indulge in self-pity or seek the Lord. Planting the flowers gave me some time to pray. Even though I didn't feel like it, I chose to intentionally press in to the Lord. That decision, as difficult as it was to make, became a turning point in my attitude. Through offering my emotionally weary self in prayer, the Lord calmed my bruised heart. Faith turned me toward God to receive His favor, His grace. Several Bible verses came to mind.

"I have loved you with an everlasting love." (Jer. 31:3a)

"I praise you because I am fearfully and wonderfully made." (Ps. 139:14a)

Slowly my spirits lifted. No matter what happened, nothing could separate me from God's love. I had to lay aside the effects of my crummy day and accept His love. These incidents weren't major events, but as the day went on, each one pulled me down. The grace of God lifted my weary heart at the end of the day.

Pressing in to the Lord means believing the promises of God in a deeper way, not just with your heart for inspiration, but also with your head for belief. It is intentionally refocusing your heart to hear the whisper of God's love even when you don't feel loved. Pressing in is resetting your mind to believe His promise to never leave or forsake you. It is grasping again that there is no condemnation for those in Christ Jesus. It is releasing a difficult situation into the hands of the One powerful enough to hold the universe. God's hands are firm and strong, yet gentle when enabling us to handle the pressures in our lives.

Comfort and assurance are found through pressing in to

the presence and promises of our loving God, His grace drawing us to Him. Faith is my response to this beckoning, believing, and trusting more in God. His unconditional favor sustains me in every situation, especially when I am weak.

Press in to God's grace if you are waiting for medical tests. He already knows what you need. Press in to the love of Jesus when you face a distressing relationship. Trust God's love as your sure foundation for strength in trials. Press in to the faithfulness of Jesus Christ when you feel uncertain about the future. He is unchanging when everything else is in flux.

God invites us to draw near to Him through His grace. "Let us then approach God's throne of grace with confidence, so that we may receive mercy and find grace to help us in time of need." (Heb. 4:16) Faith and grace are woven together through the grace impact when we press in to the Lord.

Deepening the Grace Impact

QUESTION: How can you press in and believe the promises of God today? Was there a time when you saw God's grace sustain you when you had a rough day? How can a change in focus improve your attitude when you are discouraged?

SCRIPTURES FOR MEDITATION: Isaiah 26:3; Romans 5:1-2; 1 Peter 5:10

PRAYER: Lord, in the midst of my busy life, help me press in to Your grace. I want to lean in to You and trust You more deeply, by faith, every day. Thank You for being faithful and loving when life is so changeable. Amen.

Pressing Out Fears

The LORD is my light and my salvation — whom shall I fear? The LORD is the stronghold of my life — of whom shall I be afraid? — Psalm 27:1

D riving on paved, unmarked, two-lane country roads is pleasant on a sunny afternoon, but becomes a fearful situation when navigating it late at night in a thunderstorm. Even a short drive requires more concentration because of the steep ditches flanking either side of the road with little or no shoulder.

When we lived in rural, central Illinois in the 1980s, I often chose not to drive on country roads after dark unless I was extremely familiar with the area. This was also B.T.—Before Technology like cell phones and GPS.

One night I headed to a meeting held at a home far out in the country. Because my husband was out of town, I had to take our two preschool-aged children with me. They would have other children to play with while I attended the meeting. After it wrapped up, I stayed a bit longer, visiting with friends. Although I thought I could easily navigate my way home, I soon found out otherwise.

A heavy thunderstorm rolled across the area, pelting the farmland with rain and filling ditches with water. Lighting flashed through the black night. Thick fog blanketed the countryside.

When the rain let up I dashed to the car with my kids and buckled them in their car seats. I left the muddy driveway to head home but made a critical mistake by turning the wrong way onto the paved county road. Fog eerily hung over the signposts erasing the road names. No matter what direction I turned, everything looked the same — pitch black, gray fog, with flashes of lightning in the distance.

The two-lane country road, bordered by water-filled ditches and endless flat countryside, was visible only a few feet in front of me. I hoped I was in the center of the asphalt because I could not see any highway markings or lights. I turned around to go back and start over, but became even more confused in the heavy mist. The swishing windshield wipers beat with an eerie rhythm.

Panic grew within me as I considered the possibilities of being lost, with my children in the back seat. How will I find my way home? Would I drive into a ditch? What if I hit another car? My white knuckles gripped and re-gripped the steering wheel. I slowly drove through unknown territory. The heavy fog intensified my distress.

The visibility improved a bit. I went forward cautiously, trusting and praying. Finally a few discernible road signs guided me

Fears do that to us. They make the truth of a situation hard to see, causing us to lose our way, creating improbable scenes in our mind.

through the dark countryside. It took twice as long to get home that night, but by the grace of God I eventually made it. I tucked my kids in bed and collapsed on my bed with a sigh of relief and a prayer of thanks. Even in the comfort of my own home, it took a while to calm down enough to go to sleep.

Often when we leave our comfort zones, by choice or by circumstance, we find ourselves wrapped in fear. On that perilous drive in the fog, it was hard to see, easy to lose my way, and downright scary. Fears do that to us. They make the truth of a situation hard to see, causing us to lose our way, creating improbable scenes in our minds.

But the Lord, as an expression of His grace, does not leave us alone with our fears. When the Philistines captured King David, he wrote these words…"When I am afraid, I put my trust in you. In God, whose word I praise — in God I trust and am not afraid." (Ps. 56:3-4a) Like David, we have to admit we are afraid and then choose to trust God in spite of the fear. Actively trusting God begins to melt away our fear. By looking to God, we gain courage and the power of fear diminishes. Psalm 27:1 gives us a focal point to overcome fear. "The LORD is my light and my salvation — whom shall I fear? The LORD is the stronghold of my life — of whom shall I be afraid?" Focus on the Lord, the Prince of Peace, in the midst of fears.

Trusting the Lord and His Word moves us forward into faith instead of backward into doubt and fear. Second Timothy 1:7 also offers us courage. "For the Spirit God gave us does not make us timid, but gives us power, love and self-discipline." We are promised a spirit of dynamic power to proceed when we would rather withdraw, a spirit of selfless love that overcomes our fear (1 John 4:18), and self-discipline that has the sensibility and moderation of self-control — a fruit of the Spirit. Power from God, love, and self-discipline are extended to us through God's grace.

To overcome your fears, try these three steps. First, write down your fears; don't deny they are there. Even King David admitted them. Naming specific fears begins to diminish their control over you.

Second, shred them. Put the list through the shredder. If you don't have a shredder, tear the paper into tiny pieces and throw them away.

Third, replace the fears with something positive. Meditate on Bible verses about overcoming fear until one speaks to your heart. Turn the verse into a prayer. Write it on a note card and post it where you'll see it often and replace that fearful thought. Work to memorize the verse and speak it when fear arises.

The grace impact again touches us, helping us press out fears and empowering us to go forward.

Press in to the Lord…press out fears…then you can press on.

Deepening the Grace Impact

QUESTION: What fears and doubts do you need to press out? When have you seen God calm your fears?

SCRIPTURES FOR MEDITATION: Psalm 34:4; Psalm 56:4, 11; Isaiah 41:10

PRAYER: Lord, thank You that I can approach You and receive Your grace to press out fear and doubts. Help me believe that You will help me overcome fears. Amen.

Pressing On to the Finish

Forgetting what is behind and straining toward what is ahead, I press on toward the goal to win the prize for which God has called me heavenward in Christ Jesus. — Philippians 3:13b-14

While I was putting together a presentation for a women's meeting, the Lord prompted me to create it in a way that would involve speaking, singing, and accompanying myself on the piano. It took a lot of practice and courage for me to combine all three skills. Many times I felt like giving up, but I knew this was something God would use to stretch me if I persevered. Even while performing, doubts entered my mind. Would I forget the words or melody in front of the group? Would I falter in embarrassment? I had to push those negative thoughts away and depend on God's grace and persevere to the end. It went better than I anticipated, in spite of my doubts. I was encouraged from the presentation, incorporating all three skills by the grace of God. Afterward, people told me they were blessed.

Perseverance is necessary throughout life. Young moms need it when the demands of children leave them tired. Dads need it when the pressures of work consume them. When faced with tough problems you can choose one of two things: to be discouraged and weaken your resolve, or press on with determination empowered by God's grace.

The verse in Philippians 3:14 always challenges me to press on, no matter what. It speaks of having a forward focus straining toward the end result. The apostle Paul used an athletic image to convey his message depicting runners as they stretch and strain toward the finish line. The sheer determination of the runners' faces shows us the resolve needed to press on when life gets tough.

During the 1992 Barcelona Summer Olympics, Derek Redmond of the United Kingdom was expected to be a medalist in the 400-meter dash. He had trained hard and won many impressive victories in his career.

Redmond was the lead sprinter in the first half of the semi-final race. But down the back straight, he suddenly fell in pain on the track, grasping the back of his leg. He had torn a hamstring. Later he said, "I remembered where I was and what I was doing. I was in the Olympic semi-finals — so get up and finish!"

And that's what he did. As he hobbled in agony around the last curve, race officials hurried out on the track to help him, but he insisted on finishing the race he trained for.

Then a man from the crowded stands made his way onto the track, shoving his way through the security guards. He reached out to help Derek, but was pushed away. But when the athlete realized it was his father, he put his arm around his shoulders, accepting assistance for his faltering steps. Together they moved toward the finish line, the son leaning on the father. Redmond recalled his father's words and his response:

"You can stop now; you haven't got nothing to prove."
"Yeah, I have. I've got to finish."
"Well if you're going to finish the race, let's finish it together."

Derek Redmond and his father limped across the finish line together. Although Redmond didn't medal in the Olympics, he ran a courageous race and finished to the cheers of thousands of spectators.[1]

This story of determination and perseverance illustrates our need to press on and depend on our relationship with the Lord. The athlete faltered in great physical pain and emotional agony, but persisted to finish the race he had trained for. He would not give up, pressing on through the pain, "forgetting what was behind and straining toward what was ahead." (Phil. 3:13b) Though he didn't win the physical prize, he bravely completed the task he set out to accomplish, and won the respect of thousands of onlookers.

We have a heavenly Father who is watching every step of our race. When we falter, He moves through the crowd to pick us up and help us finish. Like Redmond, we often try to resist Him. When we realize God loves us in spite of our performance, we can accept His grace and relax to let His arms support us. We can approach the finish line together. Our heavenly Father promises never to leave us. This is strongly expressed in Hebrews 13:5, "because God has said, 'Never will I leave you; never will I forsake you.'" In Greek, the intensity of this statement comes through with the use of the triple negative, two direct negatives and one implied in the word meaning. The promise is…

> "I will not, I will not cease to uphold or sustain thee." We are assured therefore of the sustaining grace of God as we go through trials and testing times…The word "forsake" means in its totality, "to abandon, to desert, to leave in straits, to leave helpless, to leave destitute, to leave in the lurch, to let one down." There are three negatives before this word, making the promise one of triple assurance. It is, "I will not, I will not, I will not forsake thee."[2]

The Amplified Bible renders it like this…

"For He [God] Himself has said, I will not in any way fail you *nor* give you up *nor* leave you without support. [I will] not, [I will] not, [I will] not in any degree leave you helpless *nor* forsake *nor* let [you] down (relax My hold on you)! [Assuredly not!]

If you face an insurmountable challenge or disappointment, trust the Lord's presence. He has not left us, even when He seems silent. If the hardest part of your day is just getting out of bed, lean into God's grace, knowing that each day is a fresh opportunity to move forward. His grace can carry you.

Press on to the finish, keeping your eyes on the goal. Part of responding to the grace impact is accepting God's grace to sustain you during trials. God will *never, never, never leave you.* Your heavenly Father is with you every step of the way and your Christian community is cheering you on to persevere.

Deepening the Grace Impact

QUESTION: What are you struggling with? What brings you hope to press on? When do you find it hardest to press on? What keeps you from seeking or accepting God's help?

SCRIPTURES FOR MEDITATION: Romans 5:3-5; James 1:3-4; 2 Peter 1:5-8

PRAYER: Lord Jesus, I look to You to help me persevere through rough trials. Thank You for being a steady arm to lean on. Only with Your help can I cross the finish line of faith, through Your grace. Amen.

"...in *all* things at all times..."

The grace impact empowers us in our relationship with the Lord, supplying us with the essentials to live the Christian life. This is evidenced by development of the fruit in us. Love, joy, peace, forbearance, kindness, goodness, faithfulness, gentleness, and self-control (Gal. 5:22-23a) are grown in our character as we allow the Holy Spirit to shape us through the events of our lives.

In all things at all times, God is present. His grace helps us manage interruptions, whether they are major life changes or small intrusions into our daily plans. God is the One who brings contentment into our hearts. We can persevere in prayer because of hope in God's faithfulness to hear and answer our prayers.

We receive encouragement through the words of the Bible. It is His grace that carries us in every situation through the daily grind of life and provides rest for our souls. Our faith in God deepens and our character grows as we seek the Lord with purpose and focus. We can lay aside perfectionism — the intense striving for flawlessness due to an unwillingness to fail — because He accepts us as we are. His grace is with us always in all ways.

The Dashboard of Life

And Jesus grew in wisdom and stature,
and in favor with God and man. — Luke 2:52

While at a conference, a speaker posed the question, "What's on the dashboard of your life?" Though he continued on with the main topic of his presentation, my mind stayed on this question. I wrestled with the implications of what he asked.

The dashboard is a complex control center. In a vehicle, it informs the driver of critical functions through the speedometer, fuel gauge, and the check engine lights. Another part of the dashboard houses the climate control center, clock, entertainment center, or possibly a navigation system. Everything is purposeful and within reach of the driver. After considering the dashboard as the control center of a vehicle, I wondered what the dashboard of my life looked like.

Some of the components of a dashboard can parallel your life's control center. In the middle is the speedometer, which shows how fast we are traveling. On life's dashboard, the speedometer represents time management. Many people start each day knowing their schedule is full, going from one appointment to another. Margins of rest aren't built into daily schedules. Everyone has the same twenty-four hours in a day, yet often we wish for more time. Trying to accomplish the unending to-do list in too little time creates more stress. We have even given our busyness a different name: multitasking. Renaming it doesn't alleviate the stress; it causes more.

To better manage your time, establish priorities, especially for small tasks. Learn to differentiate between what is vital (duties and responsibilities that must be done to accomplish what is expected of you at home and work and usually under a deadline) and what is urgent (important things that demand attention but can be temporarily delayed). One way is to create a to-do list prioritizing what is vital over what is urgent. If we spend our time always doing the urgent that screams for our attention, the vital tasks will be neglected, and we become unproductive. Look to God for insight to discern the difference. In Psalm 90:12 we read, "Teach us to number our days, that we may gain a heart of wisdom."

Another item on the dashboard is the fuel gauge. Your vehicle has to have the correct type of fuel. A diesel engine cannot run well on gasoline, and vice versa. In the Christian life, we need to have the right kind of fuel to live for the Lord. Three components make up spiritual fuel — our relationship with God, our relationship with oneself, and our relationship with others. Each of these relationships provides an important element for our mental and spiritual health.

The first component is our relationship with God, the spiritual dimension of growing in faith while loving and serving Him. Psalm 128:1 gives us a basis for how we are to relate to God: "Blessed are all who fear the LORD, who walk in obedience to him." A healthy reverence and awe of God ensures our connection with the Lord and obedience to His ways sustains the relationship. This is supported through studying the Word, prayer, and fellowship as we learn from others. Beginning the day with reading the Bible and devotionals gives your mind and soul a God-centered focus. This habit is more beneficial than checking the news or your Facebook page, as it can set your heart and mind at peace for the day.

The second component is relationship with oneself. Contrary to being a selfish idea, this is actually a selfless idea. Recall what Jesus said, "Love your neighbor as yourself." (Mark 12:31) This passage implies that we must have a healthy self-love before we can love others. As part of this self-care, each one of us has a responsibility to make sure our physical engine is running properly by taking care of the body God has given us, which involves the balance of proper nutrition, exercise, and relaxation. Even during a busy day, a simple walk or change of scenery can quiet a restless heart and allow the Holy Spirit to give us a better perspective.

Another aspect of healthy self-care is personal growth in the intellectual or mental dimension. In response to a teacher's question, Jesus replied that we are to love the Lord our God with all our minds. (Mark 12:30) Keeping our minds active can also help maintain or even improve mental sharpness. As electronics become an increasing part of our lives, they can lead to a more passive lifestyle of screen-watching. To balance this, take up a new hobby, read a different genre of book, or learn an instrument. Lifelong learning strengthens the brain, and creativity refreshes the spirit.

Relationship with others is the third component of a healthy fuel mixture —investing time with family and friends. We grow through fellowship as we learn from others how to relate in community — loving, sharing ideas, and forgiving. It is easy to neglect face-to-face communication when so much time can be spent on Facebook, Twitter, and texting. Social media doesn't offer the kind of connectedness the Lord desires for us to have with others. It is worth the effort to get to know the person on the other side of the screen. Having a large online social network is fine, but it is not a substitute for a caring fellowship of friends you can hug.

Luke 2:52 reveals to us the elements on the dashboard of Jesus' life. "And Jesus grew in wisdom *(intellectually)* and stature *(physically)*, and in favor with God *(spiritually)* and man *(socially)*." (Italics, author emphasis) Jesus showed us the correct fuel mixture *(relationships)*, and how to pace our lives. The grace impact can help us move toward a healthier balance in our relationships and more efficient time management skills to prevent the check engine light from coming on.

Deepening the Grace Impact

QUESTION: Describe your time management and the pace of your daily living. Do you have room for God's grace to work in your life? How can you improve the fuel mixture — your relationship with God, with yourself, and with others? What specifically can you do to improve the intellectual, physical, spiritual, and social aspects of your life?

SCRIPTURES FOR MEDITATION: Deuteronomy 6:5; 1 Samuel 2:26; Luke 2:52; Psalm 90:12

PRAYER: Heavenly Father, I pray for Your wisdom to guide me each day. Show me how to live a more balanced life with Your priorities. Help me live my life in response to Your grace. Amen.

Real Life Interruptions

*Let your eyes look straight ahead; fix your
gaze directly before you.* — Proverbs 4:25

Two preschool children are playing side by side on the
floor, the older boy constructing a tower with wooden
blocks, and the younger playing with his favorite car.
Without warning, the younger child runs his car into the carefully built tower. It crumbles to the floor. "Mom, he's erupting
me!" the older child yells. The interruption turned into an erup-
tion. We often handle interruptions the same way, growing ir-
ritated when someone or something else intrudes on our plans.

We don't plan for life disturbances, but they seem to happen every day. Sometimes interruptions are crisis-sized events
that occupy a period of time — dealing with aging parents, an
unforeseen loss or relocation, demanding family issues, or an
unexpected health diagnosis. These events cause us to post-
pone our dreams or delay our plans because we are dealing
with a situation for a season of life. It takes time for life to
settle down. In some cases, we may have to deal with long-
term effects, and the interruption leads to a new normal. Life
has changed and will never be the same again.

Jeremiah 29:11 gives hope during seasons of major life interruption or transition. "'For I know the plans I have for you,' declares the LORD, 'plans to prosper you and not to harm you, plans to give you a hope and a future.'" The prophet wrote these words to the exiles living in Babylon, far away from their homeland. In the midst of the darkness of their captivity, they received a word from God offering hope. He reminded them that this long season of interruption would come to an end. God was true to His Word.

Hope calms us when we rest in His sovereignty. Even when life seems out of control from unforeseen crises, we can rest in this promise from Jeremiah because God is faithful to His Word. Grace enables us to hold on to faith when there seems to be little or no reason for doing so.

Some interruptions only last for a short time, when you have to deal with an immediate problem — flooding in the house from a broken water heater or too much rain, ants in the kitchen, a sick child, car repairs, etc. Although these interruptions don't last long, they can be time and labor intensive as well as expensive. They disrupt your everyday routine. Though recovery is quicker from these interruptions, we may feel tired or stressed. While they are not as life-altering as major interruptions, attitude adjustment and great patience are needed. God's grace can enable us to handle the disruption with a positive attitude.

The words of Psalm 25:5 give us wisdom when handling these short-term situations. "Guide me in your truth and teach me, for you are God my Savior, and my hope is in you all day long." When we pray to the Lord, He gives us grace to handle the moment.

Finally, some interruptions like texting, social media, e-mail, phone calls, or television are simply distracting. The phone dings when a text arrives or a ringtone interrupts dinner conversation. Like the annoying fly, these sounds demand our attention. Our focus shifts from what we are doing at that moment to responding to the next bit of communication. We can be drawn to digital technologies and lose track of time. The continual stream of information that flows from a variety of twenty-four-hour news outlets distracts us, and can hinder our communication and productivity.

Distractions fragment our time and detract from our focus. In the story of Mary and Martha, diligent Martha was "distracted by all the preparations that had to be made." (Luke 10:40) We are just like her if we fail to consider our priorities. The common sense wisdom in Proverbs 4:25 gives direction and purposeful focus. "Let your eyes look straight ahead; fix your gaze directly before you."

C.S. Lewis had this to say about interruptions.

The great thing, if one can, is to stop regarding all the unpleasant things as interruptions of one's 'own' or 'real' life. The truth is of course that what one calls the interruptions are precisely one's 'real' life — the life God is sending one day by day; what one calls one's 'real life' is a phantom of one's own imagination.[1]

Even as I write this devotion, interruptions plague me. Thoughts get sidetracked, e-mails arrive, the computer closes the window I'm working in, and the cell phone beeps telling me it needs to be charged. C.S Lewis was right, what we call interruptions become real life.

Look to the Lord to help you manage disruptions. When you feel like throwing your hands up in frustration, reach up to the Lord. This ancient action of reaching up to the Lord is both a symbol of surrender and receptivity. Release the frustration of the interruptions to Him, pray to receive His peace in your open hands. Isaiah 26:3 offers hope and help through

God's grace when you deal with interruptions so they don't lead to emotional eruptions. "You will keep *him* in perfect peace, *Whose* mind *is* stayed *on You*, Because he trusts in You." (NKJV) The grace impact can stabilize the frustrating effect of interruptions.

Deepening the Grace Impact

QUESTION: What interruptions challenge you most often? What steps can you take to manage them with God's grace?

SCRIPTURES FOR MEDITATION: Isaiah 26:3; Proverbs 4:25-27; Luke 10:40-42

PRAYER: Lord, give us Your strength to see interruptions from Your point of view, to handle them with grace and understanding, without erupting in irritation. Amen.

The Secret to Contentment

I know what it is to be in need, and I know what it is to have plenty. I have learned the secret of being content in any and every situation, whether well fed or hungry, whether living in plenty or in want. I can do all this through him who gives me strength. — Philippians 4:12-13

Years ago an industrial company went to Central America to open a factory. The company paid a decent wage to the workers, which helped raise their standard of living.

The first paychecks were distributed on a Friday. The next Monday, none of the employees returned to work. The American supervisors were perplexed. "Why have the workers not returned to make more money?" They soon discovered that the one paycheck was more than enough for the workers to support their families for several months.

The supervisors came up with an ingenious plan. They circulated copies of the latest full-color department store catalog to everyone in the surrounding villages. The following day, workers from the surrounding area came to the factory in droves. Now workers were discontent with their paychecks, wanting more.[1]

Contentment is so elusive. For some, it is a day off spent at the lake; whereas for others, it is having enough money and time to do whatever you want. By answering the questions "If only I had…" or "If only this would happen…" you will discover what you think would bring contentment. We are content one minute, and then something happens that upsets or angers us, and our contentment vanishes. Circumstances are often beyond our control, changing so fast that contentment becomes difficult, if not impossible. If we stake our contentment on situations, we rarely find it.

> *"Give a man everything he wants and at that moment everything will not be everything."*
>
> *~ Immanuel Kant*

We need to look beyond needs or desires and bring our discontentment to the Lord. The words of Philippians 4:6-7 remind us, "Do not be anxious about anything, but in every situation, by prayer and petition, with thanksgiving, present your requests to God. And the peace of God, which transcends all understanding, will guard your hearts and your minds in Christ Jesus."

Often we try to find contentment by having more. Immanuel Kant stated, "Give a man everything he wants and at that moment everything will not be everything."[2] There is never enough time, money, desire, volunteers, etc. We see the words "collect 'em all" on toy packaging. This tells us not to be satisfied with one, but that we need to have the entire collection.

When we served with missionaries in east Africa, I saw uncommon contentment. We traveled five hours through the vast African bush to meet with a small group of new Christians. We wanted to encourage and pray with them about growing their new church.

The new believers greeted us with joy and generosity. They invited us into their home made from mud and logs. When they served us a meal on china plates, the joy of the Lord was radiant in their faces. Afterwards, the hostess asked us directly, "Why wouldn't you want to live here? We have everything we need."

Looking around, I noticed things I thought I would need — electricity and running water — to name two.

She went on to say, "We grow our own food, and we make our own houses, have friends, family, and a fellowship of believers plus opportunities to share our faith. What more could we need?" Her eyes sparkled as she laughed and said, "Oh! We need matches so we can cook."

We laughed, but I was humbled by her contentment. They didn't have much by the world's standards, but they were rich in faith.

The antidote for wanting more is learning to be thankful for what you have. When you are tempted to want more, quietly say, "Thank you, God, I have all I need." Being reminded of God's provision calms the nagging within us for more. If we wait for something to give our life meaning, we are chasing an elusive butterfly — it lands, only to resume aimless flight. Contentment is a struggle in the mind and soul.

The apostle Paul gives us the secret to contentment. "I know what it is to be in need, and I know what it is to have plenty. I have learned the secret of being content in any and every situation, whether well fed or hungry, whether living in plenty or in want. I can do all this through him who gives me strength." (Phil. 4:12-13) Look to the Lord in every situation, believing He is enough. Though the truth is simple, it is difficult to live. Paul also states, "But godliness with contentment is great gain." (1

Tim. 6:6) When contentment is found in pleasing God, godliness will increase and we'll gain an eternal perspective.

Real contentment is found in a deeper relationship with the Lord. True satisfaction that goes beyond circumstances and possessions is a gift of grace from God. With the psalmist we can pray, "Satisfy us in the morning with your unfailing love, that we may sing for joy and be glad all our days." (Ps. 90:14)

Contentment is a lifelong discovery, found by walking with God in His strength. Seek God to discover what He would have you to do in this time and place. Ultimately, God desires us to be conformed to the image of Christ. God's abiding grace helps us learn contentment.

Deepening the Grace Impact

QUESTIONS: What does contentment look like to you? Is there something in your life that leads you to be discontent? What do you need to do to change your perspective and gain contentment?

SCRIPTURES FOR MEDITATION: 1 Timothy 6:6-7; Philippians 4:11; Hebrews 13:5

PRAYER: Lord, thank You that You are all-sufficient. In You I have all I need. Give me eyes to see You, and a heart of thankfulness for all You have given me. I can rest, knowing You will provide. Calm my anxious heart from wanting more, more, more. Thank You for Your satisfying love and grace. Amen.

Persistence in Prayer

*Then Jesus told his disciples a parable
to show them that they should always
pray and not give up.* — Luke 18:1

Jana's marriage went from bad to worse. Although she prayed diligently for her husband to stop drinking, he continued, to the embarrassment of her family. Jana reached a point where she could no longer endure the tension in their marriage and decided to file for divorce. Papers were in place, ready for signatures, but the Lord nudged her to withdraw them. She obeyed and continued praying. Within the following year, finally realizing the emotional damage he was causing to himself and his family, her husband's behavior had a remarkable turnaround. Their marriage was eventually restored through prayer and forgiveness.

Giving up admits defeat, conceding the situation is over. Jana was ready to concede that her husband would not change, but the Lord directed her to persist in prayer. While not every situation like this has the desired result, prayer changes us.

Jesus knew our short sightedness and desire for quick results could cause us to stop praying until we received His answer. He was familiar with our human tendency of quitting too soon. In the gospel of Luke, verse 18:1 encourages us to continue praying and believing in faith until God answers. Because prayer is as vital as breathing, Jesus emphasizes for us to keep on praying even when we don't see results.

Romans 12:12 offers three directives for prayer. "Be joyful in hope, patient in affliction, faithful in prayer." Let's take a closer look at how these instructions can help us to keep praying and not give up.

First, we are called to have joyful hope. Hope anticipates a good future with reliance upon God's direction. By looking back and remembering God's pattern of consistent faithfulness, we can have the confidence to continue to trust Him for the future, knowing that God does not change even through the time when God seems silent. While we wait for His answer to our prayer, our faith is bolstered by the quiet joy of recalling how the Lord has answered prayer in the past. True joy looks beyond the present circumstances to the strength of the Lord.

A friend of mine, the mother of a young man dealing with the challenges of autism, maintained such a perspective while in a discouraging situation. Her son had been walking around with his eyes closed, when she discovered his left eye was bright red and severely inflamed. His mood and behavior deteriorated as he was unable to communicate about the intense pain in his eyes. Several weeks passed, but medications and blood work did not provide an answer. His condition worsened, and she feared blindness for her son. Eventually a specialist diagnosed the unusual condition and prescribed the correct medications. She waited and felt burdened for the health of her son. He could not communicate about the pain, and she agonized, waiting to see if the medications would take effect. After several more days, he began to improve and smile again. In the midst of her anxiety and fear, she focused on joyful hope. She wrote…

"Things look hopeless, yet I KNOW I have hope. This hope is not in circumstances, diagnoses, wishful thinking, or unrealistic expectations. Real hope happens in spite of and in the midst of pain and difficulties. So here is where I hang my hope today: *'The Lord is loving toward all he has made, the Lord upholds all those who fall and lifts up all who are bowed down.... The Lord is righteous in all his ways.... The Lord is near to all who call on him.... He fulfills the desires of those who fear him. He hears their cry and saves them. The Lord watches over all who love him.'" From Psalm 145*[1]

Instead of dwelling on the discouraging situation, she chose to be joyful in hope.

Second, we are to be patient in affliction. Patience is actively trusting God and resting in His sovereign care in the midst of trials. Another friend and her husband have walked through job loss, unexpected health difficulties, and financial hardship that pointed them toward possible foreclosure of their home. They prayed, believing God for His provision. Through months of wading through paperwork and continual prayer, they did not give up hope. Finally they received word that they could remain in their home. The health crisis passed and the opportunity for part-time work became available. They rested in the sovereignty of God, waiting with patient, enduring faith for His provision. During this lengthy trial of almost two years, they grew deeper in faith and reflected the joy of the Lord because He was their strength.

Affliction will happen; it is inevitable in this life. We are to wait on the Lord with hope, not to be impatient, hurried, or discouraged. And while we wait, ask the Lord to teach us the lesson He would have us learn through the trial.

Third, we are called to be faithful in prayer. We are easily tempted to give up if we don't see results in our time frame.

We get impatient, lose heart, and want to quit. Waiting for the Lord's answer and trusting His timing show faithfulness in prayer. This diligence is revealed when a mother prays for decades for her prodigal son or daughter to return to God; a missionary trusts the Lord to make a difference when there seems to be no immediate signs of the gospel's impact.

Long-term missionary friends in Kenya faced multiple setbacks. During this time the wife became seriously ill and couldn't even get out of bed because of pain. She felt discouragement for not being useful to the ministry; all she could do was pray while flat on her back. The Lord assured her that prayer was the greatest work. Eventually they had to leave the mission field because of her health. Years later, the Lord fully restored her health and they returned to Kenya to resume their work. Upon their return they were blessed and surprised to see how God had answered those prayers evidenced through many new believers and churches in the African bush. God had moved mightily throughout that area, so much that they relocated their ministry to a different, unreached part of Africa. Faithfulness in prayer is shown when we pray with hope in the middle of a crisis, believing God will use the situation for His purposes.

Throughout the Bible are many instances of believers who prayed and faithfully waited for God's answer. Abraham waited twenty-five years for the answer of the covenant prayer that he would be the father of many. Joseph prayed while in prison for several years before he was released to serve God's purposes at the right time. Jonah prayed in the belly of the whale for three days before he was delivered. Mary and Martha hoped Jesus would come and heal their brother Lazarus, but Jesus came four days after Lazarus had died. The apostle Paul prayed and faced hardship but waited for the Lord to work.

We pray and wait; nothing appears to be happening. Only

God can see the whole picture. Suddenly, we see glimpses of the Lord at work in lives and situations. He really *is* moving in this chaotic world. God's grace is at work even when we can't see it changing people's lives, drawing them to Himself. The grace impact helps us to have joyful hope, patience in affliction, and faithfulness in prayer when we would rather quit.

Deepening the Grace Impact

QUESTIONS: What longtime prayers have you seen answered? What prayers are you still waiting to have answered? How has your communication with God been affected while you wait?

SCRIPTURES FOR MEDITATION: Psalm 40:1; Isaiah 30:18; Isaiah 40:29-31

PRAYER: Lord, forgive me when I give up too quickly. Help me to pray faithfully, even when I don't see the answer. Help me to learn from You while I wait. Thank You for being faithful and forgiving, allowing me another chance to pray. Amen.

Cherish the Word

The law of the LORD is perfect, refreshing the soul.
The statutes of the LORD are trustworthy,
making wise the simple. — Psalm 19:7-8

One night, as an elderly woman was reading her Bible at home, a fierce knock came at the door. The approaching voices were ominous; the men entered to search the house and seize any Bible they might find. This was a common occurrence in communist Bulgaria during the 1930s. She hid her beloved Bible under her skirt, sitting on it for hours while her home was ransacked. The men left empty-handed.

The next day this woman went to church with the idea of sharing the Bible with others. With tears in her eyes, she tore out page after page, giving them out to the believers. A young girl named Margaret Nikol was there. She received a page containing chapters sixteen and seventeen of Genesis, the story of the promise for Abraham and Sarah to have a son. She cherished that page and did not discover the outcome of the Bible couple until years later.

Margaret Nikol's father was a pastor in Bulgaria. Although they had no Bible, her father taught about the love of Jesus. He was jailed and tortured for his faith.

Margaret, a gifted musician, was fortunate enough to learn to play the violin and studied at some of the best music schools behind the Iron Curtain. She became a prominent concert violinist in Eastern Europe. She lived her Christian faith with determination and would not renounce it. In 1981 she was forced to escape Bulgaria and made her way to the United States, traveling only with her violin and her page from the Bible.

A few days after arriving in America, Margaret visited a small church. A friendly older couple greeted her. They offered to take her shopping and buy her a Christmas gift.

"What would you like?"

"For twenty-five years I have wanted a Bible. I got only one page when I was twelve."

The couple took her to a bookstore. Wide-eyed, Margaret saw Bibles in more colors than she ever imagined! Standing in the middle of the bookstore, she wept tears of joy as she hugged a Bible to her chest. She finally had the entire Word of God.[1]

> *As we open our eyes to grace throughout the Old and New Testaments, the Word of God penetrates our souls with hope and strength.*

This true story shows the love Margaret had for the Word of God. While today many of us are blessed with access to the Bible, it is easy for us to take the Bible for granted and not even open it.

A challenge for all of us is to cherish the Word of God by reading and meditating on it. The psalmist encourages us to hide the Word in our hearts as a way to guide us in holy living. "I have hidden your word in my heart that I might not sin against you." (Ps. 119:11) When the wisdom of the Word is in our hearts, we can draw upon it to renew our inner being. "The law of the LORD is perfect, refreshing the soul. The statutes of the LORD are trustworthy, making wise the simple. The precepts of the LORD are right, giving joy to the heart. The commands of the LORD are radiant, giving light to the eyes." (Ps. 19:7-8)

As we open our eyes to grace throughout the Old and New Testaments, the Word of God penetrates our souls with hope and strength. It transforms our lives and still speaks truth to us today. "Ancient Words," a worship song by Lynn DeShazo, was written as an expression of her love and appreciation for the Bible and those who sacrificed to make it available to us today.

> "Holy words long preserved,
> For our walk in this world.
> They resound with God's own heart
> O, let the ancient words impart.
> Words of life, words of hope
> Give us strength, help us cope
> In this world where'er we roam
> Ancient words will guide us home.
> Ancient words ever true
> changing me and changing you;
> We have come with open hearts,
> O, let the ancient words impart.
> Holy words of our faith
> Handed down to this age,
> Came to us through sacrifice.
> O, heed the faithful words of Christ."[2]

Deepening the Grace Impact

QUESTION: How important is the Bible to you? What steps can you take to have more of it in your life?

SCRIPTURES FOR MEDITATION: Psalm 119:11, 30, 165; 2 Timothy 3:16

PRAYER: Heavenly Father, thank You for the Bible. Open my eyes to see Your grace throughout Your living Word. Give me a hunger and thirst to read it and apply its principles to my life. Amen.

Giving Up the Grind

"Come to me, all who are weary and burdened, and I will give you rest." — Matthew 11:28

The family's SUV carried them from place to place and became their mobile diner as evidenced by food wrappers from many drive-through restaurants. A full calendar dictated their lives, showing them when and where each family member had to be. Soccer practice, guitar lessons, and karate kept the son busy after school. Dance, piano, and scouts occupied the daughter's life. Mom became worn out just trying to keep everything at home going, as well as her career as an accountant. Dad worked overtime in his marketing business to keep finances afloat. Every day ended the same, mom and dad over-tired from the demands of life and the kids exhausted from trying to keep up with it all. Church responsibilities filled Sundays. The overcommitted family had little time to rest.

A flurry of activity has become the badge of identification for many. It states, "I have so much to do." Our time is filled with caring for our families and making a living. These are good things, but too often we leave out the most important relationship — our connection with the Lord. Our drive-thru lives leave Jesus by the side of the road as we go to the next activity.

The Lord doesn't demand us to do more, more, more. On the contrary, He teaches us to rest in Him. Even when crowds pressed in on Him, Jesus slipped away to make time with His Father. Jesus drew strength from this time.

In Matthew 11:28-30 Jesus says, "Come to me, all you who are weary and burdened, and I will give you rest. Take my yoke upon you and learn from me, for I am gentle and humble in heart, and you will find rest for your souls. For my yoke is easy and my burden is light."

We are often yoked to the burden of responsibilities to our families and the calendar full of activities. Life feels overwhelming. People are demanding, and we cry out in desperation. "How can I take on another yoke to help me out when I'm so busy? I don't have time for another thing." Jesus uses an interesting metaphor of a yoke to teach us about the Christian life.

A yoke is a wooden collar that joins two animals, usually oxen, to enable them to pull together. A yoke also refers to a team paired together. When animals are trained with a yoke, a younger, weaker ox is paired with an older, stronger one. Over time they learn to work together, walking in step with one another.

When we are yoked with Jesus, we learn to walk in step with Him. Being the stronger one, He helps carry the burden of stress and worry that is on our backs. His yoke brings relief to our overwhelmed souls.

In *The Message* Bible, Matthew 11:28-30 states "Are you tired? Worn out? Burned out on religion? Come to me. Get away with me and you'll recover your life. I'll show you how to take a real rest. Walk with me and work with me — watch how I do it. Learn the unforced rhythms of grace."

Selah, a Hebrew word of uncertain meaning, appears seventy-four times in the Psalms, and is regarded as a musical term indicating a pause or interlude. Beyond its musical implication, it can be a pause or rest for us in the activity of life. A selah moment would be a time to pause and reflect in the midst of the busyness of life, learning "the unforced rhythms of grace."

Psalm 62:5-7 explains what I call a selah moment, resting in the Lord. "Yes, my soul, find rest in God; my hope comes from him. Truly he is my rock and my salvation; he is my fortress, I will not be shaken. My salvation and my honor depend on God; he is my mighty rock, my refuge."

Choosing to rest in the Lord's sovereign grace is a remedy to the stress of busyness. Breathe deeply of His all-sufficient grace. Accept the invitation from Jesus to be yoked to Him and not to the stress of too much activity. Give up the striving and pressure of the daily grind as you rest your spirit in the Lord. Make time for selah moments.

Deepening the Grace Impact

QUESTIONS: When you are stressed, how do you relax your mind and spirit? When does your spirit feel the most at rest? When was the last time you yoked your burden to Jesus and had a selah moment?

SCRIPTURES FOR MEDITATION: Psalm 62:5; Matthew 11:28-30; Psalm 91:1

PRAYER: Lord, I come to You for rest. The busyness of life is overwhelming, but in You there is peace and rest. Take my weary heart and revive me again through Your unending grace. Amen.

Living Life Unedited

May these words of my mouth and this meditation of my heart be pleasing in your sight, LORD, my Rock and my Redeemer. — Psalm19:14

Perfectionism can be the enemy of grace. It drives you to pursue an impossible standard that is often just beyond your reach. While it is appropriate to strive for excellence in whatever you do, an intense desire for excessively high performance standards can push you to perfectionism.

As a high school piano student, I wanted to do my best to get high comments on the judge's critiques. Practice, drills, and repetition led to excellence. Scales and arpeggios trained my fingers to move with fluidity over the keys. When competition day came, I was confident and well prepared. I had put my heart and soul into memorizing the difficult music. As a senior, this would be my last contest.

Nervously, I stepped into the room and situated myself on the piano bench in front of the judge. Although she was congenial, the clinking sound of her charm bracelet on the desk rattled my nerves. I took a deep breath and positioned my sweaty hands on the keyboard.

I began…*Dissonance …*

Why didn't it sound right? Flustered, a quick glance at my

hands revealed I had placed them on the wrong keys. All those hours of practice and this happens? Unbelievable! My pounding heart sank as I thought any hope for an exceptional score had evaporated, but I had practiced too hard to come to this point and not compete.

"That's okay, just start again," the judge calmly spoke. She shook her wrist a little. The bracelet jingled. If I wasn't unnerved before, I was now.

I inhaled another deep breath and prepared to begin again. I'm sure sweat dripped from my palms; my heart throbbed against my chest. Hands in position again.

This time I got it right. Recovering from the error, I somehow performed the ten Bach masterpieces with determination and accuracy. Relieved, I exited the room to wait for the judge's comments and shook my head in disbelief at my mistake. In spite of my initial blunder, the judge extended grace and gave me high marks. I thought I deserved the worst. I was surprised that the performance was not only good enough, but had gratifying results in spite of my self-imposed stress.

I had started out seeking excellence, but was driven by perfectionism. In *The Search for Significance*, Robert S. McGee explains the performance trap of perfectionism as having to meet certain standards to feel good about oneself. It is unwillingness to fail.[1] An unrealistic, high standard is a cruel taskmaster that drives you to try harder when you've done your best. The demands of painstaking ambition altered my expectations and nearly ruined my enjoyment of piano. If perfection was the only acceptable result of performing music, I could have walked away from the piano disappointed in the realization that I am not perfect, and never played again.

But God in His grace wouldn't let me quit. Over the years, He has shown me how He delights in music that is played from the heart. Wrong notes occasionally happen, but I remember that my goal is to please the Lord, not to play with perfection.

As God has helped me tame the perfectionist within, I have found freedom in seeking excellence over perfectionism. The key is in living life unedited — living every moment in His grace, unafraid of making mistakes. Grace gives me the assurance that what I do, if I do it with the right attitude for the Lord, is good enough. God takes my effort and uses it for His purpose, regardless of the faults.

Psalm 19:14 shows David giving his words to the Lord. "May these words of my mouth and this meditation of my heart be pleasing in your sight, LORD, my Rock and my Redeemer." This is an offering of excellence, giving his best to the Lord. Likewise, our desire should be to offer our finest efforts to the Lord, not being driven by an unrealistic standard of perfectionism.

> *The key is in living life unedited — living every moment in His grace, unafraid of making mistakes.*

The Lord receives the offering of our thoughts, words, and actions when we offer our lives in worship to Him. God's grace empowers us to live confidently in the free-flowing movement of time — not in the perfect performance of life. Perfectionism has a place in professional recordings and great concert halls. However, daily life is unedited — we can't delete our mistakes. Grace allows us to accept mistakes as a part of life and not fear trying again. The grace impact grants us freedom and confidence to escape the bondage of perfectionism.

Deepening the Grace Impact

QUESTIONS: Are you driven by perfectionism? If so, how can you relax any crippling standards and temper them with grace, knowing what you do is good enough? How can you increase your awareness of offering your thoughts and actions as pleasing to the Lord?

SCRIPTURES FOR MEDITATION: Psalm 139:13-16; Romans 12:1-2; Psalm 33:3

PRAYER: Heavenly Father, thank You that I don't have to live a perfect life for You to work through me. Thank You for Your grace that accepts me as I am. Help me lay aside perfectionism and embrace Your grace. Amen.

Spiritual Cardio-Conditioning

Teach me your way, LORD, that I may rely on your faithfulness; give me an undivided heart, that I may fear your name. — Psalm 86:11

Cardiovascular workouts are important to physical health as they strengthen the heart and circulatory system. Walking, running, and swimming are all excellent workouts that increase heart strength and stamina. Often we start a fitness program with good intentions, but after a few weeks, the new motivation has disappeared. It's hard to keep lacing up the sneakers for another day's workout. We know we *should* exercise but find the discipline of effective cardio training difficult. Though it's hard work to sweat and benefit from cardio exercise, the results are worth the effort to continue.

We need to exercise our hearts for the Lord as well. This type of spiritual cardio-conditioning involves developing an undivided heart, a blameless heart, a responsive heart, and a joyful heart. The benefits lead to a stronger commitment in the Christian faith.

The basis for spiritual cardio-training is having an undivided heart. In the original Hebrew language, *undivided* has two meanings. The first meaning is *undiluted in strength*. If something is diluted, it has been watered down and weakened. If it is undiluted, it is potent and powerful when used at full strength. The second meaning of *undivided* is *pure in content*. Pollution and contaminants cause loss of quality. Contrast a pure mountain stream with an oil spill in the ocean to see the difference between corruption and purity.

This verse in Psalms about an undivided heart challenged me at the height of our family activities when lessons, practices, and appointments filled the schedule. I was struggling and asked God how I could continue to serve Him when life was busy. I sought God's strength and wisdom. The Lord whispered that all He asked from me was an undivided heart. I examined my schedule and determined what activities were necessary and which were burdensome or time-consuming. Eventually, and with the Lord's help, I made some adjustments. The result was a happier heart, knowing I was more focused in serving my family and the Lord.

Another aspect of spiritual cardio-conditioning is developing a blameless heart by checking your priorities and loyalties. *Blameless* indicates there are no divided loyalties in your heart as you seek to develop a relationship with God. Nothing else competes for your attention. The challenge is that so many things do vie for our attention and loyalty — family, children, career, sports, leisure activities, and personal wants. These in themselves are not bad, but if they distract us from following the Lord, they become idols, creating divided loyalties.

Blameless also means healing through the restoration of innocence. Steps for restoration of the heart are given in Psalm 51.

Verses 1–2 record a heart cry for God's forgiveness. In verses 3–5 a personal confession makes genuine repentance the basis for an appeal. An urgent petition for cleansing and renewal follows in verses 6–12. Assuming God's merciful answer, commitment to praise and testimony is made in verses 13–17.[1]

Only God can give us the grace to come before Him, and only His grace can restore to us a pure heart, bringing us back into relationship with Him with praise and testimony.

Developing a responsive heart to God is also an important aspect of spiritual cardio-conditioning. By drawing close to the Lord through prayer and reading His Word, we learn to respond to the prompting of the Holy Spirit. Obedience is shown in our willingness to serve the Lord. When the Lord nudges our heart to serve someone, we need to respond with willingness to take action. A responsive heart then takes action — serving meals at a shelter, visiting a lonely friend, or volunteering at church.

The last component in spiritual cardio-training is cultivating a joyful heart. The joyful heart possesses a secret stash of joy as we reflect on what the Lord has done in the past. It expresses thanksgiving for God's provision for each day. When we acknowledge our dependence on Him, we cease striving and rest in His care. A joyful heart also expresses thanksgiving for God's promises. We look to the future with hope because God is already there.

The components of healthy, spiritual cardio-conditioning are an undivided heart, a blameless heart, a responsive heart to serve Him, and a joyful heart that abides in Him.[2]

If your heart is divided by too many distractions, pray and ask the Lord to show you what is hindering your relationship with Him. Identify distractions and then remove whatever is causing you to stumble in your faith walk or diverting your attention. It will take time as the grace impact works in you. Grow toward having an undivided heart — pure, not watered down in your commitment to the Lord. Through spiritual cardio-conditioning, the Lord will teach you His ways and help you walk in His truths. The results will be well worth the effort.

Deepening the Grace Impact

QUESTION: How can you improve your spiritual cardio-conditioning? What do you need to do to have an undivided heart? Using Psalm 51, is there an area of life you need to bring to the Lord for Him to restore?

SCRIPTURES FOR MEDITATION: Psalm 51:10; Psalm 73:26; Psalm 101:2

PRAYER: Lord, I come to You asking You to strengthen my inner self. You are the strength of my heart and my portion forever. Restore my heart with Your purity so I have no divided loyalties. Give me a pure heart to serve You. Amen.

"...may have an abundance for every good work."

Grace begins with God, and then flows to us for the journey of life and through us so we can share His grace. Jesus said, "You are the light of the world... let your light shine before others that they may see your good deeds and glorify your Father in heaven." (Matt. 5:14,16)

We have a responsibility to live a life of grace, letting the love of Christ shine through us. The ripples of the grace impact extend outward to reach more people.

Section four is about living our faith journey with confidence in God. During the dark valleys of trials, the Lord strengthens us to carry on. God uses the challenges in our lives to reflect His grace to the world around us. The grace-giver forgives wrongdoings when it is difficult, sharing the love of the Lord even in the tough times. Our relationships take on new richness when seasoned with grace and forgiveness. Any act of kindness is an act of grace.

Our desire to serve God is motivated by our love for all He has done for us. We are blessed to be a blessing. We are to extend the grace impact in this grace-starved world so that others may know the ultimate life-changing grace of Jesus Christ.

The Race of Faith

Let us run with perseverance the race
marked out for us. — Hebrews 12:1b

Throughout our kids' high school and college years we spent a lot of time cheering for them in many sports. During cross country and track seasons, we became familiar with the warm-up routines of many kinds of runners. Sprinters and distance runners use differing techniques as they prepare for their races.

Athletes warm up their muscles with stretching and light jogging while dressed in sweatshirts and sweatpants. As the time of the race draws near, the warm-up clothes are thrown aside. The preparation is past and the runners will see if their conditioning and training were effective. They crouch at the starting line, anticipating the sound of the starting gun. Preparation...anticipation...BANG...and the race begins.

The writer of Hebrews 12:1-2a reminds us, "Therefore, since we are surrounded by such a great cloud of witnesses, let us throw off everything that hinders and the sin that so easily entangles. And let us run with perseverance the race marked out for us, fixing our eyes on Jesus, the pioneer and perfecter of faith." This speaks to all Christians in our race of faith — how we daily live and persevere in our faith.

Several principles of running the race of faith are shown in this passage. First, we see that we are not alone in the race. The "cloud of witnesses" — the faithful men and women who have gone before us, including grandparents, parents, and others who have prayed for us — lead the way in our race of faith. The grace impact continues in us because of their faith. I am grateful my maternal grandmother was a woman of prayer, who undoubtedly prayed for her grandchildren to live a life of faith. The prayers of others have prepared us for this moment in time, to share the grace impact today. We encourage one another with these truths, knowing we do not run alone.

One unique aspect of a cross-country race is that because the race occurs on a golf course or park, the spectators can be on the course, cheering within feet of the runners as they pass by. This is different from stadium sports where the fans are in bleachers at a distance. The cheering spectators present a picture of how Christians can inspire one another in the faith when we get weary in the race.

Another principle of the race of faith is a conscious decision to get rid of everything that thwarts our progress, throwing off the sin that entangles. In a like manner, runners remove their warm-up clothes so their movements will be unrestricted. For the race of faith, we need to throw off anything that deters us, such as the weightiness of a negative attitude, bitterness, and discontentment. Sin holds us back, like shackles that bind the heart, and keeps us from running at a smooth pace. Maybe it's the sin of self-condemnation played over in the mind, or the sin of behaviors we hope no one sees. Whatever it is, sin must be thrown aside so it won't impede progress.

Take a moment to ponder. If there is something in your life that hinders or entangles you, release it to the Lord through confession. Casting it off will bring freedom, strengthening you to run a better race.

Third, this Hebrews passage encourages us to run with perseverance. Don't give up until the race is over! The race of faith is a marathon, not a sprint. It is less important how we start, than how we finish. Too often we give up before the Lord finishes what He wants to accomplish in us. Be faithful to the finish.

Fourth, run the race marked out for *you*, not anyone else's race. A sprinter wouldn't do well in a long distance race; likewise, a distance runner wouldn't compete well in a sprint. Comparing the two is unfair to both. Your race has its own unique challenges meant especially for you.

When our daughter participated in cross-country, we learned a lot about the sport. The athletes arrived early enough to walk the golf course and see the lay of the land, locating the hills and the curves.

During one particular race, the lead runner took a wrong turn. He thought he was on the right course, but he wasn't. The other runners ran the correct path. His mistake cost him the race because he ran in the wrong direction.

When you compare yourself with someone else, you risk running a race that could take you in the wrong direction. We must be faithful to pursue what God has in mind for each of us.

Finally, keep your focus on a strong finish. During the race of faith, fix your eyes on Jesus. He is the One who ultimately cheers us on to the end. Don't get sidetracked or distracted. Persevere in His grace, being mindful of God's leading.

The faces of the runners at the end of a race show the full gamut of emotions — exuberance, weariness, happiness, and defeat. It's all evident at the finish line.

Perhaps that's the way the race of faith will finish, with everything made known. Persevere, completing the race marked out for you, focusing on Jesus.

The race of faith — this marathon — is made of many smaller races, and continues throughout our lifetime. Sometimes we struggle and sometimes we win. But our eyes must remain on the prize — heaven. It is a prize that is everlasting, that won't tarnish or fade. As the apostle James declared in James 1:12, "Blessed is the one who perseveres under trial because, having stood the test, that person will receive the crown of life that the Lord has promised to those who love him." We train for a crown that will last forever. The grace impact will undergird us in the race of faith.

Deepening the Grace Impact

QUESTION: How are you running the race of faith, with or without perseverance? Are you comparing yourself to someone else or running your own race? How can you improve?

SCRIPTURES FOR MEDITATION: Hebrews 10:35-36; 2 Peter 1:5-8; Colossians 3:1, 2, 12.

PRAYER: Heavenly Father, I need Your help to train every day in the Christian life. I desire to look to You to nourish my soul and guide me. Show me what burdens or sins I need to throw off so I can live in confident faith in You. Help me keep my eyes on You, the Author and Perfecter of my faith. Train my mind and soul to follow You effectively in the marathon of faith for Your glory, not mine. Amen.

Three Dimensional Living

*But whose delight is in the law of the LORD, and who
meditates on his law day and night.* — Psalm 1:2

Although it seems hard to believe, 3-D movies first
made an appearance in 1915.

Costly equipment and production expenses limited the advanced development of these movies. However, over the decades, 3-D movies have made a periodic resurgence with improved audio and special high-definition effects. Frequently, movies are now produced that require the moviegoer to wear stylish 3-D glasses for the best visual effect. Instead of the common two-dimensional presentations on the big screen, the three-dimensional world brings new depth and clarity.

The challenge for us as Christians is to engage in three-dimensional living so we experience the depth and clarity our Lord desires for us. Too often we settle for mediocrity or the comfort of two-dimensional living instead of going deeper in our faith walk. As C.S. Lewis reflected, the problem is that we Christians are far too easily pleased.[1] Psalm 1 describes three-dimensional living as delighting in the Lord, deepening our relationship, and developing fruit for Him.

The first D: *Delight in the Lord.* "Blessed is the one who

does not walk in step with the wicked or stand in the way that sinners take or sit in the company of mockers, but whose delight is in the law of the LORD, and who meditates on his law day and night." (Ps. 1:1-2)

It is too easy to rush past this important discipline of delighting in the law of the Lord. We can get enthused about sporting events, family gatherings, and concerts by our favorite artists, but slip into drudgery or boredom when it's time to read the Word of God. The Word commands us to "grow in the grace and knowledge of our Lord" (2 Pet. 3:18), a clear indication that growth needs to be ongoing. It is better to use a few valuable minutes reading the Word to nourish your heart than to skip it because you don't have enough time. The end result is being more equipped with God's peace and more in tune to make better choices in alignment with God's principles.

It is better to use a few valuable minutes reading the Word to nourish your heart than to skip it because you don't have enough time.

The second D: *Deepen your relationship with the Lord.* The first part of Psalm 1:3 begins, "That person is like a tree planted by streams of water."

Consider two trees. One is scraggly and the other is flourishing, each growing in different locations. The first one grows high on a rocky outcropping without a visible water source. The flourishing tree has large, shady branches with roots that go deep into a riverbank. Although both have a source of nourishment, the rockbound one is stunted while the shady one thrives.

We must choose to be planted by streams of living water and nurture our souls by connecting with God and other believers. When our souls are nourished, we grow closer to God. If we go several days without contact with the Living Water — fellowship with Jesus — our souls begin to thirst for Him. We can either become accustomed to this state of continual thirst and continue in spiritual apathy, or allow the spiritual dryness to be a catalyst that drives us toward God.

Connecting to God must be ongoing, even when we don't feel like it. As we communicate with the Lord through prayer and worship, we deepen our relationship — vertically — with Him. When we share in small groups, we gain insights and grow in our relationships — horizontally — with others.

The third D: *Develop fruit for the Lord.* Just as deeper tree roots improve the abundance of fruit, we develop more fruit for the Lord when we grow deeper in our faith. This is shown in the second part of Psalm 1:3: "which yields its fruit in season and whose leaf does not wither — whatever they do prospers."

The roots take in nutrients for the tree, which in turn help to develop fruit. As believers, our spiritual nourishment isn't just for ourselves, but for bearing fruit that will bless others.

Grace is to be shared with others. The fruit of the Spirit develops within us so we can extend the grace impact by serving others. Serving takes many forms. We might provide childcare for a single mom or volunteer at school, a nonprofit organization, church, etc. Sometimes serving involves making time in our schedules to help someone when there doesn't seem to be time available. Serving means intentionally attending to someone else's needs.

The Lord causes the development of fruit; it does not come from our own efforts. When we put our needs aside to focus on helping someone else, our faith prospers and deepens in a selfless way. Because God is so gracious, often there is a "boomerang blessing" — we receive a blessing in return when we serve.

Nurture your soul by delighting in the law of the Lord, deepening your relationship with Him, and developing lasting fruit. Three-dimensional living can continue throughout your life because of the grace impact.

Deepening the Grace Impact

QUESTION: Which of the three D's — delighting, deepening, or developing — do you need to target for growth? What steps can you take to delight in the Lord, to deepen your relationship, and to develop fruit?

SCRIPTURES FOR MEDITATION: Psalm 112:1; Psalm 119:35; Jeremiah 17:7-8; Ephesians 6:7

PRAYER: Lord, I pray for a greater desire to delight in You, to deepen my relationship with You, and to develop fruit for Your kingdom. Nourish my soul so that I can be effective for You. By Your grace help me grow in three-dimensional living. Amen.

Faith Journey

Blessed are those whose strength is in you, whose hearts are set on pilgrimage. — Psalm 84:5

Hiking is a physical pilgrimage that parallels the spiritual faith journey in challenges and adventure.

We enjoy hiking when we are on vacation. In our eagerness to start a hike in the dense forest on the Napali Coast of Hawaii, Rick and I neglected to take water along with us. The heat, humidity, and sun bore down, gradually sapping our strength, but still we pushed on to see how much trail we could walk. Sometimes we clung to trees for balance; occasionally we found a cave for a brief, cool rest.

On our return journey, we met some hikers just starting into the cliffs and valleys. They were serious hikers; each had a water pack carrier. We must have looked exhausted to them — muddy, panting, and sweating profusely.

"Need a drink?" one asked.

How gracious of them to share! I didn't want to deplete their supply, but I felt parched and desperately needed water.

Though it wasn't much, sipping tepid water infused new strength into my weary body and improved my attitude. The drink and encouragement of fellow hikers made it easier to complete our trek.

Refreshment for the faith journey is just as necessary. If this step is not taken, there can be consequences similar to not being prepared for a long hike. Spiritual refreshment comes from four sources — the Word of God, prayer, worship, and fellowship.

The Bible feeds us. Reading the Word and meditating on it gives strength to the soul. When I am feeling down, I know I can find peace in the Word. When I'm in a crisis, the Lord brings to mind Bible verses that give comfort and guidance. Understanding the Word of God isn't just for knowledge, but also for life application and transformation of our hearts. "The law of the LORD is perfect, refreshing the soul. The statutes of the LORD are trustworthy, making wise the simple." (Ps. 19:7)

Prayer connects us to God; it is the language of our relationship with Him as two friends sharing their hearts. Our words don't have to be eloquent. The power isn't in the person praying; the power comes from the Lord. He wants to hear from us, as we give our cares to Him. First Peter 5:7 offers the hope of prayer: "Cast all your anxiety on him because he cares for you."

Since several of our planned vacation activities had already been cancelled due to weather, we were concerned that the frequent rains would also prevent our hike. As we started on the muddy trail, I prayed we would see God's awesome creation, and that we wouldn't injure our knees or ankles on the slippery path. The sun brightened the afternoon sky. We were thankful for a beautiful day. God cares for us in the details of life, and answered those prayers.

When we worship, our eyes are lifted from the struggle of the journey and focus on the Almighty One. Worship gives us a new perspective as we remember the greatness of God. "Who is like you — majestic in holiness, awesome in glory, working wonders?" (Exod. 15:11b) While on our hike, we paused several times to gaze across the expanse of the Pacific. The crashing waves on the rocks below, the sun shimmering on the water, and playful whales in the distance reflected the beauty of creation. We paused to worship the majesty and wonder of the Lord and felt refreshed in our spirits. It is good to be rejuvenated by quiet moments of worship, even in the busyness of our daily lives. Praise God for who He is and remember, with thanksgiving, what He has done.

Fellowship with others gives us encouragement, both along the way and for the next stage of the journey. God created us with a need for others. A mature believer is farther along the journey than we are, and can teach us about faith. A newer believer is behind us, whom we can encourage. The experienced hikers cheered us on to finish. Near the end of our hike we met someone starting out on the trail. We encouraged them to look forward to breathtaking sights. Fellowship strengthens our resolve to progress when the way gets tough.

When we put our faith in God and decide to follow Him, our faith journey begins. We all have different starting points. Some begin walking the Christian faith as a child, while others begin later, as adults. As we continue this journey of faith, we gradually yield more of our lives to Jesus Christ. The faith journey opens our hearts and minds to the mysteries of God's love and grace. Even when we know God is guiding us on the journey, disobedience can and will happen. This was evidenced by the ancient Hebrews' forty-year wilderness trek. God's faithfulness was apparent as He waited for His people to return to Him. When they did, He led them into the Promised Land. We can also be like Paul, who followed where God led him on his missionary journeys. Each act of obedience keeps our heart tender toward God.

We are all at different places of faith. Some might be in the valley, on a level path, by a quiet stream, or on a rocky road. Throughout the days of your pilgrimage, seek the Lord as your guide. Through the grace impact, God provides what is needed for our journey.

Deepening the Grace Impact

QUESTION: How do you incorporate studying the Bible, prayer, worship, and fellowship into your faith journey? Which one is the strongest? Which is the weakest?

SCRIPTURES FOR MEDITATION: Psalm 84:5-7; *The Word:* Psalm 19:1; *Prayer:* Psalm 5:1-3; *Worship:* John 4:23-24, Psalm 145:8-9, Psalm 103:1-5; *Fellowship:* Acts 2:42, 46, 1 John 1:7

PRAYER: Lord, open my eyes to see what I lack for my faith journey. If it's time in Your Word, open my heart to Your Words of Life. If it's prayer, quiet me to rest in Your presence. If it's worship, fill me with awe for who You are. If it's fellowship, I pray for like-minded believers to encourage and support me. Thank You for providing what I need for my faith journey. Amen.

Passage through the Valley

Even though I walk through the darkest valley,
I will fear no evil, for you are with me; your rod
and your staff, they comfort me. — Psalm 23:4

Mountains are impressive and breathtaking, but a valley may not even be noticed. However, the valley gives depth to the landscape, creating rugged definition to the scenery. Passage through the valley can bring worry and uncertainty.

The steep walls of a valley can seem to close in on you as you descend into a canyon; a rocky path strewn with boulders makes hiking hazardous. It gets hard to distinguish which way the trail goes because of the rockiness. The air becomes cooler from the long shadows of the cliffs that limit sunlight, and darkness falls sooner. The descent can be rigorous, and if it is unfamiliar territory, one misstep could end in an unpleasant injury. In our lives, a valley could represent a time of great despair or loneliness, filled with uncertainty. Everything goes wrong and seems out of control.

Many people in the Bible walked through spiritual valleys. Job faced a dark and lonely valley of immense trials, but his great faith led him through the hard times. The Israelites were often in a dark valley in their wilderness experience when they turned away from God. Daniel walked through an intense valley of persecution that ended in the lion's den, and yet, he recognized the Lord's protection. The disciples walked through a valley of despair after the crucifixion, before knowing the joy of meeting the resurrected Lord.

In Lamentations 3:19-26, the prophet Jeremiah shows us how to change our focus from despair to hope. He was honest about the situation and the hopelessness he felt. "I remember my affliction and my wandering, the bitterness and the gall. I well remember them, and my soul is downcast within me." (v. 19)

But then Jeremiah changes his focus from his dismal situation and remembers several attributes of God — His love, compassion, faithfulness, and provision. "Yet this I *call to mind* and therefore I have hope: Because of the LORD's great love we are not consumed, for his compassions never fail. They are new every morning; great is your faithfulness. I say to myself, 'The LORD is my portion; therefore I will wait for him.' The LORD is good to those whose hope is in him, to the one who seeks him; it is good to wait quietly for the salvation of the LORD." (vv. 21-26, author's emphasis)

Jeremiah's action of calling to mind the faithfulness of his God led him to have hope in what looked like a hopeless situation. The Babylonians had burned Jerusalem, his beloved city, to the ground and carried its people into captivity in a foreign land.

> *Trusting the Lord while in a spiritual valley provides peace in the turmoil.*

In spite of being in this valley of despair, Jeremiah made the decision to wait on the Lord and found his strength renewed.

God's grace also sustained me when I found myself in a valley of despair. Within a seven-month period, a series of crises dominated my life. I stood by the bedside of my dying mother. Days after her funeral I had another tongue biopsy, which was cancerous. Before the week ended, my mother-in-law passed away, and then a few months later, my father-in-law breathed his last. So many devastating events happened within a short span of time, I felt helpless, as if I was trying to straighten the dominoes of my life only to have them fall into a scattered mess again. Overwhelmed with grief and physical weakness, I turned to God to receive His loving embrace.

Knowing that my life was in God's hands, even in the valley of despair, transformed my despair into peace and strength. Through those difficult months, God's love sustained me with hope. I began to see evidences of His love for me — the smile of a friend, an unexpected note of encouragement, or the beauty of a sunset. I could not have come through that intense period without the security of knowing God's love.

Trusting the Lord while in a spiritual valley provides peace in the turmoil. Remember Jeremiah's actions and refocus on the Lord's faithfulness, which gives stability when one is on a rough trail. Trusting in God's sustaining grace will carry you through the valley to a level path on the other side.

Deepening the Grace Impact

QUESTION: How have you reacted when in a valley? How can you prepare or plan to respond the next time?

SCRIPTURES FOR MEDITATION: Psalm 16:2; Psalm 73:21-26; Isaiah 43:1-3

PRAYER: Lord, help me look to You when I'm in a valley of trials. When the walls of despair press in on me, let me recall Your great faithfulness. Thank You that Your grace will see me through the valley. Amen.

Being a Grace-Giver

But grow in the grace and knowledge of our
Lord and Savior Jesus Christ. — 2 Peter 3:18a

The grace of God launches us into a life of faith when we accept Christ as Lord. We grow in our faith by the power of the Holy Spirit. The words of 2 Peter 3:18 above command us to grow in our understanding of the Savior. Through the Holy Spirit, His fruit grows in our lives. Jesus said, "I am the Vine, you are the branches. When you're joined with me and I with you, the relation intimate and organic, the harvest is sure to be abundant. Separated, you can't produce a thing. Anyone who separates from me is deadwood, gathered up and thrown in the bonfire." (John 15:5-7, *The Message*)[1]

Without the love of Jesus, joy and peace are shallow; patience, kindness, and goodness wear thin or wear out; faithfulness will turn into inconsistency; gentleness changes into harshness; and self-control diminishes. But when we position ourselves to depend upon the Lord, the fruit of His love develops in us. Gradually, the fruit of the Spirit becomes evident in our lives — love, joy, peace, patience, kindness, goodness, faithfulness, gentleness, and self-control. (Gal. 5:22-23a) The fruit matures so it can be given away and is shown when we extend the blessings of grace to others.

Unfortunately, we are sometimes stingy and withhold grace when we think someone is unworthy because of a wrongdoing. We cling to the offense instead of grasping for God's forgiveness. When the grace of God is absent, bitterness is born. The words of Hebrews 12:14-15 tell us, "Make every effort to live in peace with everyone and to be holy; without holiness no one will see the Lord. See to it that no one falls short of the grace of God and that no bitter root grows up to cause trouble and defile many."

When we hold onto bitterness, we neglect the impact of God's grace. Resentment and hostility increase bitterness until we can't see anything good in the situation or the people involved. Without grace, we judge others, label them, and let go of hope. Without grace, comparisons emerge that create unhealthy competition, and our relationships are crippled by unrealistic expectations.

Jesus gave us a new instruction — to love. "My command is this: Love each other as I have loved you." (John 15:12) He lived life as the ultimate grace-giver and invites us to walk in his footsteps.

A grace-giver lives moment by moment, in communion with Jesus. Through Him we can forgive others, even when it is difficult. Grace believes the best of people and draws it out of them. When we are aware of extending the grace of God through forgiveness, sin becomes the enemy, not people. The power of God's love fuels His grace in us.

God's grace is shown in many of our relationships — between friends, husbands and wives, parents and children, and between you and the person next to you. By sharing grace with others, people have the freedom to be themselves.

Because God's grace tempers a sour attitude when the Holy Spirit brings forgiveness in our hearts, it is possible to let go of grudges. I learn to constrain potentially harmful comments and adjust my attitude to one of love when it would be easier to yield to spitefulness. Grace and forgiveness give us the flexibility of spirit needed to deal with difficult people.

Grace is also shown when we accept others as they are, even in disappointment. This is the gift from God — grace that forgives and loves when our very nature opposes doing so. The extent of grace in daily life is amazing. Its continual pulse in big, life-changing events, as well as the small everyday events, gives us a glimpse into the depth of God's unmerited love for us. Grace is foundational for stability and strength in the Christian life.

In 1985, an earthquake struck central Mexico, bringing extensive destruction. The intensity of the huge quake was amplified in Mexico City because the metropolis is built on a dry lakebed of silt and volcanic clay sediment. When the earth shook, the soft ground beneath the city intensified the earth's movement. The absence of bedrock below ground greatly increased the devastation.[2]

The life of the Christian should be built on the bedrock of God's grace. By the power of the Holy Spirit, the fruit of the Spirit will grow so we can share it with others. With a solid foundation of grace and faith, the grace impact increases the love, joy, peace patience, kindness, goodness, faithfulness, gentleness, and self-control in our attitudes.

The benefits of being a grace-giver are many. Your heart is lighter — you readily forgive — and you are at peace with others. You become a conduit of God's love, following Jesus' teaching. Even in difficult situations, God's grace is the lubrication that keeps things flowing smoothly. Joy increases and you become more of the person God desires you to be.

Grace alone is the basis for our relationship with God and with others. Through grace God has made Himself known to us — though undeserving, we accept it, and share the gift through love with others. It's not anything we can conjure up.

God has made His grace abound through Jesus Christ. He has saved us and filled us with His Holy Spirit. But the power of grace doesn't stop there. It also enables us to "abound in every good work." (2 Cor. 9:8) We are transformed to open our hearts and pour out God's grace to others. The grace impact continues to touch even more lives.

Deepening the Grace Impact

QUESTION: How are you growing in the grace and knowledge of Jesus Christ? How can you be a grace-giver to those around you?

SCRIPTURES FOR MEDITATION: Hebrews 12:14-15; 2 Corinthians 4:7; Colossians 3:15-17

PRAYER: Lord Jesus, thank You for the precious gift of Your grace. Help me grow in grace with the fruit of the Spirit. Let me be a grace-giver, sharing Your love with the hurting world. Amen.

A New Boldness through Grace

For the Spirit God gave does not make us timid,
but gives us power, love and self-discipline.
So do not be ashamed of the testimony
about our Lord. — 2 Timothy 1:7-8a

Peter dashed out of the courtyard, gasping for breath under the weight of guilt. He paused, staring into the black sky and remembered the recent events. He hung his head, shaken by self-condemnation. Peter had promised Jesus he would not leave him, but then he had fallen asleep. He had flatly denied any association with Jesus when a servant girl approached him on the matter. Then, the sound of the crowing rooster had pierced his soul. In his mind Peter replayed these scenes, and each time the shame and regret drilled deeper into his heart as hot tears spilled onto the dust.

The days that followed were filled with fear and the horror of the brutal crucifixion of his dear friend. When Peter learned the body was taken from the tomb, he and John raced to the burial site in disbelief. Out of breath, they looked in the tomb — empty. Confusion flooded their minds.

Later that night the disciples met together behind locked doors. Questions plagued Peter and condemnation echoed within him. He rested his head against the wall. At least there was some comfort being with the other disciples, although a heavy silence hung over them. When least expected, life had changed. Their leader was gone and so was the boldness to stand with Him.

Abruptly, peace broke the dark confusion in the room. Jesus was there, showing the scars in His hands and side. Joy dispelled their fear though Peter still felt the guilt.

It was days later when Jesus approached Peter by the sea. Jesus looked right into Peter's eyes and forgave him for his actions. His burdened heart felt instant relief.

Later, Peter was present on the hillside when Jesus spoke before He was taken up to heaven. "But you will receive power when the Holy Spirit comes on you; and you will be my witnesses in Jerusalem, and in all Judea and Samaria, and to the ends of the earth." (Acts 1:8) Peter was in the room at Pentecost when the Holy Spirit came upon the disciples. From this point forward, he proclaimed salvation in Jesus.

Empowered by his encounter with the risen Lord, Peter was transformed from fearful to bold by the grace impact. He went on to live a life of power, love, and self-discipline. Peter later wrote, "Therefore be alert and of sober mind so that you may pray. Above all, love each other deeply, because love covers over a multitude of sins." (1 Pet. 4:7b-8) Referencing his actions in the garden with Jesus, Peter knew the consequences of not being alert and praying, but he also knew the depth of Jesus' forgiving love. He had received it in his encounter with Jesus by the sea after the resurrection. Peter concluded his second epistle with, "But grow in the grace and knowledge of our Lord and Savior Jesus Christ. To him be glory both now and forever! Amen." (2 Pet. 3:18) He grew in grace, and his letter commands us to do the same. Like Peter, we need boldness in our personal faith, an attitude of courage to believe, and a desire to live openly for Jesus.

Powerlessness and timidity lead to fearfulness. The spirit of timidity equates to cowardice — which does not come from the Lord. It is easy to let our internal conversation talk us out of doing something bold or difficult. We prefer to stay where things are safe and predictable. However, when we step out in faith, we can trust God because we have the promise that He is with us. God's grace is at work, and we are reminded to look to Him for our confidence.

Three things are promised in 2 Timothy 1:7. First we are promised a spirit of power. The Greek word for power is *dunamis,* the same word from which we derive dynamite.[1] This supernatural power is not a scary explosive. It is the confidence that permits the believer to go forward when the natural reaction is to withdraw.

God's power is available to us through prayer. Prayer has many forms, including praise, thanksgiving, confession of sin, and petition through intense pleading or short arrow prayers breathed for a specific need. The communication line with the heavenly Father is open if we are willing to use it. The Holy Spirit gives us the confidence to speak up or to take a stand for faith. Other times He calms us down when life is out of control. By God's grace we have access to His power.

When I felt weak in spirit and still had to carry on a ministry, God's power enabled me to do what needed done. When His Spirit empowers, the task often turns out better than expected.

Next we are promised *agape* — the highest form of love. This love, the first fruit of the Spirit, comes from God and puts others first. It is self-giving love, not the self-pitying mindset of a victim. We have the promise that perfect love casts out fear. (1 John 4:18) We rely on God's power to show His love to us in difficult situations. God's love has led me to love someone when I would rather not. When we turn to God, His divine love carries on even when our love runs out.

The final part of 2 Timothy 1:7 promises a spirit of self-discipline. This is a person with a sound mind that remains calm and uses wise judgment. Whether it's dealing with fussy children or a difficult individual at work, remember to remain levelheaded and composed. The spirit of self-discipline can curb potentially harmful words. Before reacting to a stressful situation, prayerfully consider your actions. God gives us sound judgment when we turn to Him.

The next time you feel timid, fearful, or powerless, remember Peter's transformation from timid to bold. Read the promise of 2 Timothy 1:7 for power, love, and self-discipline. This verse brings hope to live with confidence and courage. Through the grace impact, our faith can be courageous, loving, and steadfastly committed to obeying Christ.

Deepening the Grace Impact

QUESTION: Think of a situation when you have felt powerless or lacked confidence. Could the promise of 2 Timothy 1:7 have been helpful to you? In what way?

SCRIPTURE FOR MEDITATION: Jeremiah 42:11; 1 Timothy 4:11; Hebrews 4:16

PRAYER: Heavenly Father, I thank You for the promise of a spirit of power, of love, and of self-discipline. So many times I feel weak and fearful. Help me remember to turn to You for the quiet confidence of Your grace. Amen.

Be B.O.L.D. —
Believe On the Lord Daily

Have I not commanded you? Be strong and courageous. Do not be afraid; do not be discouraged, for the LORD your God will be with you wherever you go. — Joshua 1:9

With toes positioned on the edge of the wooden platform forty feet in the air, I took a deep breath to calm my mind and overcome fear. My hands gripped the top of the metal trolley as I entrusted my life to tethered straps, small trolley wheels, and a cable strung between tall fir trees. I was about to step off the solid platform and ride the zip-line to the next platform high in the trees. My feet became like cement. The guide shouted, "Now step out of your comfort zone and go!"

One step off the platform, and zzzzip! I sailed through the forest, feet dangling and holding on to the safety gear for dear life. My legs swung up onto the next platform. Getting unclipped from the cable, I felt the adrenaline rush with the realization: I did it! And was ready to do it again! It wasn't so scary after all.

Zipping through the trees taught me several things about being bold enough to leave familiar surroundings. I had to prepare my heart and mind for the task of overcoming fear. I had to have the proper equipment and trust the guide. And finally, I had to take the step of faith off the platform, looking ahead to the next landing.

Each day brings new challenges in living our faith, sometimes they are familiar and other times the trials are unknown. We are called to be *B.O.L.D.* — *to Believe On the Lord Daily.* Because of God's grace, we can live a life of bold faith. By preparing our minds and hearts with the Word of God, we can face difficulties. By listening to Jesus, we have assurance and trust Him to be with us.

Whenever God has called me to do something unfamiliar, I have felt apprehensive. However, I have the assurance the Lord will be with me in that situation. God has given me opportunities to travel and share his Word in many more places and countries than I ever imagined. Each time God pushed me out of my familiar territory, He was there.

In an earlier devotional (Day Twelve), I shared how God used the Bible studies and teaching aides in my suitcase for His glory in Russia. It wasn't my plan, but God's plan. In Africa, I saw His love in the welcoming faces of believers who had few material possessions, but they were joyful and content (Day Eighteen).

Stepping out of your comfort zone can happen every day, right where you are. Trust in God produces boldness. Many people in the Bible trusted God with a firm and resolute faith.

- Abraham negotiated with God for the fate of the righteous in Sodom. (Gen. 18:22-32)
- Moses pleaded with God on behalf of the Israelites. (Exod. 32:32)
- Ruth stayed with Naomi in unwavering loyalty. (Ruth 1:16)
- David stood before Goliath and defeated him. (1 Sam. 17:45-50)
- Esther went before the king with the mindset of saving her people. "If I perish, I perish," she declared. (Esther 4:12-16)

- Shadrach, Meshach, and Abednego boldly stood against the King's decree to worship him. (Dan. 3:16-18)
- A woman, who was subject to years of bleeding, approached Jesus in faith and dared to believe in healing when she touched the hem of his garment. (Mark 5:25-29)
- Mary, Jesus' mother, yielded to the Heavenly Father's plan to bear the Messiah through obedience. Mary said, "I am the Lord's servant." (Luke 1:38)
- Another Mary anointed Jesus in public, with humility and worship. (John 12:3-8)
- Peter and John proclaimed the Good News. (Acts 4:8-13)
- Paul preached Christ amidst opposition. (Acts 9:26-30)

Many Christ-followers in more recent history were empowered by God with love and a sound mind to take a stand for the Lord.

Elisabeth Elliot's first husband, Jim, was one of five missionaries speared to death in 1956 while attempting to make contact with the fierce Auca tribe (now known as the Huaorani) of eastern Ecuador. Elisabeth later returned as a missionary to the people who killed her husband. The leaders of the tribe eventually converted to Christianity once they understood God's forgiving love. Another evidence of grace occurred when the warrior who murdered her husband became like family to Elisabeth and the other missionaries. Elisabeth has inspired thousands through the godly wisdom of her writing and teaching.[1]

Ruth Graham, wife of Billy Graham, raised five children while her husband was away on extended, evangelistic crusades. Understanding the importance of his calling, Ruth joined Reverend Graham willingly in his ministry, though she preferred her role behind the scenes. She faithfully prayed for their son, Franklin, during his rebellious years. In time, through God's grace, he returned to faith and eventually became the president of the relief organization Samaritan's Purse. Through grace, Ruth Graham demonstrated persevering faith.[2]

Gracia Burnham and her husband Martin were American missionaries in the Philippines for seventeen years. The couple was among a larger group kidnapped by Islamist terrorists. While most of the group was freed, the Burnhams remained in captivity for over a year. A high ransom was demanded for their release. Although a partial ransom was paid, the kidnappers refused to release them. During the eventual rescue attempt by the Philippine Army, Martin was killed by three gunshots to the chest and Gracia was wounded in her right leg.

Since her release, Gracia Burnham has returned to the United States with their three children. She established the Martin and Gracia Burnham Foundation, which includes a focus of ministries to Muslims. Gracia continues to live in unwavering faith, sharing the gospel as a speaker and author.[3]

Who has bold faith? These types of people may be even more familiar to you.

- The mother who stays home with her children but wonders about her worth.
- The single mom who works hard and sacrificially gives to her family.
- The church youth worker who continues to prepare messages to reach bored teens.
- The wife who encourages her husband when he is laid off.
- The teacher who is dedicated to her students though they seem disinterested.
- The woman who invests in her marriage in obedience to the Lord.

- The office worker, who has job challenges, yet seeks to be a godly example in the workplace.
- The person who cares for an elderly parent, showing love and assisting when necessary.

We have the daily choice of being fearful or courageous. The grace of God promises His presence, His power, and His Word for us as we live with bold faith.

With a greater understanding of God's grace may you become *B.O.L.D.—Believe On the Lord Daily*. The grace impact, which originates from God, reveals His character to us. We can have a bold and courageous faith right where we are in life. As you step out of your comfort zone, the grace impact increases, touching more people for God's glory.

Deepening the Grace Impact

QUESTION: When have you stepped out of your comfort zone in faith? How did that increase your boldness?

SCRIPTURES FOR MEDITATION: Hebrews 13:5-6; Philippians 1:6, 20-21; 2 Samuel 22:33-35

PRAYER: Heavenly Father, I praise You for being the Grace-Giver. Thank You for sharing grace with me. Help me to be a channel of Your grace in this hurting world. Help me step out of my comfort zone to live for You in a bold way. Thank You for always being there. In Jesus' name, may I live a life of grace. Amen.

Endnotes

INTRODUCTION

1. *Nelson's New Illustrated Bible Dictionary*, rev. ed. R. F. Youngblood, F. F. Bruce, R. K. Harrison, and Thomas Nelson Publishers, eds. (Nashville: Thomas Nelson, Inc., 1995), s.v. "grace."

2. *Holman Illustrated Bible Dictionary*, (Nashville: Holman Bible Publishers, 2003), s.v. "grace."

3. David Jeremiah, *Captured by Grace* (Nashville: Thomas Nelson Inc., 2006), 14-15.

4. John Newton, "Amazing Grace." 1779.

DAY ONE

1. *Nelson's New Illustrated Bible Dictionary*, rev. ed. R. F. Youngblood, F. F. Bruce, R. K. Harrison, and Thomas Nelson Publishers, eds. (Nashville: Thomas Nelson Inc., 1995), s.v. "holy."

2. Charles R. Swindoll, *Growing Deep in the Christian Life* (Portland: Multnomah, 1986), 215.

DAY THREE

1. Oswald Chambers, *My Utmost for His Highest*, updated ed. James Reimann, ed . (Grand Rapids: Oswald Chambers Publications Assn., 1992), November 17.

DAY FOUR

1. Kenneth W. Osbeck, *Amazing Grace: 366 Inspiring Hymn Stories for Devotions* (Grand Rapids: Kregel Publications,1990), 348.

DAY FIVE

1. Brennan Manning, *The Ragamuffin Gospel* (Sisters, OR: Multnomah, 2005), 165.

2. S. Trevor Francis, "O the Deep, Deep Love of Jesus," published posthumously by Pickering and Inglis in 1926.

DAY EIGHT

1. *Holman Treasury of Key Bible Words: 200 Greek and 200 Hebrews Words Defined and Explained.* Eugene E. Carpenter and Philip W. Comfort (Nashville: Holman, 2000), s.v. "confession."

2. *Holman Treasury of Key Bible Words: 200 Greek and 200 Hebrew Words Defined and Explained.* Eugene E. Carpenter and Philip W. Comfort (Nashville: Holman, 2000), s.v. "repentance."

DAY NINE

1. Mary A. Kassian, *Conversation Peace* (Nashville: B&H Publishing Group, 2004), 92-93.

DAY FIFTEEN

1. "Centennial Olympic Moments, Derek Redmond," n.d., video clip, accessed July 10, 2014, YouTube, https://www.youtube.com/watch?v=OL4HRWpJmng.

2. K.S. Wuest, *Wuest's Word Studies from the Greek New Testament: For the English Reader* (Grand Rapids: Eerdmans,1997), 25.

DAY SEVENTEEN

1. Lewis to Arthur Greeves, 20 December 1943, in *Yours, Jack: Spiritual Direction from C.S. Lewis* (New York: Harper Collins, 2008), 97.

DAY EIGHTEEN

1. "God's Financial Advice-Contentment Versus Want," *Right from the Heart*, April 15, 2010, accessed July 10, 2014, http://rightfromtheheart.org/devotions/gods-financial-advice-contentment-versus-want.

2. Jerry Newcomb, "On the Origins of the Thanksgiving Holiday." http://www.truthinaction.org/November 12, 2012. Accessed August 18, 2014.

DAY NINETEEN

1. Silvia Ledon, "Prayers for Gabriel," *Like A Deer Panting for Water*...(blog), August 5, 20014, http://lgde4me.wordpress.com/2014/08/05/prayers-for-gabriel/.

DAY TWENTY

1. Nancy Leigh DeMoss, "How Much is the Bible Worth?" *Revive Our Hearts*, February 15, 2012, https://www.reviveourhearts.com/radio/revive-our-hearts/how-much-bible-worth/, accessed August 20, 2014.

2. Lynn DeShazo, *Ancient Words*, Integrity's Hosanna Music, 2001. CMG Publishing Print license no. 544248 secured June 24, 2013.

DAY TWENTY-TWO

1. Robert S. McGee, *The Search for Significance: Book and Workbook,* rev. ed. (Nashville: Thomas Nelson. 2003), 30, 34.

DAY TWENTY-THREE

1. H. F . Paschall and H. H. Hobbs, eds., *The Teacher's Bible Commentary* (Nashville: Broadman and Holman Publishers, 1972), 313-314.

2. Dr. Rick L. Grace, "Cardio-Training" (sermon series, Springdale, AR, November 2009).

DAY TWENTY-FIVE

1. C .S. Lewis, *The Weight of Glory and Other Addresses* (Grand Rapids, MI: W. B. Eerdmans, 1975), 26.

DAY TWENTY-EIGHT

1. John 15:5 (*The Message*).

2. Wikipedia, s.v. "1985 Mexico City Earthquake," last modified June 6, 2014, http://en.wikipedia.org/wiki/1985_Mexico_City_ earthquake.

DAY TWENTY-NINE

1. *Holman Treasury of Key Bible Words: 200 Greek and 200 Hebrews Words Defined and Explained.* Eugene E. Carpenter and Philip W. Comfort (Nashville: Holman, 2000), 363.

DAY THIRTY

1. "About Elisabeth," Elisabeth Elliot website, accessed August 20, 2014, http://www.elisabethelliot.org/about.html.

2. Joceyln Y. Stewart, "Ruth Graham, 87; Had Active Role as Wife of Famed Evangelist," *L.A.Times,* June 15, 2007, http:// www.latimes.com/la-me-graham15jun15-story.html.

3. "Biography," Gracia Burnham website, accessed August 20, 2014, http://www.graciaburnham.org/index.asp.

NANCY KAY GRACE

Nancy Kay Grace is captivated by God's grace and loves to share about embracing it in everyday life. She has contributed stories to *Chicken Soup for the Soul: Celebrating Brothers and Sisters, Chicken Soup for the Father and Son Soul, The One Year Life Verse Devotional, Refined By Fire: Defining Moments of Phenomenal Women* and magazine articles in *Just Between Us.*

She is married to her best friend, Rick, who is a senior pastor in northwest Arkansas. They have served the Lord for more than forty years, seeing His grace at work in many countries. Now they enjoy the stage of life with two married children and an increasing number of grandchildren.

www.NancyKayGrace.com
www.Facebook.com/NancyKayGrace
www.Twitter.com/NancyKayGrace

MORE GREAT BOOKS FROM CROSSRIVERMEDIA.COM

THIS I KNOW
Toby Holsinger

Author Tobi Holsinger has discovered that while the Bible was written two thousand years ago, our heavenly Father has some great advice and insight on some of the toughest stuff teens face including rape, gossip, suicide, and peer pressure. Whatever your teen is facing, God understands and His Word holds answers, compassion, and encouragement. Grab your Bible and get ready to take a fresh look at God's Word. – (2014 CSPA Book of the Year)

CARRIED BY GRACE
Debra L. Butterfield

If a family member, a friend, someone you know has sexually abused your child, you know the tumultuous emotions hitting you from all sides. The feelings of confusion and hopelessness. Where do you turn for help? Part memoir, part devotional, author Debra L. Butterfield offers comfort for your heartache, practical guidance for daily needs, a biblical path to healing, and encouragement and hope along the way.

THE BENEFIT PACKAGE
Tamara Clymer

Love, redemption, mercy, provision, revelation and healing… In Psalm 103, David listed just a few of the good things God did for him. His list gives us plenty to be thankful for during tough times. No matter your circumstances, God is always full of compassion, generous with His mercy, unfailing in His love and powerful in healing. When circumstances overwhelm you — unwrap His *Benefit Package* and rediscover God's goodness.

GENERATIONS
Sharon Garlock Spiegel

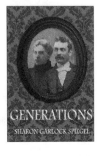

When Edward Garlock was sober, he was a kind, generous, hard-working farmer, providing for his wife and growing family. But when he drank, he transformed into an unpredictable bully, capable of absolute cruelty. When he stepped into a revival tent in the early 1900s the Holy Spirit got ahold of him, changing not only his life, but the future of thousands of others through Edward.

Made in the USA
San Bernardino, CA
15 June 2016

For Billy
with best wishes!

[signature]

Forever Contemporary:
The Economics of Ronald Coase

10-28-15

FOREVER CONTEMPORARY: THE ECONOMICS OF RONALD COASE

EDITED BY CENTO VELJANOVSKI

with contributions from

PHILIP BOOTH

STEPHEN DAVIES

MICHAEL MUNGER

MARK PENNINGTON

MARTIN RICKETTS

ALEX ROBSON

NICOLA TYNAN

CENTO VELJANOVSKI

Institute of
Economic Affairs

First published in Great Britain in 2015 by
The Institute of Economic Affairs
2 Lord North Street
Westminster
London SW1P 3LB
in association with London Publishing Partnership Ltd
www.londonpublishingpartnership.co.uk

The mission of the Institute of Economic Affairs is to improve understanding
of the fundamental institutions of a free society by analysing and expounding
the role of markets in solving economic and social problems.

A CIP catalogue record for this book is available from the British Library.

ISBN 978-0-255-36710-3

Many IEA publications are translated into languages other
than English or are reprinted. Permission to translate or to reprint
should be sought from the Director General at the address above.

Typeset in Kepler by T&T Productions Ltd
www.tandtproductions.com

Printed and bound in Great Britain by Hobbs the Printers Ltd

CONTENTS

Philip Booth

Philip Booth is Editorial and Programme Director at the Institute of Economic Affairs and Professor of Finance, Public Policy and Ethics at St Mary's University, Twickenham. He was formerly Professor of Insurance and Risk Management at the Cass Business School, where he also served as Associate Dean. He has an undergraduate degree in economics from the University of Durham and a PhD in finance. He is a Fellow of the Institute of Actuaries and of the Royal Statistical Society. Previously, Philip Booth worked for the Bank of England as an adviser on financial stability issues. He has written widely, including a number of books, on investment, finance, social insurance and pensions, as well as on the relationship between Catholic social teaching and economics.

Stephen Davies

Dr Stephen Davies is Education Director at the IEA. Previously he was programme officer at the Institute for Humane Studies (IHS) at George Mason University in Virginia. He joined IHS from the UK, where he was Senior Lecturer in the Department of History and Economic History at Manchester Metropolitan University. He has also been a Visiting Scholar at the Social Philosophy and Policy Center at Bowling Green State University, Ohio. A historian, he graduated from St Andrews University in Scotland in 1976 and gained his PhD from the same institution in 1984. He has authored several books, including *Empiricism and History* (Palgrave Macmillan, 2003), and was co-editor with Nigel Ashford of *The Dictionary of Conservative and Libertarian Thought* (Routledge, 1991).

Michael Munger

Michael Munger received an economics PhD from Washington University in 1984. He worked at the US Federal Trade Commission, then taught at Dartmouth College, Texas, and North Carolina State University before moving to Duke University in 1997. He chaired Political Science at Duke from 2000 to 2010, and now directs PPE there. He is a past Public Choice President, as well as past editor of that society's journal. His most recent book is *Choosing in Groups* (Cambridge University Press, 2015).

Mark Pennington

Mark Pennington is Professor of Political Economy at King's College, University of London. He holds a PhD from the London School of Economics and Political Science, and was the winner of the Atlas Institute for Economic Research prize for 'contributions to the understanding of spontaneous order' in 2007. His research focuses on the intersection between politics, philosophy and economics with a particular emphasis on the implications of Hayekian and public choice concepts for the comparative evaluation of socio-economic systems. He has published several books examining these themes, including *Public Choice and the Politics of Government Failure* (Athlone/Continuum, 2000) and *Liberating the Land* (IEA, 2002). He is also the author of *Robust Political Economy* (Edward Elgar, 2010).

Martin Ricketts

Professor Martin Ricketts is Professor of Economic Organisation and was formerly Dean of the School of Humanities at the University of Buckingham. He is also Chairman of the IEA's Academic Advisory Council. He has a DPhil from the University of York and was Research Economist at the Industrial Policy Group from 1970 to 1972 under the direction of John Jewkes. He was next Research Fellow at the Institute of Social and Economic Research, University of York. He joined the academic staff of the University of Buckingham in the autumn of 1977. He has published in professional journals on the new institutional economics, the theory of the firm, entrepreneurship, public choice, aspects of public finance and housing policy and has authored several books. He was Economic Director of the National Economic Development Office (1991–92).

Alex Robson

Alex Robson is Director of the Economic Policy Analysis Program at the Business School, Griffith University (Brisbane,

Australia). He was previously Senior Research Fellow at the SMART Infrastructure Facility at the University of Wollongong, Australia, and lecturer at the Australian National University in Canberra, Australia.

Nicola Tynan

Nicola Tynan is Associate Professor of Economics at Dickinson College, Pennsylvania, where she teaches courses relating to economic history, microeconomics, and environmental and natural resource economics. She holds an MS in government from the London School of Economics and Political Science and a PhD in economics from George Mason University. Her research interests and publications focus on the economic history of water in Britain, particularly London, along with topics in the history of economic thought relating to natural monopoly and institutional choice.

Cento Veljanovski

Dr Cento Veljanovski is Managing Partner of Case Associates, and IEA Fellow in Law & Economics. He was previously Research and Editorial Director at the Institute of Economic Affairs (1989–91), Lecturer in Law and Economics, University College London (1984–87), Research Fellow, Centre for Socio-Legal Studies, Oxford (1974–84), and has held academic positions at UK, North American and Australian universities. He holds several degrees in law and economics (BEc, MEc, DPhil), and is an Associate Member of the Chartered Institute of Arbitrators (ACIArb). Dr Veljanovski has been in private practice since 1990, providing economic analysis in regulatory and competition investigations, and has appeared as an expert witness in many court cases on competition and damage claims. He has written many books and articles on industrial economics, economic reform and law and economics, including *Selling the State: Privatisation in Britain* (Weidenfeld, 1988), *The Economics of Law* (IEA, 1990; second edition, 2006) and *Economic Principles of Law* (Cambridge University Press, 2007).

FOREWORD

It is an honour to be invited to write a foreword to the IEA's volume of essays on Ronald Coase. He was my hero in economics. In my 1973 inaugural lecture at the University of Aston, I selected a football team of UK Economics All-Stars. I made Coase the captain, remarking that the term 'economic insight' means roughly the same as 'ability to read the game'. However one interpreted either term, Coase was endowed with that ability. He reminded me of this honour forty years later, at our last meeting shortly before his death.

In the present volume, Coase has been well served by Cento Veljanovski and his co-authors. They amply describe his vision of economics and his remarkable contributions. In this foreword I simply try to convey something of Coase the economist that I knew.

We used to meet for lunch at the Drake Hotel in Chicago, where he would take a glass of sherry with the consommé. Later, when he was less mobile, he invited me to The Hallmark. He was invariably cheerful and good company. He had a keen sense of fun, and took pleasure in conversation, reminiscing about the past but always noting new insights into how the world works and its sometimes tenuous relationship to modern economic analysis.

I enjoyed these lunches immensely. Coase had a fund of anecdotes about economics and economists, often amusing, always telling. For example, he was in Washington, DC, at the end of the war when Keynes was negotiating loans with the US government. Keynes walked into the room and a colleague effected an introduction: 'Keynes, I don't think you know Coase?' 'No,' said Keynes, shaking his hand, 'I don't think I do,' and moved on. 'That was my life with Keynes,' said Coase wryly.

At the LSE Coase was invited to give the course on nationalised industries. He told me that he sought to identify the two or three distinctive features of each industry and to understand how and why it differed from other industries. For example, the Post Office was characterised by public ownership, monopoly and the universal service obligation. His aim was to understand how these distinctive features led to different policies in each industry. This led him to write numerous papers about the Post Office. There is surely another paper to be written, using the annual syllabuses, reading lists and examination papers at the LSE and elsewhere, explaining how his approach to teaching differed from those of his predecessors and successors.

Lionel Robbins had a graduate seminar at the LSE, where papers were given by students. In 1946–47, 'At the suggestion of Ronald Coase all the seminars were related to economics of public utilities, with the Tennessee Valley Authority as the focus.'[1] Several of the graduate students, such as Ralph Turvey, E. J. Mishan and William Baumol, subsequently became major contributors to public utility

---

1   http://archives.lse.ac.uk/Record.aspx?src=CalmView.Catalog&id
     =ROBBINS%2f4%2f1%2f2&pos=10

economics. Turvey's paper was entitled 'Mr Coase's problem'. I assume that had to do with marginal cost pricing.

In 1951 Coase emigrated to the US. He has said that 'What prompted me to take this step was a combination of a lack of faith in the future of socialist Britain, a liking for life in America ... and an admiration for American economics.'[2] His explanations to me varied, but there was also a more personal element. His famous paper on 'The nature of the firm' was published in the LSE journal *Economica* in 1937. 'Lionel Robbins, in whose department I was, never referred to the article ever.'[3] This hurt Coase. He did not feel particularly valued at the LSE. He told Ning Wang that he probably would have stayed at the LSE if Robbins had ever talked to him. Dorothy Hahn (Hayek's research assistant and wife of economist Frank Hahn) told me that he had a rough ride in a seminar he gave in Robbins's series, including at the hands of Robbins himself, and got somewhat flustered. He was attracted to a visiting post at Buffalo, having met John Sumner, a specialist there on public utilities who had visited the LSE before the war. And though he was offered Hayek's chair at the LSE before he left, it was too late.

Coase never contemplated returning to England, but he always regarded himself as British, never as American. He later wrote to me that 'American economists have a tendency to think that the truth is only to be found in their writings'. He was always deeply proud of being British.

---

2   Coase: 'My evolution as an economist' (in Breit and Spencer 1995).

3   Ibid.

Ning Wang tells me that the British tradition he valued most was tolerance. One of his students became a high official in the British Communist Party. After the war he met the chap again and had a brief but pleasant conversation. 'I never thought they would send me to the Gulag if they came to power', said Coase.

Around 1980 Jack Wiseman and I contemplated writing an economics textbook from a subjectivist perspective. It would have been congenial to the Austrian school of economics and to the UCLA tradition (see Alchian and Allen 1977). We eventually abandoned it, partly because of the time it would take, partly because we could not envisage a sufficient number of teachers and universities adopting it, and partly because we could not always agree on what to write. At one stage I asked Coase for his thoughts, and pressed him on what sort of textbook he would write or recommend. After considerable thought he suggested that each chapter should take a different type of market, and describe how competition actually worked in that market. It was a characteristic response: innovative and reflecting his interest in the real world rather than a theoretical perspective. I fear that such a textbook would require rather more knowledge of the real world, by its writers and adopters, than is commonly the case. But it still seems a project worth pursuing today.

Coase is one of the few economists to have a theorem named after them. As authors in the present volume explain, and as he himself later indicated, he didn't like the Coase Theorem. But he didn't protest at the time, or for some years thereafter. I asked him why. It was because of his respect and affection for his friend and colleague George Stigler, the proponent of the theorem. Stigler was the economist among all his contemporaries that Coase most admired: Stigler always saw things from a new and interesting perspective.[4]

In 1991, Coase was awarded the Nobel Prize in Economics. The two main articles cited were 'The nature of the firm' and 'The problem of social cost'. In one respect, these were atypical Coase articles. They address a general phenomenon rather than a specific practice. Many of Coase's most substantial pieces are studies of how particular industries work. The two Nobel-cited papers, in contrast, are conjectures about how the market as a whole works, illustrated by numerous specific examples. Coase was remarkable in that he could see both the wood and the trees.

On 20 October 1995 the IEA hosted 'A conversation with Ronald Coase' in London. I had the pleasure of introducing him. I thought a bit of Coasian research would be fun. Coase's famous 'Problem of social cost' paper focused on the 1879 case of *Sturges v Bridgman*. Bridgman was a confectioner at 30 Wigmore Street in London's West End. He and his father before him had used mortars and pestles there for more than 60 years. Sturges was a doctor who came to occupy 85 Wimpole Street just round the corner.

---

4   As he wrote in Coase (1982b): 'It is by a magic of his own that Stigler arrives at conclusions which are both unexpected and important. Even those who have reservations about his conclusions will find that a study of his argument has enlarged their understanding of the problem being discussed and that aspects are revealed which were previously hidden. Stigler never deals with a subject which he does not illuminate.'

Eight years later he built a consulting room at the end of his garden and then found that Bridgman's machinery interfered with his consultations. Sturges brought an action against Bridgman and won. Coase argued that the judge's decision in the case determined who had the property right but not what would happen, in particular whether the confectioner's machinery would continue to be used.

I thought it would be interesting to find out what actually did happen. So I paid a visit to the premises. I found new occupiers in both premises – and both seemed to be lawyers! However the property rights are allocated, the lawyers seem to come out on top.

As it happens, the very next year A. W. Brian Simpson published a paper that, inter alia, re-examined the *Sturges v Bridgman* case. He explored in some detail the circumstances of Sturges and Bridgman, and what happened after the case.[5] Some years later, Coase and I were assessing his

5   Simpson (1996: 92) observed that Sir George Jessel, Master of the Rolls hearing the case, 'guessed that Mr Bridgman would find some fairly cheap way of dealing with the problem caused by his mortars. The judge seems to have been right, for Mr Bridgman, somehow or other, dealt with the problem. The business did not move as a result of the litigation.' Simpson continued, 'we may assume that Frederick [Bridgman] died or retired in [1890]. ... At about the turn of the century, 28–34 Wigmore Street was redeveloped and became Norfolk Mansions, the building which now stands on the site.' As for Dr Sturges, 'he practiced from 85 Wimpole Street until his death [in 1894]. ... The premises at 85 Wimpole Street, however, remain just as they were at the time of the litigation and are now occupied by Adlers, a firm of Surveyors, Estate Agents, and Property and Development Consultants, who use Dr Sturges's consulting room for their meetings. If you visit there you will see the original roof light, installed no doubt to enable the doctor the more easily to examine his patients and indicating to this day the original functions of the room.'

papers for possible reprinting. One of his papers (Coase 1996a) responded to Simpson. I remarked to Coase that, despite his criticism, Simpson was a man after Coase's own heart, in that he had actually visited the premises in question. Coase agreed but regretted that Simpson's economics had not been up to the standard of his empirical investigations.

In preparing this foreword, I looked again at the historical and current records. A few small modifications and extensions might be made to Simpson's statements and conjectures.[6] In light of his paper, I may have been mistaken in perceiving lawyers at the two premises in 1995. Of most interest, however, are the inhabitants of the premises today. Dr Sturges's premises at 85 Wimpole Street are now 'The House on Wimpole Street', converted 'especially for therapy and counselling to provide a light and tranquil environment for meeting with your therapist'. Just the thing to recover from high transactions costs. And at 30 Wigmore Street, formerly home to Mr Bridgman's confectionery business, is now 'Amplifon's London branch ... offering expert advice and support with hearing loss'. For the site of a case that turned on noise: you couldn't make it up.

---

6   In 1881 Frederick Bridgman, 74, was still in business as a confectioner at 30 Wigmore Street with his son John W. Bridgman, 41. Frederick died of exhaustion at 30 Wigmore Street on 11 June 1888 (not 1890), age 82. His son was not James Bridgman, in business on the Old Kent Road in 1891, but John W. Bridgman, who in 1891 and 1901 was living on his own means at 4 Blenheim Road. 30 Wigmore Street was uninhabited in 1891. There is reference to the Norfolk Mansions Hotel in 1896.

The combination of empirical investigation and sound economics was central to Coase's research. One of the industries that he studied at the LSE was water. He researched it intensively, especially the era of the early water companies, and put together an extensive set of notes and extracts, which he kept even when he emigrated to the US. Subsequent research and publications on the Post Office, broadcasting and communications and many other topics squeezed out further work. In later years I repeatedly asked him about his research on the early water companies and he repeatedly told me that he intended to write up his notes. In October 1999 I told him it was never top of his to do list, always the bridesmaid, never the bride. In November he told me it had got to number 2. I offered to help but he declined. I had earlier commented that he had not generally worked with colleagues or research assistants; he responded that others didn't seem to see the same things in the material as he did.

A year later I sent Coase a copy of *London's Water Wars – The Competition for London's Water Supply in the Nineteenth Century* by John Graham-Leigh. It sparked his interest, and he wrote to me in a letter dated 14 November 2000:

> At first I thought that I would not need to write my piece but unfortunately on reading the book (rather quickly) I found that he did not analyse the events in a way that an economist would and was unaware of the enormous literature dealing with the problem. So I still have to write my piece although I won't be able to do this until 2002. Graham-Leigh's book is useful in bringing attention to

events of which most economists are unaware and which are economically very significant, although he does not do the job that I hope to do.

This was a man six weeks short of his 90th birthday, deferring work on his water paper for a couple of years because of other work underway. I was alerted to this book by my former OFFER colleague David Walker, who had himself carried out substantial researches into the early water companies and the nineteenth-century gas companies.[7] I sent some of his material to Coase, who said that David Walker 'is doing just the same kind of work I was undertaking in the 1930s'.

Nearly a decade ago, Philip Booth at the Institute of Economic Affairs remarked to me that Coase had been a longstanding member and supporter of the IEA, and they had published papers *about* him but they had never actually published a paper *by* him. We thought it would be good to remedy that. I approached Coase to discuss possibilities. Given his age – then in his mid-90s – my initial proposal was a collection of his reprinted papers with a brief

---

7 'Influenced by Professor Coase and yourself, I wanted to find whether there was any real evidence for the detrimental effects of competition. My initial conclusion was that competition between gas companies happened only sporadically, and the main damage was to the shareholders and (sometimes) the streets. But I could not find any reports of significant gas explosions or failures of supply. I particularly enjoyed what I regard as the success of comparative competition, based on comparative figures collected on the initiative of the radical Joseph Hume MP in 1847, and the failure of the price commissioners who allowed the Chartered Company two price increases in 1873–75'. See also Walker (1995).

introduction by himself. Coase was not keen on re-publishing his papers but promised to consider it.

However, Coase was not to be fobbed off with providing an introduction. At our next meeting a year later he suggested writing a full paper. I was surprised but naturally I agreed. A year later he proposed a monograph rather than a paper. I agreed somewhat apprehensively, conscious that this was now a man in his late nineties. A year later he proposed a book instead of a monograph. A book was more than the IEA had bargained for, or could publish at the time. What next, an encyclopaedia?

On the one hand Coase's latest proposal seemed ever more improbable. On the other hand he seemed to have a plan for delivering it. He was working with a trusted associate, Ning Wang, who had previously been a library assistant and then Coase's research associate. The book was to be on China, about which Coase had previously known virtually nothing, except what he had learned from the travels of Marco Polo. But his intellectual curiosity had been stimulated by China's fantastic growth, and Ning Wang had explained the background. Together they explored the events of the last half century. Not surprisingly, Coase saw a new and striking angle: the instigators of the reforms had not intended to transform China into a market economy, they had been trying to perfect socialism. China's transformation into a market economy was an unintended consequence rather than a deliberate plan.

Coase and Ning Wang delivered the book on schedule, Coase at the age of 102. This must be one of the IEA's proudest accomplishments.

By then Coase was devoting considerable time to encouraging the Chinese to study economics. He hoped they would study how markets actually operated, not how theoretical economics suggested they might or should operate. It was not that he thought the Chinese were better students of economics, or more inclined to his perspective. It was a more pragmatic reason: there were lots of Chinese so that even a small proportion of them sympathetic to his point of view would amount to a lot of scholars studying how markets actually worked, which in his view was the main task of economics.

In his last years I once asked Coase about his working methods. 'I think my analytic powers are as strong as they ever were,' he said, 'but I keep falling asleep.' I said that at his age he was justified in taking a nap in the afternoon. He said he also took a nap in the morning and in the evening. But with Ning Wang's assistance he still kept thinking and writing. Coase may now have fallen asleep for good, but his analytic ideas are as strong as they ever were. This volume will help to encourage an ever wider range of readers to understand and explore the thinking of one of the leading economists of our age.

STEPHEN LITTLECHILD

Emeritus Professor, University of Birmingham,
and Fellow, Judge Business School, University of Cambridge

September 2015

The views expressed in this monograph are, as in all IEA publications, those of the authors and not those of the Institute (which has no corporate view), its managing trustees, Academic Advisory Council members or senior staff. With some exceptions, such as with the publication of lectures, all IEA monographs are blind peer-reviewed by at least two academics or researchers who are experts in the field.

SUMMARY

- R. H. Coase (1910–2013), a leading modern figure in
  the classical liberal tradition, was awarded the Nobel
  Prize in Economics in 1991 for his analysis of the
  significance of transaction costs and property rights
  for the functioning of the economy.
- Before Coase's work in the 1930s, there was no real
  understanding of the relation between the theory of
  the firm and the theory of markets. Coase showed
  that the size and structure of firms, and the location
  of the border between internal exchange within the
  firm and external exchange through markets, are
  systematically related to the costs of transactions.
- These transaction costs, which Coase termed 'costs
  of using the price mechanism', include search and
  information costs (those involved in finding business
  partners, rather than having to produce your own
  inputs), bargaining costs (which rise sharply with the
  number of contractual partners) and enforcement
  costs (which, in the absence of a strong and effective
  legal framework, depend largely on trust in partners).
  When these costs alter dramatically, for example, as
  a result of introducing innovative technology, we can
  expect substantial alterations in firm and market
  structures.

- Coase was a pioneer in the modern analysis of environmental issues. He showed that, with clear property rights and low transactions costs, private solutions to many environmental problems can be achieved without government regulation. Such solutions were logically independent of the initial distribution of property rights. This is highly relevant to a number of modern economic problems which the government currently handles badly, such as land-use planning.

- His work has had a profound effect on later generations of economists, several of whom themselves won Nobel Prizes. His work on environmental issues, for example, influenced another Nobel Prize winner in Elinor Ostrom, whose work focused on how common pool resources could be used effectively with minimal government intervention. This is especially relevant to debates about environmental and ecological degradation in forestry, fishing and game animal resources – perhaps particularly in developing economies.

- Similarly his work on the firm led to the development of the 'New Industrial Economics', now associated with Oliver Williamson, which has changed our understanding of issues of economic governance. This is relevant to current concerns over corporate social responsibility.

- Coase's editorship of the *Journal of Law and Economics* over many years did much to stimulate economic analysis of legal institutions, an innovation which has had a major influence on public policy, particularly in the US. It has fed, for instance, into recommendations for accident compensation.

- Coase's insights have challenged economists' assumptions about the nature of public goods, which he demonstrated could often be provided more effectively by various forms of private initiative. He also illuminated such varied topics as the allocation of spectrum bandwith, the regulation of financial institutions and water resource management.

- Methodologically, Coase was opposed to 'blackboard economics' which relied on theory or econometric analysis at the expense of more practical investigation. He favoured careful examination of case studies and the history of industries when analysing economic policy issues.

- His work retains considerable significance in the twenty-first century. Coase's analysis of China's economic advance, published shortly before his death, sheds light on its future prospects, while his transaction cost approach can be argued to explain the new phenomenon of the 'sharing' economy which is reshaping businesses and employment. Furthermore his work should continue to be at the forefront of debates surrounding regulation, broadcasting and the environment. If policymakers and the economists who advise them ignore Coase, they are in danger of perpetuating policies which may work 'in theory' but do not work effectively in practice.

1 INTRODUCTION

Cento Veljanovski

Ronald Harry Coase (1910–2013) was a great friend and supporter of the IEA. In celebration of his life the authors of this monograph set out his contributions, and how they can frame and assess public policy in the areas in which he wrote and which are currently of importance.

A short biography

Coase was born on 29 December 1910 in Willesden, London. He was the son of a telegraphist in the Post Office and a mother who had been employed in the Post Office but ceased to work on being married. He was an only child, more academic than sporty; often alone but not lonely. At the age of twelve Coase was awarded a scholarship to Kilburn Grammar School. He then entered the London School of Economics (LSE) in October 1929 to read for a Bachelor of Commerce degree. There he took a course on business administration which, to use Coase's words, 'was to change my view of the working of the economic system, or perhaps more accurately was to give me one' (Coase 1997c: 39). This was taught by Arnold Plant, who introduced Coase to Adam Smith's 'invisible hand' and the way a competitive economic system could be coordinated by the pricing system. Plant changed Coase's life – instead of specialising in Industrial Law in his final year and 'undoubtedly' becoming a lawyer, he was set on the road to become an economist. He was awarded a Sir Ernest Cassel Travelling Scholarship to travel in the US studying the structure of American industries. His aim was to discover, mainly by visiting factories and businesses, why industries were organised in different ways. It was this that ignited his interest in transaction costs as an 'explanation of why there are firms'. Coase first formulated this idea in a lecture delivered in Dundee in the summer of 1932, when he was 21 years old. He later developed this into his 1937 article 'The nature of the firm', which helped win him a Nobel Prize in 1991.

Coase held UK teaching positions at the Dundee School of Economics and Commerce (1932–34), the University of Liverpool (1934–35) and the London School of Economics (1935–51). The LSE post was interrupted by the war and government service: he was employed to do statistical work in the Forestry Commission and then the Central Statistical Office.

In 1951 Coase emigrated to the US, disillusioned by the way the British economy and politics were developing. There he held academic positions at the University of Buffalo (1951–59) and the University of Virginia (1959–64). Most importantly he moved in 1964 to the University of Chicago as Professor of Economics in the law school, attracted primarily by the offer to become editor of the *Journal of Law and Economics.* This was a position he held until his retirement in 1982. The editorship of the journal was a source of great satisfaction to Coase, and a crucial part of his research agenda and legacy (Coase 1997: 10):

> I encouraged economists and lawyers to write about the way in which actual markets operated and about how governments actually perform in regulating or undertaking economic activities. The journal was a major factor in creating the new subject, 'law and economics'.

Coase's approach

Ronald Coase was awarded the Sveriges Riksbank Prize in Economic Sciences in Memory of Alfred Nobel in 1991 for his 'discovery and clarification of the significance of transaction costs and property rights for the institutional structure and functioning of the economy'.

Two articles were singled out by the Nobel Committee. Both made transaction costs central to the understanding of economic institutions and the workings of the economy. The first (Coase 1937b), already referred to, was an explanation of why firms exist. Coase's answer was because they economise on the transaction costs of using the market. This theme was again exploited in his second article cited in the award of the Nobel Prize, 'The problem of social cost' (Coase 1960). Here Coase showed that market failure could not arise in perfectly competitive markets. More importantly the reason why markets allegedly failed was because they were costly to use. He replaced the fiction of a perfectly competitive market with one where transaction costs were rife. Yet, paradoxically, Coase never adequately defined or studied transaction costs in any detail.

Coase's central thesis was that policy should be based on the comparison of the costs of market and regulatory solutions, not by reference to the unattainable theoretical benchmark of the perfectly competitive market. He advocated an economic framework built around the comparison of 'the total product obtainable with alternative social arrangements' (Coase 1960: 40), and 'to start our analysis with a situation approximating that which actually exists, to examine the effects of a proposed policy change and to attempt to decide whether the whether the new situation would be, in total, better or worse than the original one' (ibid.: 43). In today's language this requires a full-scale efficiency analysis not solely of the market and ideal policy solutions but of actual options. While this may seem obvious, policy continues to draw on the market failures framework which typically assumes government intervention to be motivated by efficiency and, if not costless, then at least effective. The prospect of regulatory failure is only weakly countenanced, although in recent decades there has been greater appreciation of how regulation fails.

Many have read Coase's work as a 'market manifesto' which demonstrated that the market is better than regulation. It is correct to say that Coase's analysis fostered a greater appreciation of the role of markets and market-like solutions to economic problems, and that often markets were thought to 'fail' not because they were intrinsically incapable of resolving the conflicting interests, but because of a failure clearly to delineate the underlying property and other legal rights. But it should be borne in mind that Coase was essentially studying and trying to explain the boundary between 'the market' and 'the non-market'.

Coase also pursued and advocated a particular empirical agenda: the detailed study of real-world markets, institutions and laws. His empirical approach was the case study, with its detailed analysis of how business and regulation operated in practice. This research method has more in common with economic history, and the case study approach familiar in law and business schools. Coase's work on the British Broadcasting Corporation (Coase 1950) and the UK Post Office (Coase 1961a), and later in his career Fisher Body (Coase 2000), were all detailed studies of the evolution of those institutions, and the real-world factors that explained their structure. This same approach was used to question the examples used by economists to illustrate market failure (Coase 1974b).

The world has changed considerably, as has economics, since Coase set out his original theories of the firm and public policy economics over seven decades ago. Today one would like to say that few economists would ignore institutions, or the importance of property rights, and/or fail to take into account the costs of state and regulatory intervention. It is also fair to say that transaction costs have been the focus of increasing work by economists in

5

approaches that often do not refer back to Coase – such as the economics of information, principal–agent analysis, game theory, risk analysis, and so on. The work of Coase and others has contributed to the empirical analysis of regulation and economic history, and these are now core aspects of modern economics.

Yet economics has developed in ways that disappointed Coase – the increase in abstract theorising, the mathematisation of economics, the persistence of the market failures framework, its over-reliance on econometrics as an empirical technique, the absence of an historical context or the detailed study of the functioning of markets and institutions. This has led to a certain hubris among economists, who have generally been reactive rather than innovative in their analysis of real-world problems. The failure of the profession to spot the looming global financial crisis says much about modern economics.

What of the future?

What can Coase's analysis contribute to the future development of the discipline of economics and the improvement of public policy?

Firstly, it has to be appreciated that the man was not a 'policy wonk'. He turned his back on the economics of antitrust, which he taught at Chicago, because he felt it forced economists to develop quick fixes. As he said, 'I have also suggested that this would yield the best results if conducted in an atmosphere in which the scientific spirit is not contaminated by a desire (or felt obligation) to find quick solutions to difficult policy issues' (Coase 1972a: 70).

Coase's approach puts institutions and laws at the centre of the analysis of markets and firms, both in understanding them and in developing market-based solutions based on defined property rights.

He argued that economics should be more 'microanalytical', to use the expression of Oliver Williamson (1975), who built on Coase's work to develop a transactions costs framework (Coase 1972a: 70):

> Satisfactory views on policy can only come from a patient study of how, in practice, the market, firms and governments handle the problem of harmful effects. Economists need to study the work of the broker in bringing parties together, the effectiveness of restrictive covenants, the problems of the large-scale real-estate development company, the operation of government zoning and other regulating activities. It is my belief that economists, and policy-makers generally, have tended to over-estimate the advantages which come from governmental regulation. But this belief, even if justified, does not do more than suggest that government regulation should be curtailed. It does not tell us where the boundary line should be drawn. This, it seems to me, has to come from a detailed investigation of the actual results of handling the problem in different ways.

He suggested a major research project of studying business contracts.

Contributions

The rest of this monograph considers in more depth various aspects of Coase's work.

Cento Veljanovski (Chapter 2) sets out the main tenets of Coase's approach and the way he saw economics. This identifies transaction costs and property rights as the central concepts of his scholarship, with empirical research based on a very detailed study of the institutional and economic behaviour of actual markets.

Martin Ricketts (Chapter 3) discusses the way economics has been influenced by Coase's theory of the firm. The concept of transaction costs has been useful and encouraged the economic analysis of the scope, internal governance and ownership of firms. This has fostered a rich literature in industrial organisation, focusing not only on why firms exist, but also on their governance and internal structure. It also covers different types of firms such as for-profit and not-for-profit (including cooperatives), and the hierarchical nature of different for-profit firms. Ricketts notes that omitting consideration of the full range of responses to transactional hazards through private governance as well as state regulation is potentially a significant cause of regulatory failure.

Alex Robson (Chapter 4) expands on Coase's approach to natural monopoly and industry regulation. The hallmark of Coase's work is the careful attention he paid to institutional arrangements and historical details such as legal rules and property rights, motivated almost always by 'real-world' commercial issues or policy questions.

Mark Pennington (Chapter 5) looks at the impact and relevance of Coase's work on environmental control. This work fostered an increasing recognition of the importance of property rights and market-like response to environmental problems. Yet, as Pennington observes, the relationship between Coase's ideas and those who study environmental policy is 'a perplexing one' – Coase's 'Problem of social cost' is one of the most widely cited articles in environmental political economy, yet his ideas are routinely ignored as interesting, but unrealistic, and ethically problematic. Pennington argues that both practical and ethical objections are misguided. Far from being unrealistic, Coase's analysis suggests a pragmatic case for a greater reliance on market processes and property rights to tackle environmental issues. Far from being unethical, Coase's arguments point toward the importance of moral pluralism and respect for individual differences in the process of environmental valuation. Pennington goes on to set out a Coasian framework supporting a greater scope for bargaining between individuals and organisations and stresses the importance of government action in enforcing property rights and resolving disputes where such rights are contested. He points to the strength of Coase's 'comparative institutions' approach, where the costs and benefits can assist in identifying the boundaries between 'private solutions', 'public solutions' and 'no solutions'.

Nicola Tynan (Chapter 6) looks at the insights Coase's work can generate for the pressing problem of water scarcity, and the role and evolution of water rights across the world. Water resource management today must determine, to quote Coase (1960: 27) whether 'the gain from preventing the harm is greater than the loss which would be suffered elsewhere as a result of stopping the action which produces the harm.' Full-cost pricing and clearly defined rights for all water resources can help make this determination. One important technique is the definition of rights in water, allowing them to be traded in a market. Tynan notes that the acceptance of property rights, water pricing and water markets is happening slowly but surely.

Stephen Davies (Chapter 7) examines private solutions to the collective and public goods problems. The concept of a public good, non-rivalrous in consumption and non-excludable (Samuelson 1954), has been central to the market failure framework and the consequent call for state intervention and production. The archetypal public good is said to be defence, but the category has often been extended to areas where it is deemed that the state should fund, supply and produce a good or service. The concept has been pushed much too far, for example, the treatment of broadcasting as a public good. According to Davies, Coase set out an extensive research agenda for empirical economic and economic historical research of public goods. Davies shows that this is a grossly under-researched area, and that historically individuals and private enterprises, without the assistance of the state, have found solutions to the public goods problem. Moreover, not all public goods are the same. Some are 'club' goods, where individuals can organise collectively to find a solution to the excludability and pricing issues. Other public goods issues have been resolved by more innovative solutions with the assistance of collective organisations, as with the funding of lighthouses in the past. To quote Davies's fitting words to describe Coase's research agenda:

> When he published his article on public goods and the example of the lighthouse all those years ago, Ronald Coase did what all good social scientists should do. He refused to take for granted and assume without question something that seemed self-evidently correct to most of his colleagues. Instead he looked at the empirical evidence of history and asked pointed and important theoretical questions – in this case granting that there was a public goods problem, why assume that the only way to address it was through government? This generates a very rich and fruitful research agenda, and investigating these matters reveals things such as the contemporary growth of private governance and the plethora of historical private means of solving public goods challenges. We may actually come to very radical conclusions such as that most so-called public goods are actually club goods and that the very need for government is contingent and historically specific rather than essential. All this comes from simply asking questions.

In Chapter 8, Philip Booth looks at financial markets using Coase's discussion of the private provision of lighthouse. Coase showed that while 'blackboard economics' indicated that the private provision of lighthouses was impossible in theory they were in fact provided in England. There is, Booth contends, a similar logic evident in the development of financial regulation today – a widespread belief that market failure is endemic and that the state regulation of financial markets is necessary. But the historical evidence shows that the participants in financial markets developed self-regulatory institutions, rules, codes and penalty structures. There are still several examples of club-based financial regulation operating internationally, for example, the International Swaps and Derivatives Association, and examples of private regulation though very much under state supervision – such as the UK's Alternative Investment Market. Based on historical analysis in the tradition of Coase, Booth concludes that the two key issues for the future development of financial regulation are (a) the empirical question of the comparative effectiveness of state and private regulation, and the nature and mix of each; and (b) whether private regulation (and one should add state regulation) gives rise to market power intentionally or unintentionally when dealing with a perceived market failure.

Finally, Michael Munger (Chapter 9) sets out a thought-provoking discussion of how transactions costs are the driving force of the 'sharing economy', and more. One cannot avoid being infected by Munger's application of Coase's insight. He argues that we are at the frontier of the 'third human entrepreneurial revolution, the "Transactions Costs Revolution"'. In the new economy the key economic activity is 'selling reductions in transactions costs'. This is what Munger says middlemen do, what the new communications platforms facilitate, and what apps bring to the consumer. Uber, Amazon, AirBnB and other online services and apps reduce transaction costs by (in brief) supplying relevant information, assuring safety and quality, and providing a reliable transactional system. Whether this is all about the sharing economy is moot, but one can see the portent of his 'buy or rent' discussion of power tools. If the owners of power tools were able to rent them easily – to develop a market in power tool sharing – then not only would the utilisation of existing power tools go up rather than lying in garages, but the production of new power tools would dramatically fall. The economic consequences of this for power tool firms, their employees, suppliers and distributors would be profound. The hostile reception recently given the Uber ride sharing app by the taxi industry indicates the disruptive and transforming effects of this type of innovation. Munger goes further to suggest, provocatively, the death of the firm and the long-term employment contract – trends which are already in play in many economies as a result of the disruptive effects of technology. It would be paradoxical if Coase's fundamental insight about transactions costs last century led in this century to the demise of large firms and insti-tutions, and a return to a much more atomistic, perhaps even anarchistic, economic structure which we know as the market. If we go along with Munger's thesis, then in the second century of Coase's economics it will be used not to explain institutions but the death of institutions; to become anti-institutional economics – a fitting tribute to the resilience of Coase's work.

2 THE ECONOMICS OF RONALD COASE

Cento Veljanovski

Ronald Coase based his economics on the real world, on the study of the firm and the market, and his application of simple economics artfully applied to came to novel conclusions which he said were 'so simple' as to make them 'truths' which were 'self-evident' Coase (1988: 1).

I trace here the development of Coase's economics, describing his contributions (a full list of his publications appears at the end of this volume), and the essence of the law and economics enterprise he fostered.[1]

What Coase did

In two articles separated by over two decades, the last written over half a century ago, Coase used one theme to change the way economists and lawyers think about the nature of economics, and how it should be applied.

---

1 While at university in Australia in the early 1970s, reading law and economics, I was much impressed by Coase's ideas and the debate they gave rise to. This influenced my research and my first published article was on the Coase Theorem (Veljanovski 1977, 1982). The exchange between Ng, Walsh, Swan and me in the *Economic Record* during the 1970s was one of the first debates outside the US (Medema 2014).

In his 1937 article 'The nature of the firm' Coase asked the elementary question: Why are there firms? Economics provided no convincing explanation since in perfect competition tasks carried out by the firm could just as easily be undertaken in the market by means of contracts between independent suppliers, manufacturers and jobbers. The firm was simply represented as a cost schedule as in Marshall's 'representative firm'. The answer Coase offered was that the firm was a cheaper way of organising production. In the market there were transaction costs – the costs of negotiating, bargaining and enforcing contracts. When these costs became excessive, the market was replaced by the firm (the 'non-market') because it was cheaper. Other institutions arose for the same reason. Coase's article was largely ignored for the ensuing three decades.

In 1959 and 1960 Coase wrote two articles, 'The Federal Communications Commission' and the follow-up 'The problem of social cost', respectively. Transaction costs again featured prominently. 'Social cost' is the more important of these articles, although Coase's study of the FCC could be said to have had the greater policy impact, as I show below.

'Social cost' is one of the most cited[2] and most misunderstood of articles. It develops a number of themes in an informal way, using simple descriptive economic logic. But at its heart is an attack on the concept of market

---

2   According to Shapiro (1996), by the late 1990s it was the most cited article in US law journals, outstripping the next most cited article by two to one. A more recent assessment by Landes and Sonia (2012) shows Coase's work remains much cited and durable.

failure as a framework for policy analysis, which at the time was associated with A. C. Pigou's *The Economics of Welfare* (1920). Economists then habitually used, and still use, the competitive market as a benchmark to evaluate economic performance. They declared that a market has failed when there is any departure from the competitive model's assumptions, and recommended corrective government intervention. Coase criticised this approach on several grounds – that it was wrong in theory, failed properly to diagnose the cause of 'market failure', and assumed costless efficiency-motivated government intervention. In highlighting these issues he offered a profound critique and alternative to the market-failure approach which Demsetz (1969) called the 'comparative institutions' approach.

Coase's first criticism was that at the heart of the textbook model of perfect competition was a contradiction – it implicitly assumed zero transactions costs – which ruled out the possibility of market failure. If coordinating economic activity was costless, then markets could not fail; just as costless central planning, socialism and regulation could not fail. Indeed, subsequent research showed that many of the examples used by economists to illustrate market failure – such as bees pollinating apple orchards (Chueng 1973), trespassing cattle and the provision of lighthouse services (Coase 1974) – were completely misleading, as in the real world firms and individuals had negotiated solutions (see the articles collected in Spulber (2002)).

Coase went on to show that in the unreal world of zero transactions costs the initial legal position, or property rights, did not affect the efficient outcome. The parties would bargain to efficiently resolve otherwise putatively external harmful or beneficial incidental effects. This became known as the 'Coase Theorem', a term coined by George Stigler (1966: 113) though disdained by Coase, which said that 'under perfect competition... private and social costs will be equal', or to use the words Coase's words (Coase 1959: 27):

> the delineation of rights is an essential prelude to market transactions; but the ultimate result (which maximizes the value of production) is independent of the legal decision, when transactions costs are zero.

The logic of the Coase Theorem rides on the rails of the opportunity cost concept 'that a receipt foregone [sic] of a given amount is equivalent to a payment of the same amount'. This concept, while central to modern economics, derived from a different view of costs then circulating at the London School of Economics (LSE) which had not influenced mainstream economics at the time.[3]

---

3   Coase wrote a series of twelve short articles published in *The Accountant* in 1938, where he stated that: 'The notion of costs which will be used is that of "opportunity" or "alternative" cost. The cost of doing anything consists of the receipts which could have been obtained if that particular decision had not been taken... This particular concept of costs would seem to be the only one which is of use in the solution of business problems, since it concentrates attention on the alternative courses of action which are open to the businessman' (Coase 1938). He said this concept of costs encompasses non-monetary elements, implied profit maximisation, was forward-looking and must be calculated by reference to a specific decision. A shorter version appears in Buchanan and Thirlby (1973).

The theorem is easy to explain. Suppose that there is a factory belching out smoke causing discomfort, illness and irritation to the surrounding residents. If the law bans the factory emitting smoke without the agreement of the residents, the polluting factory must negotiate permission from the residents or pay compensation. The factory's profit and loss account directly takes into account the monetary costs of the harm. If the factory owner has the right to belch out smoke, the market failure approach claimed that he would not bear the costs of the harm – there would be a divergence between private and social costs, and the market will have failed. Coase pointed out that if bargaining was costless and the parties acted rationally, the victims would pay the factory to reduce the level of smoke to the point where the payment offered equalled the marginal profit that the factory gained from belching out less smoke. At the margin the factory owner would face the costs of the incremental harm in terms of the forgone payment from the residents to reduce the level of smoke a further unit. In each case the social costs of smoke are taken into account by the factory owner and residents.

The Coase Theorem generated considerable controversy (Veljanovski 1977, 1982)[4]. It strikes nearly everybody on

---

4   Coase said that this was the argument that convinced economists at the University of Chicago who first rejected his claim (Coase 1997a):

   I said I'd like to have an opportunity to discuss my error. Aaron Director arranged a meeting at his home. Director was there, Milton Friedman was there, George Stigler was there, Arnold Harberger was there, John McGee was there – all the big shots of Chicago were there, and they came to set me right. They liked me, but they thought I was wrong. I expounded my views and then they questioned me and first hearing as wrong, and subsequently as a tautology or theoretical special case. But its logic is impeccable. Most commentators never got beyond treating the theorem as an extreme market manifesto – that markets would resolve all social evils – so long as government clearly defined property rights. While Coase is largely known for the Coase Theorem, a fact that perplexed and disappointed him, and as setting out a market manifesto,[5] his work points to the power of private solutions, and against the abstract and unreflecting support for government intervention.

Notwithstanding the counterintuitive and novel nature of the theorem, it was emphatically not central to Coase's

---

questioned me. Milton was the person who did most of the questioning and others took part. I remember at one stage, Harberger saying, 'Well, if you can't say that the marginal cost schedule changes when there's a change in liability, he can run right through.' What he meant was that, if this was so, there was no way of stopping me from reaching my conclusions. And of course that was right. I said, 'What is the cost schedule if a person is liable, and what is the cost schedule if he isn't liable for damage?' It's the same. The opportunity cost doesn't shift. There were a lot of other points too, but the decisive thing was that this schedule didn't change. They thought if someone was liable it would be different than if he weren't.

Stigler (1988) describes the initial reception to the Coase Theorem by twenty Chicago economists at Aaron Director's home: 'We strongly objected to this heresy. ... In the course of two hours of argument the vote went from twenty against and one for Coase to twenty-one for Coase. What an exhilarating event!'

5   Joseph Stiglitz, for one, boldly set out a 'Generalized Coase Fallacy' that 'private solutions can do just as well as government, no government is needed' claiming outrageously that 'This view is loosely attributed to Coase' (Stiglitz 1989: 37, 36). He then posited the 'Fundamental Non-decentralisation Theorem' that 'market allocations cannot be attained without government intervention' and 'it is only under exceptional circumstances that markets are efficient' (ibid.: 38).

economics. He was merely showing that the standard approach was flawed. As Coase (1998: 174) said: 'The world of zero transaction costs has often been described as a Coasian world. Nothing could be further from the truth. It is the world of modern economic theory, one which I was hoping to persuade economists to leave'.[6]

The 'world of zero transactions costs' was the springboard for a more profound and, as Coase argued, fairly obvious reorientation of applied economics (Coase 1960: 27):

> A better approach would seem to be to start our analysis with a situation approximating that which actually exists, to examine the effects of a proposed policy change and to attempt to decide whether the new situation would be, in total, better or worse than the original one. In this way, conclusions for policy would have some relevance to the actual situation.
>
> It would clearly be desirable if the only actions performed were those in which what was gained was worth more than what was lost. But in choosing between social arrangements within the context of which individual decisions are made, we have to bear in mind that a change in the existing system which will lead to an improvement in some decisions may well lead to a worsening of others. Furthermore we have to take into account the costs involved in operating the various social arrangements

---

6   Coase hated the theorem: 'I never liked the Coase Theorem', he claimed in an EconTalk podcast in 2012. 'I don't like it because it's a proposition about a system in which there were no transaction costs. It's a system which couldn't exist. And therefore it's quite unimaginable.'

(whether it be the working of a market or of a government department) as well as the costs involved in moving to a new system. In devising and choosing between social arrangements we should have regard for the total effect. This, above all, is the change in approach which I am advocating.

'Social cost' developed other very important propositions and implications which have, in my view, largely been overlooked.

The first is the *principle of reciprocality*. Coase emphasised that the typical problem of law and economics is a reciprocal one. Resources are scarce, activities clash; interests conflict, and to protect A's interest is to limit B's interests. 'The problem we face in dealing with actions which have harmful effects,' stated Coase (ibid.: 1), 'is not simply one of restraining those responsible for them. What has to be decided is whether the gain from preventing the harm is greater than the loss which would be suffered elsewhere as a result of stopping the action which produces the harm'.

A corollary of the principle of reciprocality is the *irrelevance of causation*. The question 'who caused the harm or accident' is from an economic viewpoint irrelevant. Both parties 'caused' the harm, in the sense that if one withdrew from the interaction there would have been no harm. Harm is the result of the confluence of two or more activities at a particular point in time. This contrasts with the approach of economists prior to Coase's analysis (and still today) who based their policy prescriptions on physical cost (or benefit) causation. The Pigovian approach took the view that if A harmed B, then the external costs were attributable to A. This overlooked the fact that the better response may be to remove B from being a victim. For example, a bridge collapses onto a house. It would be extreme to suggest that the victim was responsible or could have prevented the accident. But the issue is not the immediate question of who could have prevented the accident but whether the losses would have been less had the house not been built close to the bridge. This is not to dispute the importance of physical causation or moral precepts surrounding harm, only that from an economic viewpoint causation is not the key factor in determining whether the two incompatible activities should co-locate, and which party should take any avoidance action.

This view of the legal and economic problem leads to two important subsidiary tenets:

- Joint costs. Since an accident or harmful activity is jointly caused, the loss is the joint cost of both activities. The implication is that efficiency requires both activities, either explicitly or in the opportunity cost sense, to bear the full costs of external harmful actions.
- Cheapest cost avoider need not be the cost bearer.[7] The party who can most efficiently avoid harm need not be the one who bears the cost of doing so. This falls out of the Coase Theorem, which shows that the efficient outcome occurs irrespective of which party

---

7   This concept was brought home to lawyers by Guido Calabresi (1967, 1970).

must pay for the reduction in harm. In the pollution example above, the party best able to reduce the level of pollution did so whether required to pay compensation or offered payment by the victims. That is, there was an economic symmetry between the polluter pays and victim pays approaches. Real-world examples of the latter abound: governments pay subsidies to industry to abate pollution, and bounties to farmers to cut back excessive production. In this sense economics has no notion of 'harm' and 'benefit', suggesting that these notions really reflect distributional values.

Coase's impact

Coase's work did not lead to a revolution in economics or public policy in the same sense that Keynes' General Theory did. Yet it did progressively stimulate two distinct intellectual developments: New Institutional Economics[8] on the one hand and the economic analysis of law on the other. As Coase commented in his 1991 Nobel Prize acceptance speech, while Social Cost had a considerable impact on legal scholarship, it had been largely neglected by economists.[9] Nonetheless, even though Coase

---

8   Coase co-founded the International Society for New Institutional Economics (www.isnie.org). See Williamson (2000) and Menard and Shirley (2005).

9   Coase (1992: 717) said: 'I now turn to the other article cited by the Swedish Academy, "The problem of social cost," published some thirty years ago. I will not say much about its influence on legal scholarship, which has been immense, but will mainly consider its influence on economics, which has not been immense, although I believe that in time it will be'.

effectively stopped writing over four decades ago and his contribution rests on two articles, he remains the most cited economist in law and economics, and his influence the most durable.

Notwithstanding this, arguably one of Coase's greatest contributions came as editor from 1964 to 1982 of the *Journal of Law and Economics*, where he fostered a generation of scholarship based on his research agenda. In March 1993 the *Journal of Economic Literature*, published by the American Economic Association, introduced 'Law and Economics' as a separate classification formally recognising the field among economists.

New Institutional Economics (NIE)

Coase's work was picked up most notably by Douglass C. North (1999) and Oliver Williamson (1975, 1985, 2009a,b), both of whom went on to receive Nobel Prizes in 1993 and 2009 respectively; North with Fogel 'for having renewed research in economic history by applying economic theory and quantitative methods in order to explain economic and institutional change' called the New Economic History or Cliometrics; and Williamson (and Elinor Ostrom) 'for his analysis of economic governance, especially the boundaries of the firm'.

Williamson's work in particular examined the organisational structure of firms and contracts through the prism of transaction costs. He observed that Coase had left his central transaction cost concept 'non-operational'. Although Coase gave transaction costs a practical definition,[10] they remained something of a theoretical artefact, almost tautologically defined as the frictions that prevented efficient outcomes. Coase (1998b: 6) later said that: 'Dahlman crystallized the concept of transaction costs by describing them as "search and information costs, bargaining and decision costs, and policing and enforcement costs"' (Dahlman 1979). Williamson expanded the taxonomy of transaction costs (to include information costs, risk and uncertainty, asset specificity, strategic behaviour and opportunism) in order to investigate firm behaviour and institutional arrangements. Like Coase's work on the firm, his analysis showed that real-world institutions and contracts could be explained as efforts by the parties to reduce transactions costs. This has led to the type of 'microanalytical' empirical research advocated by Coase.[11]

It should be added that others contributed to the NIE agenda, in particular the work on property rights associated with Furubotn and Pejovich (1974), Demstez (1964, 1968), Alchian (1961, 1967), Alchian and Demsetz (1973), Dale (1968), and others.

---

10 Coase (1960: 18) defined transactions costs in the following terms:

In order to carry out a market transaction it is necessary to discover who it is that one wishes to deal with, to inform people that one wishes to deal and on what terms, to conduct negotiations leading up to a bargain, to draw up the contract, to undertake the inspection needed to make sure that the terms of the contract are being observed and so on.

11 Masten (1995: xi) states: 'Progress in the application and testing of transaction cost economics can only be described as phenomenal' and Williamson (2002) described it as 'an empirical success story'. See surveys by Macher and Richman (2008) and Carter and Hodgson (2006).

Even within the NIE school, Coase proved a renegade. The work of Oliver Williamson expanded Coase's work on the firm and contract to focus particularly on asset specificity, which he argued led to 'large switching costs', 'lock-in', 'holdout' and 'opportunism'. Williamson's idea is simple. Assume that in order to win a contract a firm must invest in capital equipment specific to its customer's requirements – such as a specialised press which can only be used to make a component for this customer. Ex ante the parties negotiate and reach a set of terms and price which reflects a commercial balance between the two. During the negotiations the supplier has committed no funds and has the option of walking away. But once the firm invests in the specific asset, it is locked into the arrangement in the sense that the salvage value of the asset is much less than its initial capital costs. Anticipating lock-in, the parties should frame their contract to reduce ex post opportunism, but the supplier will always be vulnerable with a real risk of contract failure and inefficiency.

Coase was sceptical about the real-world importance that Williamson (1985, 2009) and Hart (1995) attached to asset specificity. This was graphically seen in his reaction to the work of Klein et al. (1978) and Klein (1988, 2000), who used the acquisition of Fisher Body by General Motors (GM) to illustrate 'market failure' caused by asset specificity. They claimed that contractual opportunism by Fisher Body forced GM to eventually acquire it to replace inefficient market transactions (contract) by ownership (vertical integration). GM had signed a 10-year contract with Fisher Body to purchase closed car bodies, and acquired a 60% interest in Fisher Body in 1919. The contracts contained a price clause designed to protect Fisher Body from a holdout arising from the need to commit significant asset-specific investment to fulfil the contract in the form of presses, dies and stamps. In the 1920s the demand for closed bodies increased, and Fisher Body allegedly took advantage of this to charge high prices, which, it was said, made GM uncompetitive. By 1926, the situation was described as intolerable, and GM acquired Fisher Body. Klein and his associates claimed that the contractual problems arising from asset specificity were resolved by GM's acquisition of Fisher Body.

In his last substantial article, Coase (2000) argued that this analysis misrepresented the facts (also Casadues-Masanell and Spulber 2000). Contrary to the version just outlined, there was in reality close collaboration between the two companies. The initial acquisition in 1919 was accompanied by substantial investment by GM in Fisher Body, there was equal representation on the Board by GM and Fisher Body, Fisher Body did not price opportunistically, many Fisher Body plants were located near GM plants and, perhaps most damaging of all to the argument, there was no large transaction-specific investment in metal presses and dies because the technology was wood-based and labour intensive. The full acquisition of Fisher Body had little to do with contractual failures. The alternative explanation for the merger was that the growth in the car market and the increasingly complex technology made close coordination necessary and vertical integration efficient. For Coase the work of these economists, who sought to use a transaction cost approach, illustrated the failures of what he called 'blackboard economics' and the value of the case study approach he advocated (Coase 2006: 275–76):

> If it is believed that certain contractual arrangements will lead to opportunistic behaviour, it is not surprising that economists misinterpret the evidence and find what they expect to find. That the belief in the truth of a theory leads to a lack of interest in what actually happens is not uncommon in economics is suggested by the work of … Paul Samuelson … Samuelson felt able to make statements about the finance and administration of lighthouses without having made any serious investigation of the subject.

Economic analysis of law

'Social cost' also attracted the interest of lawyers because it used the English and US laws of trespass and nuisance to illustrate the effects of legal rules when transaction costs were negligible, and when they were prohibitively high. To many, Coase appeared to be (and arguably was) saying that common law judges had a better grasp of economic theory and reality than economists. The legal notion of 'reasonableness' which runs through Anglo-American common law was, suggested Coase, a version of economists' concept of opportunity costs and the approach he was advocating (Coase 1960: 19):

> it is clear from a cursory study that the courts have often recognised the economic implications of their decisions

and are aware (as many economists are not) of the reciprocal nature of the problem. Furthermore, from time to time,
they take these economic implications into account, along
with other factors, at arriving at their decisions.

(Ibid.: 38):

it seems probable that in the interpretation of words and
phrases like 'reasonable' and 'common or ordinary use',
there is some recognition, perhaps largely unconscious
and certainly not very explicit, of the economic aspects
of the question at issues.

(Ibid.: 27–28):

It was argued that the courts are conscious of this and
that they often make, although not always in an explicit
fashion, a comparison between what would be gained
and what would be lost by preventing actions which have
harmful effects.

The idea that the common law might have an underlying economic logic was picked up by a number of lawyers,
and, in particular, by Richard A. Posner (1972, 1973) and
Posner and Landes (1988). Posner, a colleague of Coase at
the University of Chicago, used economics in a doctrinal
way to explain the rules and procedures of the law. Beginning with his paper 'A theory of negligence' (Posner 1972)
and refined in later articles and books, a new branch of
the economic analysis of law was ushered in, one that the

lawyer could use to analyse and rationalise the hotchpotch of legal doctrines which made up the common law. Posner's approach differed from Calabresi's (1967, 1970) earlier normative economic analysis, which suggested reforms of the law; Posner offered a positive theory of law designed to 'explain' the common law. Posner advanced the radical and highly controversial thesis that the fundamental logic of the common law was economic (not a new claim even before Coase) and that its doctrines and remedies could be understood 'as if' judges decided cases to encourage a more efficient allocation of resources. The idea that economics could unlock the logic of the common law raised its profile among legal scholars, who were either attracted or repelled by the proposition.

The 1970s and 1980s were the growth decades of the economic analysis of law, at least in the US (Veljanovski 2006, 2007).[12] Increasingly, North American legal scholars began to use economics to rationalise and appraise the law, and by the 1980s the economic analysis of law had firmly established itself as a respectable, albeit controversial, component of legal studies. In the US many prominent scholars in the field (Richard Posner, Guido Calabresi, Robert Bork, Frank Easterbrook, Antonin Scalia and Robert Breyer) were appointed judges, and economics – especially supply-side economics – was thrust to the forefront of the political agenda by reforming governments in both West and East.

---

12 Landes and Posner (1993) find that the influence of economics on US law was growing through the 1980s but that the rate of growth slowed after the mid-1980s.

While in North America this application of economics grew rapidly and is now well established, it was not something Coase contributed to or approved. Coase's (1978a) concern was how institutions affected economic activity, not what he saw as an imperialist pursuit by economists to conquer law and other disciplines. Coase was out of step here with his Chicago colleagues, and the tensions often erupted.

Economics

Coase was iconoclastic: a fully paid-up member of the 'awkward squad', not in his demeanour and personal relations, but intellectually. He started out as a socialist influenced by among others Abba Lerner, and ended up an advocate of the inherent logic of markets. He was a classical liberal economist in the tradition of Adam Smith, Alfred Marshall and the less well-known economist Arnold Plant, his mentor at the London School of Economics in the 1930s to 1940s.

His view of economics was clear. Economics was defined principally by its subject matter: 'the working of the social institutions which bind together the economic system: firms, markets for goods and services, labour markets, capital markets ... and so on' (Coase 1978a: 206–7).

Coase adopted what today is called a supply-side approach focused on 'the institutional nature of production' (the title of his Nobel acceptance speech). The consumer, and demand analysis, did not feature much in what he wrote.

His building blocks were the transaction, transaction costs, gains from trade, 'total' as opposed to 'marginal' analysis, and property rights. He argued that markets traded principally not in goods and services but legal rights (Coase 1988e: 656):

> Economists commonly assume that what is traded on the market is a physical entity, an ounce of gold, a ton of coal. But, as lawyers know, what are traded on the market are bundles of rights, rights to perform certain actions. Trade, the dominant activity in the economic system, its amount and character, consequently depend on what rights and duties individuals and organizations are deemed to possess – and these are established by the legal system. An economist, as I see it, cannot avoid taking the legal system into account.

Coase's (1960: 40) policy framework is built around the notion of opportunity cost, which compares 'the total product obtainable with alternative social arrangements'. His approach is 'to start our analysis with a situation approximating that which actually exists, to examine the effects of a proposed policy change and to attempt to decide whether the whether the new situation would be, in total, better or worse than the original one' (ibid.: 43).

His empirical approach was the case study, with its detailed analysis of how business and regulation operated in practice. This research method has more in common with economic history, legal analysis and that of the business school (where his theory of the firm has had more impact than in economics).

For Coase economic research involved immersing oneself in the details of markets and their institutions, and carefully examining why the institutions which existed, did exist. The presumption was that they arose in response to economic factors, and the first effort should be to reveal why this was so. He wrote (Coase 1988a: 71):

> An inspired theoretician might do as well without such empirical work, but my own feeling is that the inspiration is most likely to come through the stimulus provided by the patterns, puzzles, and anomalies revealed by the systematic gathering of data, particularly when the prime need is to break our existing habits of thought.

Despite his move to the US, Coase was not influenced by US economists or the Chicago School, with the exception of Frank Knight. Remarkably, while he was a professor in a great law school, he was not interested in influencing lawyers or legal scholarship. Coase was at Chicago, but not of Chicago. He was attracted to the university primarily by the prospect of becoming the editor of the *Journal of Law and Economics*, which he saw as an opportunity to implement his research agenda among economists. It was from Arnold Plant at the London School of Economics that he received his economic perspective (Coase 1988b: 6–7):

> Plant also explained that governments often served special interests, promoted monopoly rather than competition, and commonly imposed regulations which made matters worse. He made me aware of the benefits which flow from an economy directed by the pricing system. Clearly, I did not need Chicago.

Coase's approach strikes the modern economist as literary and old school. Indeed, his focus on institutions and transactions had more in common with the American Institutionalist School (Commons 1920), which surrounded the New Deal, but there is no suggestion from Coase that he was influenced by or endorsed their approach. His economics was solidly neoclassical and he did not eschew theory or the fundamental tenets of demand and supply. But he did rail against the way economics was developing. He was forthright in his criticism of the increasing tendency to:

- *Abstract theory*, which he described as 'blackboard economics'. ('When economists find that they are unable to analyse what is happening in the real world, they invent an imaginary world which they are capable of handling' (Coase 1988c: 29).)
- *Mathematics*. (He said that 'In my youth it was said that "what was too silly to be said may be sung". In modern economics it may be put into mathematics.')
- *Econometrics*. ('If you torture the data enough, nature will always confess.')
- *Rational agents*. While he accepted that people were self-interested, he was unconvinced they were rational or that the assumption assisted economists. Quoting Ely Devons, an English economist, Coase (1999) noted: 'If economists wished to study the horse, they wouldn't go and look at horses. They'd sit in their studies and say to themselves, "What would I do if I were a horse?" And they would soon discover that they would maximize

their utilities.' He would have had sympathy with the belief of today's behavioural economists that people are not rational – but they would have then quickly parted ways.

Coase's view of economics as defined by its subject matter was not accepted by his colleagues at the University of Chicago. Indeed the complete opposite was the case, with many – such as Gary Becker, George Stigler and lawyer Richard Posner – intent on pushing the frontiers of economics towards the subject matter of law, political science, sociology, administration and any topic (divorce, the family, capital punishment) where choice was involved. Coase was highly sceptical of these efforts (Coase 1978a: 203):

> The reason for this movement of economics into neighbouring fields is certainly not that we have solved the problems of the economic system; it would perhaps be more plausible to argue that economists are looking for fields in which they can have some success.

It is ironic that Gary Becker received the Nobel Prize the year after Coase for his contribution to expanding economics to the 'non-market', which was so at odds with Coase's conception of economics.

The tension between Coase and his fellow Chicagoans flared in the Posner–Coase–Williamson exchange in the *Journal of Institutional and Theoretical Economics* in 1993. Posner (1993a,b) dismissed the New Institutional Economics as atheoretical and derivative of his economic analysis of law, claiming that Coase had 'declared war on modern economics'. He went further, and somewhat comically, to claim that the key to Coase's economics 'lies in his Englishness' (Posner 1995: 409):

> His Englishness expresses itself in a number of ways, one superficial: the wit, feline in its subtlety and sharpness, that he occasionally turns on his fellow economists is vintage English academic acid ... The other aspects of Coase's Englishness have deeper significance. He writes in an English economics tradition shaped by Smith and Marshall, by Coase's teacher Arnold Plant, and by the nineteenth-century lassiez faire movement ... The mathematical and statistical movement in economics, which is primarily American (or at least primarily non-English), has passed Coase by completely and indeed is an object of scorn. He writes the limpid prose of the accomplished English essayist. Its self-conscious plainness, modesty, commonsensicality, and rejection of high theory make Coase the George Orwell of modern economics.

This passage reveals more about Posner's sensitivity (presumably to Coase's 'feline wit') and parochialism – Smith was a Scot; Marshall an accomplished mathematician – and the English continue to combine wit and irony with mathematics and statistics.

No doubt part of Coase's approach and view of economics was generational. 'The nature of the firm' was published before Posner was born. Economics on both side of the Atlantic was a very different subject then, and not mathematical. The mathematical movement in economics only gained hold in the 1960s, by which time Coase had made his major contributions.

Coase was not an isolated critic of 'modern economics', nor does 'modern economics' share or exclusively adhere to the positivist approach espoused by Becker and Posner. Posner (2011) himself has acknowledged the failure of modern economics in the face of the global financial crisis and suggests that perhaps there is something in the 'English' approach of Coase and Keynes (although Coase would not have liked the pairing).

Regulation

Coase has also been accused of being anti-regulation and having no theory of regulation. In this regard he could be seen to reflect Adam Smith's view of government. But Coase's views were not abstract or based on prejudice, but rather on the detailed study of British state-run monopolies – the British Broadcasting Corporation (Coase 1950), the UK Post Office (Coase 1939, 1961a) – and the US Federal Communications Commission (Coase 1959). In these he found intervention based on flawed claims of market failure.

His move to the US in 1951 was in large part because of 'a lack of faith in the future of socialist Britain' (Breit and Spencer 1985: 239). This may have been a catharsis since Coase was a socialist in his earlier years. After World War II the Labour Government of Clement Atlee embarked on a massive nationalisation programme and growing state intervention. The intellectual climate changed. He, like Plant and a number of other economists, was swimming not only against the political but also the intellectual tide in Britain. Economists in Britain were for much of the latter part of the twentieth century socialistic, ready to see market failure everywhere, and government as a benign force motivated by the public interest. They were more than ready to become the technicians and theorists for government intervention.

Coase's editorship of the *Journal of Law and Economics* was characterised by the publication of articles which showed the failure of government regulation. Yet he had no real theory of regulation such as was later spelled out by Stigler (1988a,b) and Posner (1974), or by public choice theorists such as James Buchanan and Gordon Tullock (1962) (see, generally, Veljanovski 2010). Why Coase thought regulation seemed to fail he spelt out later in life (Coase in Hazlett 1998):

> When I was editor of the *Journal of Law and Economics*, we published a whole series of studies of regulation and its effects. Almost all the studies – perhaps all the studies – suggested that the results of regulation had been bad, that the prices were higher, that the product was worse adapted to the needs of consumers, than it otherwise would have been. I was not willing to accept the view that all regulation was bound to produce these results. Therefore, what was my explanation for the results we had? I argued that the most probable explanation was that the government now operates on such a massive scale that it had reached the stage of what economists call negative

marginal returns. Anything additional it does, it messes up. But that doesn't mean that if we reduce the size of government considerably, we wouldn't find then that there were some activities it did well. Until we reduce the size of government, we won't know what they are.

Antitrust

One would have thought that given Coase's work on the firm and the industrial organisation that he would have taken a greater interest in antitrust, especially as his Chicago colleagues were revolutionising thinking about antitrust policy and laws. Yet he remained aloof from these developments. William Landes, who succeeded to Coase's Chair in the law school after his retirement, reports that:

Ronald [Coase] said he had gotten tired of antitrust because when the prices went up the judges said it was monopoly, when the prices went down they said it was predatory pricing, and when they stayed the same they said it was tacit collusion. (Landes 1983: 193)

It is true that US antitrust of the 1960s and 1970s was an intellectual disgrace. Yet, however amusing Landes's quote, it does not convincingly explain Coase's lack of interest. In 1972 Coase gave a far more reasoned explanation, consistent with his approach to economics (Coase 1972a: 66):

I have said that the character of the analysis used by economists has tended to conceal the fact that certain problems in industrial organization are not being tackled. But I think there is a much more important reason for this neglect: interest in industrial organization has tended to be associated with the study of monopoly, the control of monopoly, and antitrust policy. This is not a recent development. When in the late nineteenth century, economists came to be interested in problems of industrial organization, they were confronted with the problem of the trust in the United States and the cartel in Germany. It was, therefore, natural that with the development of antitrust policy in the United States, interest in antitrust aspects of industrial organization came to dominate the subject.

This has had its good and its bad effects but, in my opinion, the bad by far outweigh the good. It has, no doubt, raised the morale of many scholars working on problems of industrial organization, because they feel that they are engaged on work which has important policy implications. It has had the salutary result of focusing these scholars' attention on real problems concerning the way in which the economic system operates. It has also led them to utilize some sources of information which might otherwise have been neglected. Still, in other respects, the effects seem to me to have been unfortunate. The desire to be of service to one's fellows is, no doubt, a noble motive, but it is not possible to influence policy if you do not give an answer. It has therefore encouraged men to become economic statesmen – men, that is, who provide answers even when there are no answers. This tendency has discouraged a critical questioning of the data and of the worth of the analysis, leading the many able scholars in this field to tolerate standards of evidence and analysis which, I believe, they would otherwise have rejected. This association with policy – and antitrust policy in particular – gave a direction to the study of industrial organization which prevented certain questions from being raised or, at any rate, made it more difficult to do so. The facts as stated in antitrust cases were accepted as correct (or substantially so). The ways in which the problem was viewed by the lawyers (judges and advocates) were accepted as the ways in which we should approach the problem. The opinions of the judges often became the starting point of the analysis, and an attempt was to make sense of what they had said. This so tangled the discussion that most economists were, apparently, unaware of having failed. ...

One important result of this preoccupation with the monopoly problem is that if an economist finds something – a business practice of one sort or other – that he does not understand, he looks for a monopoly explanation. And as in this field we are very ignorant, the number of ununderstandable practices tends to be rather large, and the reliance on a monopoly explanation, frequent. ...

I have suggested that what is wanted is a large-scale systematic study of the organization of industry in the United States. I have also suggested that this would yield best results if conducted in an atmosphere in which the scientific spirit is not contaminated by a desire (or felt obligation) to find quick solutions to difficult policy issues.

Coase made forays into areas of industrial economics such as the marginal cost controversy (Coase 1946a), and monopoly and durability (Coase 1972b). The former attacked the optimality of marginal cost pricing in decreasing cost industries and the distortions created by the state funding of the consequent losses. His analysis of durability and monopoly garnered him a second 'theorem' known as the 'Coase conjecture'. This says that a monopolist's very act of selling a durable good dissipates its monopoly power. This is because new sales compete with its own previous sales, which can be resold in secondary markets. Coase argued that the ability of a monopolist to charge a supra-competitive price depends on its ability to make a credible commitment to limit future output.

Spectrum: from wireless to mobile phones

One area where Coase (1959) has had a major policy impact is the adoption of pricing and market allocation of spectrum bandwidth.

Since the 1920s, when wireless communications started to gain in popularity, it was firmly believed that a market in spectrum was not possible or was inefficient, giving rise to bedlam on the airwaves. Famously, the then Chief Economist at the US Federal Communications Commission (FCC), Dallas Smythe (1952), held this view. As result throughout the world spectrum was allocated by fiat and was highly regulated and rationed, with large chunks of spectrum allocated to government and the military without being used. It also resulted in restriction in the services that could be provided and thus encouraged the creation in Europe and farther afield of state-run monopoly broadcasters such as the BBC (Coase 1950). Coase was prompted into print by the 'feebleness' of Smythe's response to an article by a law student, Leo Herzel (1951), who wrote that if property rights were clearly established in bandwidth, then firms would trade spectrum and allocate it to its highest valued user and use.

Coase's work on spectrum markets was badly received by fellow economists and policymakers. After his article was published, the Rand Corporation asked him together with Bill Meckling and Jora Minasian to write a report on radio spectrum allocation. Rand's internal reaction to the draft report was scathing. Coase (1998: 579) quotes one internal reviewer as writing: 'I know of no country on the face of the globe – except a few corrupt Latin American dictatorships – where the "sale" of the spectrum could even be seriously proposed'. Another said spectrum was a public good so that a market solution was not on the cards, and the project had been a 'waste of Rand resources' (ibid.: 580).

As Hazlett (1998) reminds us, it took 67 years for the FCC to finally adopt the market. It is now accepted that markets and prices can be used to allocate spectrum, and that congestion and radio interference were due to the absence of clearly defined and enforceable property rights. Today the use of market solutions has become accepted but not always as a fully fledged market in spectrum. Across Europe and elsewhere auctions have been used to allocate spectrum to third (3G) and fourth (4G) generation mobile (cell) phones. This was regarded as a more transparent and fairer way of allocating spectrum than the earlier 'beauty parades' of aspiring users, which lacked transparency. It is no doubt that one of the main reasons for this was to generate revenue for governments but it has also been appreciated that this is a fairer, more transparent and more efficient way of allocating valuable bandwidth. Reforms are afoot to allow limited trading in spectrum, known as secondary trading in the UK and Europe, as already exists in New Zealand and Australia. A few countries have gone as far as Guatemala, which allocated spectrum bandwidth on a 'first-in-time' basis to those who file claims with the regulatory agency (Spiller and Cardilli 1999).

Coase's legacy

Ronald Coase was a great economist who left an enduring legacy. He based his economics on the real world, on the study of industry, and his application of simple economics artfully applied to come to novel conclusions – which he would have said were obvious.

Coase did not reject economics or theory. A large amount of what he wrote was on economic theory – whether on the nature of costs, the problem of monopoly, or the gaps in welfare economics. That he did this in plain English and without the aid of mathematics is not a source of criticism but of admiration. That he could have formulated not one but two theorems, changed the minds in two hours over drinks of twenty of Chicago's leading economists, encouraged a generation of scholars to take institutions seriously through his editorship of the *Journal of Law and Economics*, and provide the launch pad for not one but at least two major new fields of research, and capped this with being the progenitor of the use of market methods to allocate radio spectrum, is astounding. George Stigler (1963) once remarked that economists' most common error is to believe other economists. It was not an error committed by Ronald Coase.

3 OWNERSHIP, GOVERNANCE AND THE COASIAN FIRM

Martin Ricketts

The nature of the firm

When Coase (1937) advanced his essential idea that the firm was a response to 'the cost of using the price mechanism' and that it acted as a substitute for market transactions when these were accompanied by higher transactions costs, he laid the foundations for the entire later edifice of the New Institutional Economics. Like some ancient medieval cathedral this new approach to microeconomics has taken several generations to take shape, and its different parts reflect the preoccupations and tastes of very many different contributors over a long period of time. The founding insight – that transacting was not a costless activity – led, with considerable lags, to detailed analysis of the economics of contract, the economics of property rights (the entities being traded), the economics of information, legal economics (the processes and rules under which exchange takes place) and the economics of collective decision making (public choice). Of direct concern to this paper it also led, in the 1970s and 1980s, to the study of *'Markets versus Hierarchies'* and the *'Economic Institutions of Capitalism*' to use the titles of two celebrated books by Oliver Williamson (1975, 1985).

Coase's paper on the firm was seminal to an astonishing degree because its observation that there was a cost of using the price mechanism was simple, obvious and (perhaps because of these characteristics) carried implications that had been entirely overlooked. It was the basis upon which economics could once more become a 'social science' concerning how human beings come to agreements and thereby coordinate their actions and gain the advantages of division of labour and exchange. This range of enquiry had been subtly undermined by a rather formal theory of 'price determination' that emphasised individual rational choice among technically available alternatives and which could be studied almost without recognising that the social activity of exchange was what underlay it. Indeed this highly focused attention on rather rarefied zero cost market transactions had proceeded so far that there was no particular rationale embedded in the theory itself for organisational forms such as 'firms' to exist at all.

Transactions cost, as a theoretical concept, thus opened up the prospect of using economic reasoning to study institutions other than perfect markets. It did not, however, immediately suggest a theory of ownership or of 'governance' more generally. Coase's original approach reflected his research agenda at the time. He wanted to explain why some industries consisted of vertically integrated firms while others relied far more on market transacting between independent firms at the various stages of production. His answer that transactions would be integrated within the firm when it was less costly to treat them that way than to use 'the price system' (i.e. to negotiate contracts with independent suppliers) led to a simple bifurcation. Within the firm, resources were allocated by management decision and (within limits) suppliers agreed to abide by these instructions in return for an agreed remuneration. Outside the firm it was necessary to choose a supplier and negotiate terms. The firm was thus conceived as a set of contracts of a particular nature – durable and not very highly specified – with a central contractual agent. Market contracts, in contrast, were conceived of as short term, requiring frequent renegotiation and with more detailed provisions.

At first sight this conceptual foundation does not seem to tell us much about the ownership and governance of firms. The firm is simply a set of contracts of a particular type with a central agent which enables a mini-plan to be implemented by the 'entrepreneur-coordinator'. It seems to give us a theory of the single proprietorship or the entrepreneurial firm but not to help us understand larger firms with shared ownership – partnerships, the public limited company, cooperatives, mutuals, labour-managed firms, not-for-profit firms and so forth. Developments during the years since the appearance of Coase's paper have shown, however, that the transactions cost framework provides a means of analysing not merely the size and scope of the firm, as initially proposed, but also questions relating to its 'constitutional structure'.

In essence, Coase explains 'the firm' as a response to transactional hazards. It does not remove these hazards but mitigates them at the margin by substituting 'internal governance' for 'the market'. He did not investigate the internal governance of the firm in detail, but by making the firm a social organisation dependent upon the nature of the contracts observed within it, rather than a technological entity dependent upon the laws of engineering, Coase opened the door to further analysis of its economic structure. Ownership and governance could be regarded as the outcome of a competitive selection between institutional forms. Instead of a single 'ideal' model of the firm emerging from this analysis, the Coasian research paradigm suggested that firms might differ according to the contractual hazards they encountered and to which they are a response.

'Ownership' in the Coasian theory of the firm

In the rudimentary Coasian firm, the entrepreneur-coordinator would seem to be the implied 'owner'. Coase does not discuss ownership explicitly, however, and the reasons for assuming that the central contractual agent 'owns' the firm require elaboration. Someone has to formulate and then implement the activities that will be undertaken within the firm. An incentive is required to provide these services. How can such an incentive be provided? One possibility is for the central agent to hold a complementary set of residual control rights and profit rights. Owners have the right to determine how assets will be used providing these uses do not infringe any contractual rights of others in the same asset. The owner's return from the use of the asset is a residual rather than a contractual return. It is what remains after contractual claims have been settled.

This is the argument presented by Alchian and Demsetz (1972) in their rationalisation of the classical firm. In circumstances where the contribution of individual members to a joint team output is hard or even impossible to observe, contracts with team members will be unverifiable. All that can be observed is the result of the entire team's effort, and sharing the proceeds of this effort between team members will give rise to a moral hazard problem. Any gains from higher individual effort will be shared with the entire team and, conversely, the losses from poor effort will be felt only partially by the shirker. Where mutual monitoring of effort is possible and peer pressure can be brought to bear, this difficulty can be reduced, but in other conditions the alternative is to use a residual claimant to hire and fire members of the team, direct activities, monitor effort and act as the single contractual agent.[1]

Alchian and Demsetz thus provide a rationalisation for ownership of the firm – defined as possession of rights to claim the residual and to exercise 'control' – by the central

---

1   Coase is at pains to make the point, in his criticism of Frank Knight (1921), that the ability actively to direct the allocation of resources is not a necessary condition for paying someone a definite reward. The main requirement is simply that the promised outcome is easily observed, in which case there is no need for the price system to be superseded. Neither is the existence of uncertainty per se the crucial factor in giving rise to the firm because entrepreneurs could still in principle pursue their particular judgements through contracting in the market. Alchian and Demsetz set up conditions in which the direction and monitoring of inputs is required because individual output is unobservable and they thereby explain the advantage achieved by bringing the contract within the firm.

contractual agent. It is worth noting, however, that alternative ownership arrangements are conceivable even in the context of the simplest firm. For example, the central agent might be hired by the team members rather than the other way round. A specified reward could be paid after the planning and monitoring services have been carried out successfully. Note that this would produce a sort of inverse Coasian firm in which all the cooperating inputs hire the central coordinator. It would require some collective arrangement by which team members are able to choose the monitor/coordinator – a potentially costly process in itself. McManus (1975) considers this possibility when he recounts 'the fable of the barge'. When, in the nineteenth century, a team of straining barge pullers was observed on the Yangtze being cruelly treated by an overseer, the horrified onlookers were informed that the team owned the rights on this stretch of river and had hired the overseer. Presumably this arrangement would only work where close proximity of team members would give some assurance that the overseer was doing the job properly and not capriciously; where the team is not too big so that a share in the outcome would anyway give some positive incentive to effort; and where the end product was something fairly simple such as the completion of a trip within a specified time.

This example, apocryphal or not, provides a Coasian basis for the workers' cooperative even if it also illustrates the difficulties of that particular form. It requires that transacting over monitoring, managing and coordination services faces lower hazards than transacting over the services of other inputs. It relates to Coase's definition of the firm as the supersession of the price system in that contracts between the barge pullers are suppressed and are replaced by shared ownership – the possession of control rights (to determine what trips are undertaken and to appoint the overseer) and claims to the residual. The moral hazard associated with agreements to cooperate in a team enterprise where individual outputs are unobservable can therefore be countered in two ways. A monitor can acquire ownership rights and employ each member of the team (as in the argument of Alchian and Demsetz), or the team can share ownership rights and employ the monitor (as in one interpretation of the fable of the barge). There is no single correct way of assigning the rights or contracting with the team. Everything will depend on the circumstances and the transactional difficulties to which they give rise. All that can be said is that where mutual monitoring and peer pressure are not possible, the sharing of ownership rights will be less effective and the single proprietorship is more likely to prevail.

The hazards of transacting

The Coasian firm that we have so far been considering is clearly a rather rudimentary and pared-down conception comprising an entrepreneur-coordinator and a team of employees. Coase's insight, however, in no way confines the firm to such a structure. His point is that the firm will economise on the cost of transacting, and this is an observation that is applicable to its relations with all its

potential contractors – labour, management, intermediate inputs of various descriptions, capital and even
its customers. Contractual hazards abound in all these
areas.

In labour markets services are traded that are not
merely hard to define with outcomes that are often difficult to measure, but labour skills can be impossible to
assess in advance and some can be highly specific to the
operations of a particular firm (often acquired gradually over an extended period of employment). All these
conditions give rise to contractual problems. Inability
to attribute output to the activities of a given individual
gives rise to *moral hazard*[2] as pointed out by Alchian
and Demsetz. Inability to assess the generic skills of a
person – or indeed the quality of any other input before
its purchase – makes trade in high quality inputs hard
to achieve in the face of *adverse selection*.[3] Firm-specific skills that raise the productivity of particular people
within the firm (but not outside) create problems of bargaining over the resulting rents and lead to dependency
on the firm if remuneration rises above levels achievable
elsewhere. In all these cases procedures and rules within
the firm can be seen as ways of mitigating the hazards.
Over time, information is revealed within the firm about

2   Moral hazard arises when individuals are motivated to take part in risky
    activity because they know that someone else will bear any resulting costs.

3   Adverse selection can occur when users of a service know more than sup-
    pliers about the use to which the service is put. People who know they are
    'bad risks' are more likely to take out insurance, for example, than those
    who know they are 'good risks'; consequently the price of insurance rises,
    possibly to prohibitive levels.

an employee's effort and skill levels, and hierarchical (promotion) and other incentive devices (pay scales) are instituted, many of which require mutual trust to be effective. The firm becomes a 'governance structure' for hazardous contractual relations.

The same transactional problems are found in the firm's relations with its suppliers of intermediate inputs. Where quality is hard to measure but can be linked to care in the actual process of production, the firm must decide whether its own internal monitoring and control mechanisms will be superior to alternative market-based incentives such as the supplier's fear of contract termination or loss of reputation in the event of failure to meet the required standards. Similarly, if suppliers are required to invest in highly specific equipment or human capital that has little value in serving alternative customers, fear of dependency and possible opportunistic behaviour might lead to the supersession of contract and integration within a single firm. One of the most famous case studies in business history (Klein et al. 1978) of the eventual merger of Fisher Body and General Motors in 1926 concerns these issues, although Coase (2000) doubts that fear of opportunism was the primary factor. Rapidly changing technical conditions are themselves likely to lead to integration as novel requirements are often costly to communicate to suppliers through relatively arm's length arrangements (Kay 1979; Silver 1984).

Coasian explanations of multinational expansion by the firm are also based on transactions costs. If firms have developed reputations for high quality, or if they have access to knowledge that has been generated internally and which cannot itself be traded (either because it is inherently difficult to codify or because property rights are costly to enforce and police in foreign jurisdictions), the value of these assets can only be fully realised by internal expansion (Dunning 1973; Casson 1987). This approach to the scope of the firm has much in common with theories that emphasise the firm as a repository of 'competences' – the ability to undertake tasks differently or more effectively than others – that form the basis of its competitive advantage. If these advantages could be traded at low cost the firm could expand into management consultancy or even license the information to independent management consultants. In fact some of the capabilities of a firm may be so linked to its history, culture and ownership that they become impossible simply to replicate elsewhere and derive from a form of corporate 'knowledge' that is effectively untradeable.

Hazards in the capital market are particularly hard to circumvent. The Coasian entrepreneur-coordinator will find it difficult to act at the hub of the firm's set of contracts without financial resources. If the entrepreneur is already endowed with personal capital the problem can be assumed away. But in the more general case, attracting funds requires that the transactional problems associated with the use of instruments of debt are overcome, or alternatively that claims to the residual are diluted and that ownership rights are extended to the providers of capital. Linking pure entrepreneurial talent with finance is clearly hazardous because the entrepreneur will fear the theft of any ideas disclosed to the financier, while the financier will fear that the talent of the entrepreneur is unknowable and that his or her promises will be effectively unverifiable.

Where 'the firm' has an independent legal personality and there is limited liability, entrepreneurs will be expected to increase risk taking as the proportion of debt finance increases because bond holders (lenders) will lose their capital in the event of bankruptcy and failure, while the entrepreneur will experience all the additional gains from extremely favourable outcomes. Diluting ownership confronts a rather different hazard. An entrepreneur-co-ordinator receiving only a small fraction of the residual will be expected to work less and to indulge in more non-pecuniary benefits with a consequential reduction in the value of the firm. These losses are sometimes referred to as agency costs on the grounds that the entrepreneur-coordinator can be regarded – in a loose rather than a legal sense – as an agent of his or her financiers. Jensen and Meckling (1976) used this Coasian reasoning to establish their theory of the optimal financial structure of the firm, where the marginal agency cost of more outside equity is just equal to the marginal agency cost associated with more debt.

In general, the dispersion of residual rights of control across larger and larger numbers of people will reduce risk-bearing costs, but it will make the actual exercise of control over the assets of the firm more difficult because each owner will have a much reduced incentive to acquire information or to invest resources in managing the firm. Actual day-to-day business decisions will be made by managers who owe fiduciary duties to the owners but who are not monitored closely by them. This separation of ownership from control is particularly associated with the large joint stock firm, but it is actually a characteristic of any structure with widely dispersed control rights and residual claims. Large cooperatives, limited partnerships, mutual enterprises and even not-for-profit firms will face similar agency problems between those with shared control rights and those with decision rights and fiduciary duties.

Competition and the selection of governance structures

Given the variety and extent of transactional hazards, it is evident that there will be no single governance structure for firms that will always represent the best response. Firms will vary not only in size and scope but in the arrangements that are introduced to govern transactions with their inputs and in the location of the residual and control rights that accompany ownership. Some firms will use 'higher powered' incentives than others to motivate effort, or adopt looser franchise arrangements rather than close managerial oversight. This will be likely when qualitative outcomes are relatively easy to define and observe and where the dangers of moral hazard are considered to be low. Other firms might tolerate quite 'low powered' incentives – payments dependent on rudimentary observations of effort but not linked strongly to particular measures of output. This will be likely where there are extensive opportunities for shading on quality or for meeting targets by cutting back on other unobservable[4] or hard to measure components of output.

Where the gradual accumulation of firm-specific capital is important and suppliers therefore become dependent on the firm and differentiated from potential alternative contractors on the outside market, the firm develops procedures for handling disputes and resolving bargaining problems. Williamson (1985) refers to this as the evolution of 'unified governance' to handle frequent contracting with resources that are 'idiosyncratic' and operating in an uncertain environment. The nature of these arrangements, involving procedures for inducing cooperation and trust over time instead of rent seeking and conflict, might vary between firms. But there is a clear competitive advantage available to firms that can create conditions conducive to exchange rather than in-fighting, and competition is as much about the successful development or protection of effective internal governance as it is about the production of better goods and services. Firms compete to economise on the costs of transacting and thus achieve outcomes that other firms cannot match.

---

4   These components of output might be unobservable to managers but not necessarily to customers. It is worth emphasising that Coase, even in his 1937 paper, permits a range of contracts to appear within the firm although he does emphasise the active direction of resources rather than independent decision-making by employees. He comments, for example, with respect to the entrepreneur-coordinator, that 'the payment to his employees may be mainly or wholly a share in profits' (Coase (1937: 392) although he does not speculate about the conditions under which this form of payment might emerge.

One important method of reassuring vulnerable firm-specific assets that their dependency will not be exploited is to offer them some control rights. As Alchian and Woodward (1987: 119–20) express it, 'In general, whoever has a value that has become firm-specific will seek some form of control over the firm'. The word 'control' here presumably is intended to imply a sufficient degree of influence to prevent opportunism on the part of the firm's owners. This might be accomplished, for example, by seeking representation at board level, by restricting changes in ownership to reduce the risk that new owners might renege on existing understandings, or by forming staff associations to monitor the firm's compliance with its own governance arrangements. Ultimately, however, the fear of opportunism can only be removed entirely by the firm-dependent resources actually becoming the owners of the firm. In this case, contract is suppressed and the dependent resources become holders of residual claims and control rights.

The transactions cost view of the firm thus leads to the idea that property rights in the firm will be structured and assigned in such a way that the gains to coordinated effort are maximised. It follows that residual control rights and profit rights are likely to be assigned to those parties who would otherwise face the highest costs of transacting with the firm.[5] This could be because of a whole range

---

5   Transactions costs here are relative to the costs exercising the rights of ownership and control. Parties facing high transactions costs relative to other patrons of the firm will not become owners if they also face the highest costs of collective decision making and control.

of transactional hazards and not merely the problem of firm-specificity. We observed above that depending upon the assumed relative costs of contracting for monitoring services and barge-pulling services it was possible to derive a single proprietorship or a workers' cooperative. Similarly if lack of trust on the part of consumers deriving from severe information problems discourages trade in high quality goods, one response is to give ownership rights to consumers. The firm uses contracts to employ its workers and attract its capital but control is exercised by the buyers of its output. Retail cooperatives developed originally as a protection against local monopoly power and as a means of reassuring customers that their ignorance was not being exploited. Middle-class cooperatives such as the Army and Navy Stores were established as the complexity, durability and range of available products presented great information problems to consumers with rising disposable incomes.

Some financial contracts are so hazardous that the mutual or 'club' principle evolved to permit these services to be provided within the firm. In nineteenth-century England, for example, fire insurance companies that did not have the local knowledge to tell good from bad fire risks or to specify and police suitable precautions would find their position undermined by clubs of factory owners providing mutual insurance. These mutual arrangements took advantage of the possibility of much greater understanding of the risks and the possibility of peer pressure to comply with required standards. Life insurance companies all took the mutual form when they evolved in the eighteenth century. In an age before good statistical information about mortality rates and life expectancy was available, the financial calculations were so speculative that mutual ownership was the natural response. Premiums could be kept prudently high and any surpluses distributed among the policy holders. The provision of loans for the construction or purchase of domestic housing also developed initially along mutual lines. Membership of a building society could be controlled in such a way to ensure the reliability of borrowers and to reassure lenders that their deposits were secure. Initially, members of the club would save regular amounts with the accumulating funds being lent to house buyers until all were housed and the society could be wound up. Later 'permanent' building societies operated more like banks. Mutual status meant that control was in principle exercised by depositors and borrowers – groups with diverging interests. However, both would plausibly be concerned to maintain a prudent and cautious policy and to prevent the taking of excessive risks on the part of managers.[6]

Although, in the evolving history of institutional forms, consumer and producer cooperatives, mutual enterprises and even not-for-profit and charitable firms have played an important role, the modern corporate world is dominated by the public limited company. In this form of enterprise ownership rights are held by the suppliers of equity capital. The very term 'capitalist system' as distinct from the more neutral 'system of free enterprise' suggests the particular

---

6   The history of mutual and non-profit banks and insurance companies in the UK as well other forms of enterprise is reviewed in Ricketts (1999).

importance of the suppliers of capital to the control of industry. An explanation for this domination in the spirit of Coase would concentrate on the particularly hazardous nature of contracting in financial markets and on the financing of firm-specific capital. Where the firm requires relatively small amounts of non-specific capital, it is possible, as we have seen, for transactional problems in labour or product markets to dominate and give rise to other forms of enterprise. In general, however, the provision of very long term capital is likely to be associated with the demand for control, unless the capital is of a very non-specific type and easily reallocated to alternative uses outside the firm.

An additional consideration emphasised by Hansmann (1996) is that the shareholders of a public limited company are likely to face lower decision-making costs than other groups. Wherever ownership rights are shared it will be necessary for actual day-to-day decision rights to be delegated and for general policy to be set by a collective choice mechanism. Any such mechanism will be easier to operate the more homogeneous are the aims of the group holding the control rights. Very heterogeneous owners might never be able to exercise control as one subgroup opposes another – high-income consumers against low-income consumers in a retail cooperative; lenders against borrowers in a building society; skilled versus unskilled workers in a workers' cooperative (though not in a 'professional' partnership, where a more homogeneous group has control); and so forth. Shareholders in a public limited company will no doubt differ in some respects – individual compared with institutional, 'patient' versus 'impatient', long-term holders or short-term traders – but their ultimate interest in protecting the market value of their shares is likely to be a dominant consideration and managers pursuing this objective will be more secure than those who do not.

There are circumstances, however, in which control rights are dispersed widely and profit rights are suppressed. Not-for-profit and charitable enterprises are common in sectors such as health, education and the arts. In higher education, for example, surpluses are not usually distributed to owners but used for the further development of teaching and research. Academic control is usually exercised by academic staff through a senate, but other interests are also represented on governing bodies including non-academic staff, the alumni (who will be keen to maintain a good reputation for the institution) and donors. Ownership by investors would enable them to raise fees and appropriate some of the rents associated with the social and intellectual environment generated by the academic staff and students. It would also be extremely unattractive to donors, who would expect resources to be distributed to owners rather than used for charitable purposes. The non-distribution constraint simply ensures that resources are not dispersed as cash but are used within the institution. Non-profit hospitals, for example, would be expected to be more lavishly equipped than investor-owned ones as the gadgetry is a form of non-pecuniary benefit to the medical staff who work there.[7] For consumers, however,

---

7   Newhouse (1970) presented a model of a non-profit hospital along these lines. More generally, Hansmann (1980) considered the role of non-profit enterprise in several different sectors including the arts and education.

this bias might not be unwelcome (at least up to a point) in the sense that, if all institutions give rise to agency costs, patients would prefer that these should take the form of the over-provision of up-to-date equipment rather than (say) the payment of inflated dividends to investors. Where the aims of an institution are more contractible, however, and consumers see fewer potential advantages in the over-provision of particular inputs, as in the case of schools for teaching languages or for offering training in particular skills, investor-owned businesses can flourish against competition from non-profit enterprise.

Public policy towards the governance of enterprise

From a Coasian perspective the ownership and governance of the firm is the outcome of trial-and-error processes in a world of competition between alternative assignments of property rights, arrangements for collective choice and contracts for motivating managers and employees. However, these matters frequently give rise to public policy interventions (or recommendations for intervention) on the grounds that 'systems competition' cannot be relied upon to operate in the public interest. Recent examples, in the wake of the financial crisis, include criticism of the governance structure of commercial banks (including the Co-operative Bank); criticism of the pay structure of senior executives in financial institutions and in other businesses (including the BBC); general disquiet at the idea that the interests of investors should be paramount in the public limited company and recommendations for control to be extended to a wider group of 'stakeholders'.

It is clearly not possible here to give close attention to each of these examples. As a matter of general principle, however, a Coasian policy towards such matters would concentrate on encouraging experiment and competition between differing arrangements rather than trying to impose a single ideal model. Any reform, for example, that required control rights to be granted to wide stakeholder interests in all corporate entities would implicitly be ignoring the problem of transactions cost or asserting that other considerations are more important. In other words, the firm is often treated not as an economic but as a political entity – a microcosm of the state itself – in which all citizens have an interest; and its governance is viewed not as a question of transactional efficiency but of wider democratic control or even of some conception of social justice. Coase's view of the firm is social rather than technological, but it is not political in the sense that its constitution must reflect that of the state itself. People are free to choose the terms upon which they are prepared to transact with the firm or hold its residual claims, and can adjust these terms to suit changing or local circumstances.

A second important element of a Coasian policy towards the governance of firms is to avoid introducing distortions into organisational choice through the tax system or the regulatory framework. Any tax system is likely to have unintended consequences for firm structure and governance. Even a system that levied taxes entirely on people living in a jurisdiction on the basis of their individual flows of income or expenditure or their personal asset holdings, and which left legal entities such as firms out of the system entirely, might still distort the competitive advantage of different organisations. Some organisations such as public limited companies will have tradable residual claims which give rise to taxes on distributions and capital gains to shareholders. Cooperatives or partnerships with non-tradable rights will distribute surpluses in the form of higher wages or lower prices with potentially different tax implications depending on the details of the tax code. Where taxes are levied on firms themselves, subsidies to certain types of organisation are often observed. Non-profit enterprises in the US, for example, are exempt from federal corporate income tax[8] as well as sales and property taxes. In the UK, eligible not-for-profit bodies such as those supplying educational services are exempt from value added tax. Profit-making organisations are not eligible bodies even if they provide similar educational services.[9]

It is in the field of state regulation, however, that unintended effects on firm governance are particularly likely. If firms are structured in differing ways in order to respond to contractual hazards, direct intervention addressing (or appearing to address) these hazards by state regulators will make differences in private governance less important to commercial survival. Consumer protection regulation to ensure the quality of goods and services will undermine the consumer cooperative. Financial regulation to

---

8   Section 501 (c) (3) of the Internal Revenue Code.

9   HMRC Reference: Notice 701/30 (February 2014).

ensure the safety of financial intermediaries will reduce the attraction of mutual or non-profit banks or insurance companies. Employee protection will cut the ground away from worker control. Utility regulation makes cooperative or municipal enterprise solutions to natural monopoly unnecessary. State regulation will often substitute for private governance and does not necessarily simply represent a supplement to already existing structures. Mutual savings banks and building societies, for example, have declined in relative importance over a long period,[10] but in the UK demutualisation accelerated greatly in the 1990s as new regulators eroded the competitive advantage of building societies.[11]

From a Coasian perspective, widespread state regulation addressing every variety of hazard is most unlikely to be efficient. Transactors are relying on a publicly provided service rather than assessing the hazards of the environment themselves. Of course a perfectly informed and socially motivated regulator could indeed improve on the imperfect governance mechanisms that evolved over time through gradual and decentralised organisational experiment. But no such informed and motivated regulator exists and the dangers of subverting existing mechanisms are substantial. The much criticised behaviour of banks

---

10 In the US, for example, the number of mutual savings and loan associations peaked in 1928. See Hansmann (1996: 254).

11 Abbey National (in 1989), National and Provincial (1996), Cheltenham and Gloucester (1995), Alliance and Leicester (1997), Halifax (1997), Woolwich (1997), Northern Rock (1997) and Bristol and West (1997) all demutualised over this period.

in the run up to the recent financial crisis – the excessive risk-taking and the high-powered incentives and large bonuses for managers – would not have surprised observers of the financial scene in the nineteenth century. Protection from such risks in non-profit firms or mutual banks and life insurance companies derived not so much from the ability to exercise close control as from the reassurance given to customers from the low-powered incentives faced by managers. Historically, the greater safety of mutual banks compared with investor-owned banks is well established (see Hansmann 1996: 254–58), but regulators in the early twenty-first century faced an industry dominated by investor ownership and in which it was hard to countenance allowing a large bank to fail because of risks to the system as a whole.[12]

Conclusion

Nearly 80 years have elapsed since Coase introduced the concept of transactions cost into economics. It has proved a very fertile innovation that has encouraged the economic analysis of the scope, internal governance and ownership of firms. The policy relevance of this strand of analysis in the history of economic thought is still not widely appreciated, probably because of its complexity and because

---

12 The temptation now is for regulators to specify limits to the incentive arrangements permitted in all banks. A systems competition approach would recommend ensuring that failing banks can be wound up without compromising the system as a whole. Over-aggressive pay policies should then be penalised by the loss of investors, depositors or policy holders.

estimates of transactions costs are conjectural and a matter of business judgment rather than exact calculation. Omitting to consider the full range of responses to transactional hazards through private governance as well as state regulation, however, is potentially a significant cause of regulatory failure.

4 COASE'S CONTRIBUTIONS TO THE THEORY OF INDUSTRIAL ORGANISATION AND REGULATION

Alex Robson

Introduction

Ronald Coase's analysis of the boundaries of the firm (1937b) and his examination of externalities (1960) – both of which were built upon the key concept of transaction costs – have implications for a range of topics in microeconomic theory and economic policy analysis.[1] One obvious example from industrial organisation and antitrust that immediately comes to mind, but which Coase did not develop in any great detail, is the application of Coasean bargaining to the theory of corporate takeovers and mergers. Economies of scale, scope and sequence, 'synergies' (that is, positive externalities) and the reduction of transaction costs via vertical integration all figure prominently in modern explanations of merger and acquisition activity (see, for example, Betton 2008). Although Coase later stated that he had not written his 1937 paper with the intention of revolutionising microeconomic theory (Coase 1988d),

---

1   For an overview of some of Coase's more widely cited work, see Robson (2014).

transaction costs have today become a lens through which many economists view the commercial world. Transaction costs help organise one's thoughts, and can be used as an aid to guide empirical analyses of real-life economic phenomenon. As he wrote (Coase 1998a: 73):

> Even if we start with the relatively simple analysis of 'The Nature of the Firm,' discovering the factors that determine the relative costs of coordination by management within the firm or by transactions on the market is no simple task. However, this is not by any means the whole story. We cannot confine our analysis to what happens within a single firm. This is what I said in a lecture published in Lives of the Laureates (Coase 1995: 245): 'The costs of coordination within a firm and the level of transaction costs that it faces are affected by its ability to purchase inputs from other firms, and their ability to supply these inputs depends in part on their costs of coordination and the level of transaction costs that they face which are similarly affected by what these are in still other firms. What we are dealing with is a complex inter-related structure.' Add to this the influence of the laws, of the social system, and of the culture, as well as the effects of technological changes such as the digital revolution with its dramatic fall in information costs (a major component of transaction costs), and you have a complicated set of interrelationships the nature of which will take much dedicated work over a long period to discover. But when this is done, all of economics will have become what we now call 'the new institutional economics'.

This chapter reviews some of Coase's work on industrial organisation and regulation, and demonstrates that it spanned – and remains highly relevant for – a wide range of economic policy issues. Because Coase wrote a number of papers on the broadcasting industry, we pay particular attention to applications in the economic analysis of telecommunications and related industries. The chapter argues that, even though the pace of technological change in these industries has been (and continues to be) very rapid, Coase's work on the economics of the broadcasting industries in Great Britain and the United States published more than 50 years ago continues to influence and enhance our understanding of modern policy issues concerning telecommunications networks and their regulation. Many of the policy issues in this area that arose in the last century are still with us in some form or another, and hence this work provides a number of valuable policy lessons, particularly regarding economic institutions and the interaction between regulators and the private sector.

The chapter is structured as follows. Section 2 explores the Coasean theory of the firm from an industrial organisation perspective, paying particular attention to Coase's authoritative critique of the field in the early 1970s. Section 3 examines a piece of Coase's work which has had the most significant impact upon modern regulatory economics: his analysis of marginal cost pricing. Section 4 summarises Coase's critique of one of the most famous 'fables' in economics – GM's acquisition of Fisher Body – and explores some of the implications for regulatory economics. In Section 5 we change direction slightly, and briefly survey

Coase's work on the communications industry, spanning a broad range of topics and countries over several decades. Section 6 concludes with a brief account of his editorship of the *Journal of Law and Economics*.

The nature of the firm: implications for the theory of industrial organisation

Coase's approach to industrial organisation was a natural extension of ideas explored in 'The nature of the firm'. Transaction costs not only determined the boundaries of the firm; they also influenced the firm's overall costs, consumer prices and ultimately the competitive landscape of particular industries. Since business organisations which survived and prospered would be those which minimised the costs of internal and market transactions, understanding how these costs were managed was critical to understanding the 'organisation of industry' as Coase understood it.

This Coasean approach to industrial organisation has a number of implications. Certain kinds of commercial behaviour (for example, price discounting and sales) which might otherwise be regarded as anti-competitive could actually be a necessary and economically desirable manifestation of healthy competition. Similarly, mergers which might increase market power could be justified on efficiency grounds if the alternative was that the merging firms were forced to tolerate high transaction costs in the absence of any deal.

Unfortunately, the exploration and analysis of these implications were very slow in coming, because according to Coase the profession basically ignored 'The nature of the firm' for thirty or forty years after it was published (Coase 1988d: 33). It was against this background of indifference from the profession that Coase wrote his 1972 article 'Industrial organisation: a proposal for research'. This paper provided a powerful critique of the field of industrial organisation as it stood at the time, and set out an ambitious research agenda for the National Bureau of Economic Research in the US.

The Coasean critique of the state of industrial organisation theory in the early 1970s consisted of three strands. First, he argued that while the focus of the post-1930s literature on 'industry structure' was important, it missed a number of vital ingredients. Before one could hope to understand what firms did and why they did it, Coase argued, one needed a theory of why firms existed in the first place. The transaction cost theory of the firm introduced by Coase in 1937 was, of course, such a theory, and so he reintroduced that framework in the context of the existing industrial organisation literature and demonstrated how it could be applied.

Coase's second theme was that industrial organisation scholars were far too narrow in their outlook. Perhaps as a way of previewing what would turn out to be one of his most well-known papers, 'The lighthouse in economics' (Coase 1974b), which appeared in the *Journal of Law and Economics* just two years later, Coase urged industrial organisation economists to tackle a range of other issues. These included the choice between private and public provision of services such as police protection, garbage collection, utilities, education and hospitals. Such analyses, as we show below, were a common feature of Coase's work.

Interestingly, Coase went even further and called for the integration of public choice analysis into industrial organisation, arguing that (ibid.):

> It seems to have been implicitly assumed that the same considerations which led welfare economists to see the need for government action would also motivate those whose active support was required to bring about the political changes necessary to implement these policy recommendations. In this, we are wiser than we were, in large part because of the new 'economic theory of politics'. We are beginning to perceive the nature of the forces which bring about changes in the law – and there is no necessary relationship between the strength of forces favoring such changes and the gain from such changes as seen by economists. It suggests that economists interested in promoting particular economic policies should investigate the framework of our political system to discover what modifications in it are required if their economic policies are to be adopted, and should count in the cost of these political changes. This presupposes that the relationship between the character of the political institutions and the adoption of a particular economic policy – in our case, government operation of industry – has been discovered. We do not know much about these relationships, but uncovering them seems to me a task to be assumed by students of industrial organization.

The inclusion of public choice analysis was a common theme running throughout Coase's work.

The third main strand in Coase's critique of industrial organisation theory related to the economics profession's overly narrow focus on monopoly and antitrust issues. Coase preferred to start with a competitive paradigm – and this is yet another common theme than can be found throughout his writings. For example, in a 1988 article revisiting the nature of the firm, he states that (Coase 1988c: 26):

> The literature on industrial organization was largely American and laid emphasis on the effects of monopoly, and it must have had an influence on our thinking ... I have no doubt that while in America I took seriously what was said in the reports of the Federal Trade Commission. But my basic position was (and is) the same as Plant's, that our economic system is in the main competitive. Any explanation therefore for the emergence of the firm had to be one which applied in competitive conditions, although monopoly might be important in particular cases. In the early 1930s I was looking for an explanation for the existence of the firm which did not depend on monopoly. I found it, of course, in transaction costs.

In Coase's view there was a tendency for industrial organisation scholars to rely too heavily on monopoly as an explanation for any phenomenon which could not be understood within the narrow confines of the (transaction-cost-free) theoretical ideal of perfectly competitive markets. This method of thinking not only led to poor economic analysis and unreliable predictions; it could potentially have widespread negative economic consequences if it was taken seriously by the antitrust enforcement authorities. Any behaviour that could not be fitted in to the simple competitive paradigm could risk being seen as an abuse of market power.

Regulating utilities: the Coasean critique of marginal cost pricing

One commonly encountered feature of public utilities (such as electricity networks, communications networks, water and gas pipelines) is that fixed costs are significant when compared with incremental production costs. Products with large fixed costs and low marginal costs are likely to have average costs declining over a significant range of their output. The standard textbook analysis argues that allowing more than one firm in such an industry risks wasteful duplication of fixed costs, but that restricting the market to a single firm enables the firm to charge inefficiently high monopoly prices. Thus the question arises: what is the efficient pricing rule in these circumstances?

Prior to Coase's (1946a) paper, a standard response was that the firm should set its output price equal to its marginal cost (see, for example, Hotelling 1938). In this way, it was argued, consumers would consume up to the point where incremental willingness to pay equalled incremental opportunity cost, ensuring an efficient allocation of resources. To the extent that this scheme produced an

Figure 1   Marginal cost pricing can produce a socially inefficient outcome

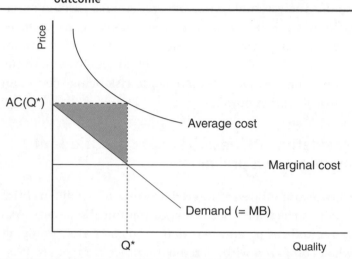

economic loss for the firm, the government could provide an offsetting subsidy.

Coase's analysis demonstrated that this policy recommendation was highly inadequate as a matter of theory, and that it could lead to economically damaging results in practice (see also Coase 1947a, 1970b). His main argument is illustrated diagrammatically in Figure 1, which features a single firm with a constant marginal cost curve, everywhere declining average costs (due to the presence of large fixed costs) and a downward-sloping demand curve (which reflects social marginal benefits). In this example, the marginal cost pricing rule produces a quantity equal to Q*. Gross social benefits are equal to the entire area beneath the demand curve, whereas gross social costs are equal to the rectangle $AC(Q^*) \times Q^*$, which exceeds benefits by the shaded triangle. Note that applying the marginal cost pricing rule here produces a sizeable social loss, equal in magnitude to the size of the consumer surplus. Note also that the average cost pricing rule is of no assistance either: since the average cost curve does not cut the demand curve, there is no average cost pricing rule that will cover costs.

The reason for these two outcomes in this particular example is straightforward: in Figure 1 it is simply uneconomic to produce the good, with total costs exceeding total benefits at all levels of production. The efficient outcome is zero production, but under both marginal cost pricing and average cost pricing there is not enough information for a government agency to compare total willingness to pay with total costs. As Coase later argued in a response to one of his critics (Coase 1947: 150):

> If the Hotelling–Lerner solution is adopted, there is only one way out of this difficulty. This is for the State to decide whether or not each consumer should be supplied with the particular good concerned. This would be done by estimating whether or not each consumer would be willing to pay an amount equal to the total cost of supplying him, if he was called upon to do so. I argued that no Government could estimate individual demands accurately; that if all pricing were on a marginal-cost basis, there would be less information available by which such an estimate could be made; and that the incentive

to correct forecasting would be diminished if there were no subsequent market test of whether such estimates of individual demand were correct or not.

Coase proposed a straightforward solution to this problem in the form of a two-part tariff, which is well known to modern microeconomists. Under this pricing scheme the firm charges each consumer an access fee to cover its fixed costs, and a marginal price to cover incremental production costs. Not only does this scheme have the advantage of allowing the firm to cover all of its costs; it also supplies the government with the information to encourage efficient production choices at the extensive margin. Indeed, Coase noted that (ibid.: 151):

> Simply to equate marginal cost and the marginal valuation is not to determine, in conditions of decreasing average cost, whether the total supply should be undertaken or not. The advantage of multi-part pricing is that consumers can be asked to pay an amount which is equal to 'the total' cost and therefore it is possible to discover whether consumers value the total supply at more than the total cost of supplying them.

The hold-up problem: implications for regulation

Coase recognised in 'The nature of the firm' that in a world of incomplete contracting, if firms make sunk, relationship-specific capital investments there is a risk that the 'hold-up' or 'holdout' problem may arise. This occurs if, after such investments are made, circumstances change in an unanticipated way and one of the parties finds itself in a monopoly position and can act opportunistically, exploiting the fact that the other firm cannot simply end the relationship and take its capital elsewhere. Such expropriation of specific investments can arise frequently in network industries (for example, in the telecommunications industry a downstream service provider may rely on an upstream network owner for access to an essential network facility (see, for example, Laffont and Tirole 2001: 75)). One possible consequence of the hold-up problem is inefficiently low investment: if, at the investment stage, the downstream firm anticipates that expropriation may be likely, it is less likely to make such an investment in the firm place.

Direct regulation of access prices and other contractual conditions has been proposed as a solution to the hold-up problem.[2] Long-term contracts (quasi-vertical integration) or full vertical integration (a takeover or merger) are alternative, market-based solutions which are consistent with Coase's transaction costs theory of the firm. However, if the upstream network owner also competes in the downstream retail market, this can lead to other problems.[3]

In neither case are transaction costs completely eliminated, but it is far from obvious that access regulation (which can create a highly adversarial, litigious

---

2   For example, Australia implemented a national access regulatory regime in the mid 1990s.

3   For a survey, see Armstrong and Sappington (2007).

environment between parties) in practice leads to lower transaction costs.[4] The belief that such hold-up problems are ubiquitous – let alone the theory itself is rarely questioned. One likely explanation is that there are some very good historical, real-world examples of hold-up problems that economists have been able to point to. Perhaps the most celebrated example is the acquisition of Fisher Body by General Motors in 1926, first analysed by Klein et al. (1978) (and which, incidentally, was published in the *Journal of Law and Economics* under Coase's editorship).

The basic Fisher Body story has been outlined in Chapter 2. The view set out by Klein and colleagues was that the transaction took place because of concerns over relation-specific investments and contractual hold-up problems (Klein et al. 1978). However, in an important paper, Coase (2000) argued that the standard account was incorrect.[5] In typical Coasean fashion he carefully traced the history of the Fisher–GM commercial relationship and noted that the standard account was wrong for several reasons, including the fact that the Fisher brothers (who controlled Fisher) were members of the board of directors of GM and were unlikely to have advocated the use of inefficient production methods by Fisher Body.

Furthermore, Coase showed that Fisher did not locate its body plants far away from GM assembly plants. There

---

4   This point is made by Ergas (2009).

5   Coase's paper was accompanied in the same issue of the *Journal of Law and Economics* by two other papers which had independently come to the same conclusion. See Freeland (2000) and Casadesus-Masanell and Spulber (2000).

was no contractual hold-up: the prevailing view was implausible.

While this refutation of the canonical example of the hold-up theory in action in no way defeats the theoretical possibility of contractual hold-up leading to inefficiently low investments, it has important implications. First, vertical integration may be motivated by a range of factors, and is not always implemented to eliminate hold-up problems. Secondly, and more importantly for the theory and practice of regulation, behaviour that appears superficially to resemble a hold-up problem may be nothing of the sort. Indeed, an upstream network owner may reject an offer from a downstream service provider simply because the terms of that offer would result in both a commercially unprofitable transaction for the network owner *and* a socially inefficient outcome – the two are not mutually exclusive. The main lesson of Coase's analysis of the Fisher Body acquisition (a lesson which he had provided earlier in 'The lighthouse in economics') is that economists should carefully check their facts before jumping to conclusions – advice that regulators would also do well to follow.

Regulation and industrial organisation of the communications industry

Private and public telecommunications networks – the internet, radio, television and fixed and mobile telephone networks constitute one of the 'commanding heights' of the modern economy. The economic and social importance of the ability of businesses and households to store and access information (cloud computing), engage in ecommerce and send emails and upload and download products and services (apps) at fast speeds is difficult to overstate.

Modern regulatory economists frequently grapple with the problem of designing appropriate institutional arrangements to ensure that the value of network access, speeds, coverage and mobility reach their full potential. The sheer breadth and variety of economic issues associated with regulation is almost overwhelming, and includes problems associated with optimal spectrum management and the allocation of broadcasting licence fees; the regulation of fixed and mobile network access and usage prices; the efficient rollout of new networks, technologies and user platforms; the interaction between various modes of delivering information (known today as 'convergence'); the consequences of privatisation (or re-nationalisation) of public broadcasters and/or postal services; content and programming restrictions; and issues surrounding advertising and freedom of speech.

Remarkably, Coase's work spanned all of these issues and more. For example, he published a historical analysis of the British television industry in the 1950s (Coase 1954), while in the 1970s he developed an economic approach to advertising and free speech (Coase 1974a, 1977c) and published a detailed account and analysis of the practice and regulation of payola in the US (Coase 1979a). He also published a number of papers on the radio broadcasting industry in Great Britain and the United States, to which we now turn.

The development of the radio broadcasting industry in Britain

Coase's papers on British radio broadcasting were a formidable blend of regulatory analysis and economic history. His first paper (1947b) was a fascinating and detailed history of the development of the British Broadcasting Company, the private sector predecessor of what would in 1927 become the government-owned British Broadcasting Corporation (BBC). The early twentieth century was, as today, a time of rapid technological progress, innovation and entrepreneurship in the communications industry. Coase's analysis showed that a number of factors (including the fact that the Marconi company owned most of the relevant wireless broadcasting patents) ultimately led to the development of a private monopoly in broadcasting in Great Britain. However, he concludes that the most important influence in the development of this monopoly was related to public choice considerations: the Post Office simply wanted to deal with one broadcasting company instead of two or more, fearing that it would appear to be granting favours if it had to issue licences to multiple broadcasters. In other words, Coase argued that this monopoly was borne out of desire on the part of the Post Office for administrative and bureaucratic convenience.

Coase showed that the argument that the broadcasting monopoly in Britain was somehow good for the public on moral grounds using its 'programme monopoly' doctrine came much later, but that it had deleterious economic effects. In his 1948 paper he traced the history of the wire broadcasting industry in Great Britain from its private sector beginnings in 1924 to the British Government's release of its White Paper on Broadcasting Policy in 1946 (Coase 1948). Coase concluded that the monopoly enjoyed by the British Broadcasting Company (whose wireless service would have been forced to compete directly with wire broadcasting) had an important negative influence on this new industry. In particular, the BBC's ability to lobby for restrictions on the private sector's development of wire relay exchanges over the period had negative effect. The nationalised BBC was aided and abetted by the British Post Office, which placed heavy restrictions on the issue of wire relay exchange licences. Coase showed how the BBC's efforts to protect its programme monopoly on moral grounds (the argument that domestic and foreign wire broadcasts could have had a corrupting influence upon the British public) were ultimately more successful than any economic argument derived from economic theory.

The allocation of radio frequency spectrum in the United States

One of Coase's better-known contributions is his detailed history of the US Federal Communications Commission (Coase 1959). Much of the analysis in this paper would form the basis of arguments that also appeared in 'The problem of social cost', which appeared soon afterwards.

After providing his usual comprehensive historical and political overview (in this case, of how the FCC was formed), Coase analysed the way in which it regulated the radio frequency spectrum and found the existing system sadly wanting. Coase's economic critique stemmed from what he regarded as the flawed way in which policymakers had conceptualised regulation in this important area. While conceding that questions of anti-competitive behaviour, the regulation of potentially monopolistic broadcasters and control of programme content were important, Coase argued that these were conceptually separate from the narrow economic issue of how licences should be allocated.

For Coase, the questions faced by policymakers regarding the management of radio frequency spectrum were essentially questions regarding the allocation, clarification and enforcement of private property rights in a scarce resource. His main proposal for reform was that instead of issuing licences for free (which Coase, anticipating the modern theory of rent seeking, argued would create incentives for lobbying and corruption) the US government should auction spectrum rights to the highest bidder and allow those property rights to be traded between broadcasting firms. Coase argued, as he would later demonstrate in more detail in 'The problem of social cost', that this would result in an efficient allocation of spectrum, with the scarce resource moving from low-valued to high-valued uses. Moreover, assuming that the costs of private bargaining were sufficiently low, issues that arose around conflicting or overlapping spectrum rights (where one broadcaster might broadcast on a frequency that interfered with another's signal) could be readily dealt with by negotiation between firms, rather than requiring heavy-handed regulation by government agencies. Crucially, Coase further argued that government bureaucracies (such as emergency services) should also be forced to pay for spectrum, as this would encourage a more rigorous assessment of incremental social costs and benefits of alternative methods of achieving similar policy goals.

These ideas were nothing short of revolutionary at the time, a fact which Coase's article ably demonstrated along the way, as he set out a depressingly large number of quotations from public officials and other commentators who either didn't understand the basic economics of markets, or who opposed them outright on political and ideological grounds. As Coase would later point out (Coase 1965: 162):

> As we all know, scarce resources are normally allocated in the United States by means of the pricing mechanism and a price emerges which is sufficiently high to reduce demand to equal the available supply. The question is: why isn't this done in the case of the radio frequency spectrum? The answer, extraordinary though it may seem, is that the possibility of using the pricing mechanism is something which never occurs to those responsible for policy concerning the use of the radio frequency spectrum.

Despite early scepticism and opposition these market-based proposals gradually caught on in the communications industry and elsewhere. Today the notion that the government should simply establish or clarify private property rights where none previously existed, auction off these rights and then enforce voluntary contractual agreements to exchange these rights – but otherwise engage in light-handed regulation – forms the basis of a significant number of modern regulatory policies, including spectrum auctions, tradeable fishing quotas, hunting licences and emissions trading schemes.

Conclusion

This chapter has reviewed Coase's work on industrial organisation and regulation. As I have noted elsewhere (Robson 2014), his writings tended to pay careful attention to institutional arrangements and historical details such as legal rules and property rights, and his analyses are almost always motivated by 'real world' commercial issues or policy questions. These characteristics are certainly apparent in the publications surveyed in the present chapter. They are also evident in the *Journal of Law and Economics*. Coase served as the editor of this journal for 18 years, beginning in 1964. During this period the *Journal of Law and Economics* established itself not only as a distinct and prestigious academic journal, but also helped to create and maintain momentum in what was then a very young new field of study: law and economics.

Under Coase's editorship the *Journal of Law and Economics* published a number of important papers in industrial organisation and regulation, including valuable contributions to the theory of predatory pricing and collusion, as well as utility regulation and antitrust. To take just one well-known example, the journal published Harold

Demsetz's classic article 'Why regulate utilities?', in which Demsetz argued that instead of directly regulating the prices of natural monopolies using standard mechanisms like average cost pricing rules, governments could instead create competition for the market by inviting firms to bid for customers, where the bids would involve prices and other contractual terms (Demsetz 1968b). This approach was to later become 'the dominant approach to the modern theory of regulation'.[6]

It is appropriate to close this chapter with a quote from Coase's colleagues on the occasion of his resignation from the journal's editorship. They wrote that (Landes et al. 1983: iii):

> Coase was the editor as intellectual leader. His editorship meant much more than managing the flow of manuscripts submitted to the Journal. He used it to nudge and influence economists, and lawyers with a strong interest in economics, to work on problems that Coase thought were both important and neglected. Coase sought out and encouraged faculty members at Chicago and elsewhere to examine how particular markets actually worked, what factors determined the types of transactions and contracts that parties entered into, and the role of laws and legal institutions in shaping markets. Coase recognized that encouragement would be insufficient. As a strong believer in the power of self-interest, he offered

---

6 See Demsetz's entry at the American Economic Association website: https://www.aeaweb.org/honors_awards/bios/Harold_Demsetz.php

the prospect of publication in the Journal. He prodded authors to finish their papers, he commented extensively on drafts, he urged authors to make the papers readable. Coase's efforts resulted in a distinctive journal.

The qualities that Coase brought to his editorship of the *Journal of Law and Economics* were the same as those that he had displayed throughout his academic career. There will never be another economist like him.

5 COASE ON PROPERTY RIGHTS AND THE POLITICAL ECONOMY OF ENVIRONMENTAL PROTECTION

Mark Pennington

Introduction

The relationship between Ronald Coase's ideas and those who study the allocation of environmental resources on a professional basis is a perplexing one. On the one hand his seminal article 'The problem of social cost' (Coase 1960) is one of the most widely cited works in environmental political economy.[1] On the other, however, Coasian ideas are routinely ignored in discussions of environmental problems because they are deemed unrealistic. 'Interesting, but irrelevant' would probably be an accurate description of the way that the vast majority of environmental policy analysts see Coase's work. Others question the ethical foundations of the key Coasian idea

---

1   Google Scholar currently registers over 25,500 citations to 'The problem of social cost', whereas A. C. Pigou's arguably more influential 'The economics of welfare', first published in 1920, has just over 9,000 citations. The higher figures for Coase here may reflect the influence of his work in fields outside of economics – and especially in the domain of legal studies predominantly in the US.

that environmental values should be brought within the scope of market exchange, preferring instead a greater reliance on democratic deliberation and 'command and control' regulation. It will be my contention in this chapter that both the practical and ethical objections to Coase's perspective are misguided. Far from unrealistic, Coasian analysis suggests a highly pragmatic case for a greater, though by no means exclusive, reliance on market processes and the specification of private property rights, as the best way to tackle environmental issues. Far from being unethical, Coasian arguments point towards the importance of moral pluralism, and respect for individual differences, in the process of environmental valuation.

In order to explicate these points, my analysis is divided into three sections. The first sets out the core Coasian idea that externalities are 'reciprocal' in nature and examines how the specification of property rights can help to reduce resource use conflicts by facilitating a process of contractual bargaining. It highlights the critique of Pigovian welfare economics and outlines the case for the comparative transaction costs approach to environmental policy that flows from Coasian analysis. The second section uses a loosely Coasian framework to categorise different sorts of environmental issue with respect to the character of the transaction costs problem they may engender and the scope for the development of environmental markets. The third and final section considers and rebuts some of the primary ethical objections levelled against the Coasian approach.

Coase on the problem of social cost

Many discussions of environmental problems pertaining to habitat destruction or pollution of various kinds proceed from the implicit assumption that all environmental damage is inherently 'bad' and are apt to depict the structure of these problems as reflecting the struggle between a 'perpetrator' and 'victim' of this damage. A little reflection, however, reveals that this analysis may not always be appropriate. Those who pollute or damage the environment may not typically do so for the sake of 'imposing costs' on their 'victims' but because the activities concerned may be necessary to generate benefits that people in general also value. Pristine ecological conditions may be associated with human lives that are impoverished, with few opportunities for travel, low living standards, limited or non-existent access to health care and modern drugs, and low life expectancy. Decisions to protect habitats and to reduce or eliminate pollution, therefore, need to account for the benefits that may be *lost* as a consequence of such decisions. We should not then necessarily see 'polluters' as the only agents seeking to 'impose costs' and those demanding protection from environmental damages as the only potential 'victims'. This recognition that what environmental economists call 'externalities' are a 'double-sided' or 'reciprocal' phenomenon is a fundamental insight of Ronald Coase's work. As he explained (1960: 2):

> The question is commonly thought of as one in which A inflicts harm on B and what has to be decided is: how

should we restrain A? ... The real question that has to be decided is: should A be allowed to harm B or should B be allowed to harm A?

Though Coase deals with 'externality' issues, his seminal 'The problem of social cost' does not use the term. For Coase, natural resource and environmental protection problems typically arise when there are diverse and often competing demands for the use of environmental assets and when there is a need to balance these conflicting interests. Whether an actor or group of actors is the 'victim' or 'perpetrator' of an 'externality' is fundamentally a question of who has the rights to engage in the activity concerned and if they wish to trade such rights for compensation. If property rights reside with those wishing to preserve habitat or clean air then those wishing to use these assets can offer to pay compensation to the relevant owners for any damages that may result. Whether the owners accept these terms will depend on their assessment of how the losses of value with respect to anticipated property values and benefits such as peace, tranquillity, cleanliness, etc., compare to the monetary compensation on offer. The extent, to which those who wish to engage in 'damage' are willing to offer compensation meanwhile, will be proportionate to their production costs and the benefits they expect to derive from the customers who buy their products. Similar calculations will be considered if property rights reside with 'polluters' and it is those with a preference for environmental protection who must compensate the agents concerned for agreeing 'not to pollute'. If rights to use different aspects of the environment are specified in this way then strictly speaking externalities do not exist. Or, if problems arise, they can be tackled via the usual processes of tort law through injunctions against transgressors.

It was recognition of the reciprocal nature of externalities, and appreciation for the manner in which private bargaining might determine the trade-offs between environmental protection and other objectives, that led to Coase's critique of the then (and still) dominant Pigovian approach to environmental problems. According to the Pigovian view (Pigou 1920), the divergence between private and social costs owing to the unaccounted externalities that may occur in a free market created a strong prima facie case for government intervention in the form of taxes to discourage environmental pollution or subsidies to encourage resource conservation. For Coase, however, if property rights to assets have been specified then there is in fact no divergence between private and social costs because *all* relevant costs and benefits will be accounted for in the bargains struck between different rights holders – resort to Pigovian taxes or subsidies is thus wholly unnecessary. However the initial rights are assigned, the processes of private negotiation in the market will ensure that the rights move towards those who value them most. As Coase explained in his Nobel acceptance speech, discussing 'The problem of social cost' (Coase 1992):

> What I showed in that article ... was that in a regime of zero transaction costs, an assumption of standard economic theory, negotiations between the parties would

lead to those arrangements being made which would maximise wealth and this irrespective of the initial assignment of rights ...

For Coase, therefore, the existence of any unaccounted costs and benefits in 'real world' conditions must reflect that transaction costs are *not in fact zero* and that markets for the relevant goods are 'incomplete'. When the courts assign rights and liabilities in a context of *positive* transaction costs, then there is no inherent tendency for a welfare-maximising result to emerge, because the existence of these costs may block potentially beneficial exchanges between the respective parties. Transaction costs are those costs associated with the definition and enforcement of property rights and of negotiating contracts – costs which may be high in the case of environmental assets that are often associated with problems of 'non-excludability' or 'public good' characteristics (Anderson and Libecap 2014).

The recognition that environmental problems are a consequence of *positive* transaction costs is perhaps *the* central Coasian insight, yet strangely enough this very idea has often led to the dismissal of Coasian policy ideas. According to a common characterisation (for example, Kelman 1987; Stiglitz 1994), the Coase theorem (see Chapter 2) offers an ideological apologia for a laissez-faire or free-market approach to environmental protection, rooted in the assumptions of neo-classical equilibrium theorising that simply cannot be reflected in the real world. The implication is that Pigovian taxes and subsidies or even direct regulation or control of economic activity by the state are the only realistic possibilities for environmental management. Yet, far from being impractical or ideological, the purpose of Coase's analysis was to highlight the policy implications that flow from recognising the significance of transaction costs. Imperfections or frictions in markets may result in less than optimal outcomes – but these imperfections or frictions exist under *any* institutional alternative which involves direct government intervention. Deciding whether to rely on one mechanism or another requires a comparative institutions approach which considers the *extent* of the likely transaction costs under different types of 'solution'. Within this context, Coase identifies four mechanisms for approaching externalities: (i) relying on individual bargaining within a process of market-based negotiation; (ii) internalising externalities by bringing decisions within the structures of pooled decision structures such as firms or other private corporate bodies; (iii) direct government regulation, with the state acting as a 'super-firm' which imposes prices or regulations via administrative fiat; (iv) doing nothing.

In view of the variety of options that Coase highlights it is often those who oppose markets and private sector solutions (options (i) and (ii) in the above typology) that are guilty of an excessively ideological approach. Having noted that transaction costs may prevent the emergence of fully efficient markets, there is often an assumption that a state-centric alternative is immune from the very same costs. 'Real world' governments, however, face positive transaction costs as much as real-world private decision-makers and indeed, in many though by no means all instances the transaction costs that face imperfect governments may be *higher* than those involved in the private sector. Absent the profit-and-loss signals to which individuals and firms have access in markets, decisions by the state to impose taxes, subsidies or regulations are not subject to any obvious feedback mechanism that can weed out erroneous interventions and lead over time to an improved set of decisions.

Insofar as politicians and regulators are subject to feedback mechanisms, these are derived from political bargaining. But these processes are subject to high negotiation costs and problems of non-excludability which can introduce significant bias into decision-making. To achieve benefits from political activity requires collective action, but the larger the numbers that might benefit or bear the costs from such action, the greater the incentives to act as free riders on the non-excludable good of successful political lobbying. Policies that concentrate benefits on a relatively small number of actors may attract well-organised lobbies that face lower costs of monitoring and disciplining free riders. By contrast, measures that diffuse benefits across large groups may not bring forth organised support proportionate to the numbers affected, owing to the higher costs of controlling free-rider behaviour in large-number situations (Olson 2000).

While the Coasian approach offers no panacea for environmental conflicts, it is true that Coase's own policy preferences were weighted towards a greater reliance on markets and property rights than is typically the case. However, this preference arose not from assumptions about zero transaction costs but from a 'real world' comparison of these costs in different settings. In many cases it is the intellectual dominance of the belief that markets *cannot* work that has locked in institutions which *prohibit* the emergence of private, contractual solutions. In addition, it was Coase's sensitivity to the importance of transaction costs that led him to recognise that both 'market failures' and 'government failures' may be so extensive that 'doing nothing' may sometimes be the best that can be hoped for because 'it will ... commonly be the case' that the costs of allowing an externality to persist may be less than the costs of trying to enforce private property rights or governmental regulations (1960: 18).

In what follows I offer a loosely 'comparative institutions' analysis to consider the prospects for solutions to a variety of environmental problems drawing on Coasian reasoning. The subsequent section responds to some of the ethical objections that have been raised against the perspective.

Coasian analysis and the scope for environmental markets

'Easy' problems

Although transaction costs arise in the context of most markets for environmental goods these costs tend to be at their lowest in the case of land-based issues such as the management of forests, mineral extraction rights, and wild game conservation, which can be subject to various fencing technologies. Other stationary resources, such as oyster beds and water-based assets such as rivers and in-shore fisheries that are excludable with existing technology also exhibit relatively lower bargaining and enforcement costs. Although in many cases such assets are amenable to private ownership of one form or another, the political/ideological framework often prevents the development of environmental markets even where they have considerable potential to improve resource allocation. Prices can work to signal the demand for environmental quality and com-municate the scope for mutually advantageous exchanges. By contrast, when governments own assets or regulate dir-ectly the terms on which they can be used, incentives often weigh against a proper consideration of relevant costs. On the one hand, without private property rights bureaucrat-ic managers lack strong rights of residual claimancy which would enable them to weigh the costs and benefits of al-ternative uses and to face the costs of the trade-offs they make. On the other, the bureaucratic process is frequently subject to the vagaries of political lobbying which tends to favour concentrated and highly visible interest groups to the detriment of less organised taxpayers and consumers.

The contrasting performance of private and public resource management regimes is well illustrated with the case of river management. Evidence suggests that where private property arrangements have been allowed to emerge, there have been considerable improvements in terms of the maintenance of fish stocks and the reduc-tion of pollution. In Britain, for example, private fishing rights to rivers are widespread and an extensive angling market has developed. Riparian owners are able to charge angling clubs for the right to fish and in some cases clubs have purchased stretches of the rivers themselves. In turn, the prices generated in such markets have provided an important way of communicating environmental values – signalling to owners the demand for well-stocked and clean water. As a consequence, from a position in the 1950s where trout and salmon fishing was the preserve of an elite few, by the early 1990s such opportunities had become readily available in and around most British towns. Correspondingly, there have been substantial improvements in water quality with owners, such as the Anglers Cooperative Association,[2] taking successful legal actions against instances of non-contracted pollution (on this see Bate 2001). In the US, by contrast, the 'public trust' doctrine has in many states often forbidden the private ownership of water rights and has thus thwarted the development of markets. The resulting command-and-control approach to river management has continued to be reflected in periodic overfishing and relatively poor water standards (Anderson and Leal 2001).

The differential results that have emerged in the context of contrasting regimes for the management of wild game further illustrate the potential of property rights solutions to improve outcomes and to internalise external costs. In a context where people cannot capture the benefits from conserving wild game, there are then few incentives for them to reduce activities such as poaching and habitat

2 Now known as Fish Legal.

destruction. By contrast, where property rights enable people to capture the gains – and to face the losses – of their resource management decisions, they are more likely to consider the benefits of resource conservation than would otherwise be the case. Within this context, elephant populations have grown significantly in countries such as Botswana, which have allowed individuals and tribal groups to establish ownership rights to herds and to participate in the legal ivory trade or to receive revenues from tourists participating in various eco-tourism schemes. Elsewhere in Africa, however, where the state has retained ownership rights via national parks and where international treaties have banned the trade in ivory and other wild game products, the population has failed to recover from decades of rampant poaching. Though there is some evidence that the elephant population has started to recover following more rigorous internationally funded efforts to enforce the ban on ivory trading, these achievements pale in comparison to the results where property rights have been established (ibid.: Chapter 6).

'Middle-range' problems

Though many environmental assets are more amenable to allocation via bargaining in markets than is commonly recognised, in other cases the extent of the transaction costs problems involved in defining and in enforcing property rights reduces the scope for bargaining between individual agents. This can be a particular problem where there are relatively large numbers of affected parties and where external effects occur across a large territorial scale. In these contexts, however, decentralised and private solutions are still possible through the creation of 'firm-like' structures, which can reduce bargaining costs by imposing rules to which the members of 'the firm' must subscribe – and which exist in a meta-level environment of competition between different hierarchical structures. Just as conventional business firms can reduce the transaction costs involved in monitoring production processes based on 'spot-contracts', so people can pool property rights so as to reduce the costs of individual bargaining by ceding control to a private, but collective, organisation that internalises costs by developing rules at the relevant territorial scale. Within this context, the 'common property regimes' discussed by Elinor Ostrom provide a useful illustration of the kind of institutional innovations that are likely to emerge to deal with such problems. In the case of managing river catchments Ostrom shows that successful governance structures have often arisen in 'nested arrangements' where relatively small groups of water users at the level of individual water basins have created associations to manage intra-basin issues, but where these have 'contracted up' to form higher-level associations to address *inter*-basin externalities (Ostrom 1990: Chapter 5).

Ostrom's work suggests that many resource conflicts may be dealt with effectively through the bottom-up emergence of rules, but that the potential for such institutional innovations is often thwarted by government actions which impose regulation from above. In cases such as the European Union Common Fisheries Policy, for example, a one-size-fits-all approach has superseded the efforts of private fishing associations that had previously developed their own rules to manage stocks. In these cases, central regulation frequently suffers from higher transaction costs than the relatively more decentralised structures it has replaced. In particular, there are huge enforcement costs and principal–agent problems created where fisherman have little personal incentive to adhere to rules developed by regulators whose livelihood is not significantly affected by the decisions taken. In this instance, it is the determination to treat the entire fishery as a common asset rather than a separable resource that raises the costs of coming to an effective solution. If associations of fishermen were allowed greater scope to enforce exclusion rights to particular parts of the fishery such that they could profit directly from managing stocks effectively themselves – or sell the rights to outsiders – then incentives would be better aligned and transaction costs, though still positive, could be reduced.

'Tougher'/ 'insoluble' problems

Though the analysis presented thus far has highlighted cases where there are grounds to favour decentralised non-state solutions, the Coasian perspective does not rule out a role for the state. Rather, it urges that attention is paid to comparing the transaction costs involved under different institutional arrangements. Thus, government can have an important role to play in reducing the transaction costs that face private agents by providing for effective enforcement against property rights violations and allowing for clear and transparent processes of dispute resolution where an ownership claim is contested. State action may also help to facilitate the emergence of private solutions by laying down the terms by which private agents can acquire ownership rights to resources that have been held in an 'open access' situation.

Outside of these cases, however, there may also be a role for more direct state regulation where private bargaining is too costly and where 'firm-like' structures cannot emerge on a sufficient scale to internalise the relevant environmental costs. This is especially likely to be so in cases of regional, national or international air pollution problems. In some instances state agencies themselves may engage in acts of bargaining with other such bodies to internalise costs or states may 'contract-up' decision-making responsibilities to an overarching agency or treaty that devises and monitors a set of rules at the supra-national scale – such as those enforced in the Treaty of the Rhine.[3]

To recognise the scope for state action in these situations, however, should not be taken as an endorsement of state action whenever and wherever a more decentralised or private alternative is unavailable. Though state action may be desirable in some circumstances, it may also be the case that when the transactions costs involved in state solutions are factored in that 'doing nothing' – and thus

---

3   The Convention on the Protection of the Rhine, which came into force in 1998, was signed by Switzerland, Germany, France, Luxembourg, the Netherlands and the EU. It reinforces earlier cooperation towards the sustainable development of the Rhine ecosystem.

failing to internalise the externality – may be the best available option.

Consider the case of anthropogenic climate change. This represents a problem where there is no private market solution and, given the global trans-boundary character of carbon dioxide and other greenhouse gases, and the difficulty of identifying individual polluters, inter-jurisdictional bargaining between states may also face insurmountable barriers. On the face of it, therefore, a strong theoretical case might be made for the creation of a global governance mechanism that could implement and enforce a global carbon tax or an emissions trading regime. Before supporting such an argument, however, it is crucial to consider the transaction costs that would be involved in operating such an arrangement.

First, there would be huge monitoring costs facing such an authority in seeking to discover whether its own regulations are being enforced – and significant enforcement costs in imposing fines and sanctions against recalcitrant nations. Second and perhaps more important, there would be an unprecedented principal–agent problem in holding the authority itself to account should it abuse its powers or be captured by particular interests seeking to impose costs on others. Early results from the European Union emissions trading system, for example, suggest that it has failed to reduce emissions while producing higher prices for consumers and conferring anti-competitive benefits to incumbent energy firms (Helm 2010). Given the difficulties that voters face in holding to account existing regional and international structures such as the European

Union, the costs they would face in controlling global level structures may well be insurmountable. We cannot draw an unequivocal conclusion on this front, but at the very least on Coasian comparative institutions grounds there is no clear-cut case to suppose that the costs associated with 'doing nothing' and relying primarily on adaptation and national mitigation strategies to climate change are likely to be any worse than those resulting from imposing a costly transnational 'cure'.

Ethical objections to the extension of environmental markets

Though the economic case for extending, where possible, the role of property rights and market solutions to environmental resource conflicts is a powerful one, the lack of appreciation for the comparative transaction costs approach is by no means the only reason why the Coasian perspective has not had greater policy impact. An equally important reason underlying resistance to environmental markets arises from ethical claims that the nature of environmental goods is such that they should not be subject to bargaining procedures or to analyses in terms of transactions costs. According to this view, willingness to pay and bargaining are invalid forms of decision-making in the context of goods which reflect moral and ethical values – and many environmental goods are deemed to reflect such values (Anderson 1990). The use of a common denominator such as money is judged to be inappropriate where there are potentially incommensurable moral ends involved and where the aggregation of conflicting values into a 'social welfare function' is impossible. Markets are said to undermine non-commercial values by encouraging people to see goods which are traded as 'mere commodities'. Just as one may devalue friendship if one tries to buy it, so on this view we devalue the non-material values associated with environmental protection if we subject them to contractual bargaining. Instead of trying to commodify environmental values therefore, resource use conflicts should be matters for democratic deliberation by the political community.

A related objection (see, for example, Barry 1999; Dryzek 1987) contends that market-based approaches take the preferences which form the context for environmental resource conflicts as 'given' and ignore the possibility that people may have their preferences educated and transformed in a more environmentally sensitive direction through the processes of public debate. Such debate should be relied upon to arrive at a considered moral judgement in which values accord with the common good of the community – and once these values have been decided they should be enforced by command-and-control regulation that reflects an agreed conception of 'right' and 'wrong' rather than as commodities that can acquire a market price. In the same way that it is considered inappropriate to judge the merits of rival scientific theories according to willingness-to-pay criteria, so decisions pertaining to the ethical status of environmental goods should not be determined by monetary bargaining.

A further ethical objection to environmental markets is a distributional one. The Coase theorem suggests that decision rights will flow to those who value them most highly *irrespective of the initial allocation of rights*, but this neglects the fact that the distribution of income *will* be affected by the initial assignment of rights since this determines who must compensate whom. Failure to pay attention to the distributional dimension can lead to regressive consequences, such as the prospect of relatively poor people having to pay relatively wealthier corporate shareholders not to pollute, or of relatively poor environmentalists having to bid directly in markets to prevent logging companies from cutting forests. Even where it is the relatively poor who are granted the initial property rights there is a concern that they will be prone to 'sell too cheaply' since their relative poverty is likely to mean that lower-income people will place less weight on environmental protection issues than they will on more materially focused concerns.

Though these ethical objections to Coasian analysis and to environmental markets are frequently made, they are at root misguided and it is unfortunate that few economists including Coase himself have rebutted them directly. The first point that should be made here is that the case for a greater reliance on market prices makes no claims about the possibility of aggregating preferences into a utilitarian social welfare function. Though Coase spoke of 'wealth maximisation' as arising from a context of private bargaining, it is important to specify what this means.

The generation of prices in a market for goods, environmental or otherwise, enables people to spot opportunities for mutually advantageous exchange and facilitates mutual adjustment among those pursuing a diversity of different and perhaps incommensurable goals. These adjustments help to reduce imbalances between the supply and demand of particular goods and to increase the possibility that people in general have the possibility of achieving their separate ends – *whatever these ends may be*. There is therefore no implication that one can determine whether the 'environmental costs' of a particular decision are outweighed by the 'economic benefits' to 'society' and that market prices somehow tell us what these benefits and costs 'to society' actually are because no such social welfare function exists. On the contrary, the entire point of allowing markets and of specifying property rights is to enable, as far as possible, individuals to reflect their own subjective environmental valuations and not to have these decisions made according to the calculations of planners and bureaucrats or by majorities of other citizens. Just as one may refuse to sell the family home to the highest bidder because of personal identity or history, so a property right to a stretch of forest or a waterway would allow individuals not to sell extraction rights if the monetary gains offered are judged inappropriate to the attachments concerned. Thus, the suggestion that allowing something to be bought and sold in a market devalues or undermines non-commercial values is false. If it were accurate, it would imply that being allowed to buy and sell a home makes it impossible to see the place that one lives in as anything more than a 'mere commodity'. Yet, the fact that some people never sell the family home, or if they need to do so because of more pressing priorities they often feel a sense of great loss, demonstrates that being able to buy and sell an asset need not reduce or 'crowd out' recognition of non-commercial values.

Crucially, decisions over environmental protection matters are not like scientific truths that can be judged right or wrong on the basis of reasoned argument, and it is precisely the different subjective weightings that people may place on environmental objectives relative to other valuable ends that may give rise to prices reflecting what the marginal buyer is willing to give up to secure the good concerned. Money is a medium of exchange between individuals *not* a measure of 'social value'. The choice therefore is not between 'commodified' and 'non-commodified' forms of environmental valuation but between those that rely on voluntary agreement and those that rely on the coercive imposition of a particular scale of values – coercion exercised either by planners and regulators or by majorities of other citizens.

Seen in this light, the argument that public deliberation should be preferred to property rights and markets must be recognised for what it is – the illiberal notion that individual valuations of environmental goods should be superseded by those of 'the community'. Of course, insofar as environmental goods are indivisible goods, then resort to collective, majoritarian decision-making may be the only viable option. As has already been noted, however, many environmental goods though they have 'publicness' characteristics can be supplied on a private or decentralised basis. It is not clear, therefore, why these goods should not be allocated by mechanisms that allow individuals to choose their own preferred level of environmental protection – by buying and selling particular assets or moving into jurisdictions which offer different levels of environmental quality.

The suggestion that preferences are not 'given' and can be shaped towards more environmentally beneficial outcomes by the process of public debate should also be challenged – on two grounds. First, it seems to imply that preferences should be 'shaped' towards the outcomes that the more environmentally conscious might prefer – a suggestion which should not sit well with any society that claims to stand for moral and evaluational diversity. And second, it assumes that, if placing a greater weight on environmental protection is indeed desirable, this may best be achieved under collective or democratic processes. On the contrary, the expression of alternative lifestyles is more likely to be facilitated in a context that allows people the greatest possible scope for minorities to take decisions *without* requiring the permission of large numbers of other citizens – and this is precisely what secure private property rights allow for. It is because property rights enable minority individuals to stand out against the crowd and to live out their preferred ideals – rather than just talking about them – that more and more people may emulate such role models if and when the benefits of their lifestyle choices become more evident.

Objections to environmental markets which focus on social justice or distributional issues fare little better than those emphasising the supposedly deleterious consequences of commodification. There are legitimate grounds for dispute as to whether the achievement of social justice requires a focus on the fortunes of those on lower incomes – and if it does, whether improving their position is best achieved by direct redistribution. Nonetheless, assuming that one should focus on the fortunes of the least well off, the recognition that assigning property rights has distributional consequences does not undermine far the case for markets. It would seem to imply, though, that when 'privatisation' occurs it should do so in a way that is sensitive to these distributional effects. This might require for example that, when the state divests itself of environmental assets instead of auctioning decision rights to the highest bidder, rights should be assigned in a way which will advantage the relatively poor. Offering preferential terms or simply giving the assets at stake to those who may be in a weaker bargaining position would offer a way of securing support from those on lower incomes.

The recent failure to build political backing for the privatisation of the Forestry Commission in the UK may offer some possible lessons here. At least some of the opposition to privatisation arose from the concern that the bidding process would allow commercial forestry companies to acquire most of the assets to the exclusion of those relatively poorer actors wishing to maintain woodland for recreational or conservation purposes. Though some safeguards were offered to ensure the protection of recreational access, these were insufficient to assuage public concern about the privatisation process. Assuming that the purpose of the privatisation was to ensure a more diversified forestry management system, rather than just a revenue-raising exercise for the state, then a better approach might have been to give the assets directly to environmental organisations such as the Woodland Trusts who could then have been in a position to determine on what terms, if any, commercial logging could be balanced with recreation or conservation uses.[4]

The more general concern that the poor will 'sell too cheap' can also be addressed without blocking the scope for environmental markets. If the demand for environmental quality is income-elastic (as people become richer they place more value on environmental protection concerns), then the key issue is to take those measures that will enable the least well off to reach the income required for them to place a relatively higher weighting on environmental goods. Within this context, there may be a case for redistributing income towards the poor – but if this redistribution goes too far, the danger that incomes in general may stagnate as a consequence of lowering of productivity must also be taken into account. Whether income redistribution is best placed to avoid the problem of 'selling too cheap' is thus largely an empirical matter, and the answer may vary according to different cultural and economic circumstances.

---

4   Though this example illustrates that the distribution of bargaining power can influence the character of privatisation, the opposition to privatisation of the Forestry Commission arose primarily from predominantly middle-class groupings rather than the ranks of the least advantaged. Given the relative wealth of these groupings, a case can be made that organisations such as the National Trust and the Royal Society for the Protection of Birds might have been in a position to buy up part of the Forestry Commission estate.

Either way, this issue does not count against the case for environmental markets. On the one hand, the problem of selling too cheap will not be addressed under a non-market form of allocation. If a significant proportion of voters are too poor to afford environmental quality and if the political process is at all responsive to their interests, then there is no reason to suppose that political or bureaucratic allocation processes will deliver better environmental quality – unless, that is, they deliberately ignore the preferences of the poor. On the other hand, once the level of income that people have is sufficient for them not be 'forced' into sacrificing environmental quality owing to economic necessity, if they then choose to opt for a lesser level of environmental protection than is preferred by others this must be seen as a genuine reflection of their preferences and not as a problem of 'selling too cheap'. To override such preferences on the basis that people *should* value environmental protection more highly would be an act of paternalism showing scant respect for the individuality and decision-making autonomy of those with relatively lower incomes.

Conclusion

I have sought in this chapter to set out some key features of a Coasian approach to environmental protection issues. Though the nature of the analysis does not suggest a prescriptive route to addressing all environmental dilemmas, it offers nonetheless some broad-brush principles that can guide policy makers. On the one hand, it suggests the need for a framework that allows greater scope for bargaining between individuals and organisations and of the importance of government action in enforcing property rights and resolving disputes where such rights are contested. But though it recognises that government regulation may sometimes represent the option that lowers the burden of transaction costs, it also calls for much greater awareness that the scale of the costs generated by government action may be so great that 'doing nothing' may be the least bad option. In the final analysis, the precise boundaries between 'private solutions', 'public solutions' and 'no solutions' will be determined by matters of political judgement, but these lines will be drawn very differently if this judgement is informed by the comparative institutions approach that Ronald Coase inspired, and its ethical foundation in liberal individualism.

6   COASE AND WATER

Nicola Tynan

Introduction

Water is a scarce resource. While this may sound obvious today, a century ago it was not. A recurring criticism of London's private water companies during the nineteenth century was that they failed to provide a sufficiently large quantity of water for flushing and street-cleaning at a time when water was considered unlimited in supply, if not from the Thames then from Wales. Globally, the majority of institutions for water resource allocation were developed on similar assumptions, though the institutional details differ between countries and even regions within countries (Glennon 2009: 122). For water in rivers and lakes, legal institutions implicitly assumed that surface water could be allocated to consumption uses without a negative impact on the quantity or assimilative capacity of the instream water. Similarly, groundwater rights were often tied to land ownership on the assumption that water withdrawals would remain below recharge rates so use by one landowner would not negatively impact a neighbour.

Though not universally true even in the nineteenth century, for many places the assumption of unlimited water resources was reasonable. More recently, the tide has turned. Driven largely by population growth, water use has increased and water stress – defined as withdrawal in excess of available renewable supply – has increased globally, not only in arid and semi-arid regions.[1] Groundwater aquifers are being depleted in many locations – from Mexico, where groundwater pumping has resulted in a clearly observable sinking of Mexico City, to India, the world's largest groundwater user.[2] Shortages of surface water are causing more frequent conflict in the western and southern US and more frequent water use bans in the UK. We now have to face the reality that one person's use of water often has a negative impact on others, either today or in the future, and, increasingly, the impact is being felt today.

Flush toilets capture this change in our understanding of water. We have moved from the competition between toilet brands on the basis of how much they could flush – with names such as 'Niagara Falls', 'The Deluge' or 'The Dreadnought' – to today's low-flush toilets competing on how efficiently they can flush using the least amount water. Flushing accounts for nearly one third of domestic water use. Households with water meters who pay a volumetric fee have an incentive to reduce water use; low-flush toilets can deliver long-term savings at relatively low cost. Water meters help us move closer to full-cost pricing for domestic water.

---

1   For a map of global water stress, see http://www.wri.org/our-work/project/aqueduct/aqueduct-atlas (accessed 3 July 2015).

2   World Bank (2010). For example, according to the Water Governance Facility (2013: 5) 'governing the groundwater has become a growing challenge in large parts of the country where the water table is steadily sinking'.

It takes time to change indoor plumbing. It takes even longer to change long-established institutions. The problem presented in Ronald Coase's 'The problem of social cost' (1960) is one where the actions of one user have harmful effects on others but where the relevant costs to be considered are the joint costs of preventing the harmful effects.[3] This is exactly the situation we face with water resource management today. In improving water resource management policies, we need to determine whether 'the gain from preventing the harm is greater than the loss which would be suffered elsewhere as a result of stopping the action which produces the harm' (ibid.: 27). Full-cost pricing and clearly defined rights for all water resources can help make this determination.

Clearly defined property rights

One challenge facing the water sector globally is the weak or now inappropriate definition of property rights. Coase explained that, as long as property rights are clearly defined and transactions costs are low, market transactions will result in the most efficient outcome. He also argued that clearly defining property rights and reducing uncertainty will itself reduce transactions costs.

For surface water, property rights tend to be use rather than ownership rights, often connected to land-ownership (riparian), first use (prior appropriation) or state licence.

---

3   For further discussion of this tenet of Coase's argument, see Veljanovski's introduction to this book.

Even in the western United States, where property rights are seemingly well-defined under a prior appropriation system, there is significant uncertainty because rights were over-allocated in ways that make it uncertain who has the right to use water from a particular source, and there was a failure historically to recognize the value of instream flows. The problem is exacerbated in locations where surface water rights are not tradable, which prevents them being transferred to the highest value user.

Groundwater is more frequently connected to land ownership, in some places as use rights, in others as full ownership rights to the water. Because the difference did not matter too much when withdrawals were below aquifer recharge rates, there is often uncertainty regarding water rights. Robert Glennon highlights this uncertainty within the western US (Glennon 2009: 128):

> Property-rights advocates often argue that property owners have an inherent right to drill wells on their property. Restrictions on this right, it is claimed, would violate the takings clause of the U.S. Constitution and require government compensation. But groundwater is not a private resource owned by the overlying landowner. It's a public resource owned by the state. Citizens can use it, but use rights differ profoundly from ownership rights.

Even use rights can call for compensation if restricted in ways not allowed for in advance. A bigger barrier to the creation of water markets and compensation through the purchase of water rights results from the requirement, in many locations, that landowners use their water themselves.

Water is essential for life. This fact underlies the resistance to water pricing and water trading that has resulted in numerous books, documentaries and public protests attacking 'water commodification' in recent years. Making sure that everyone has access to sufficient clean water for survival and general well-being is a crucial policy goal. It is also a goal that some countries have failed to achieve under any institutional structure for water provision. Private participation in domestic water provision has been introduced to improve quality, extend access and improve the efficiency of failing utilities. While poorly implemented policies have made access to water more difficult for some people and communities, private participation elsewhere has improved access for many. In all cases the problem, as explained by Coase, 'is to devise practical arrangements which will correct defects in one part of the system without causing more serious harm in other parts' (Coase 1960: 34). To do this we need to 'compare the total social product yielded by these different arrangements' rather than focus on a less-than-ideal outcome in one part.

Some instances of conflict surrounding the introduction of private participation in water treatment and distribution have resulted from either ill-defined rights to water or water rights defined in such a way that prior users of water are excluded without compensation. This was a major issue in the notorious case of water privatisation in Cochabamba, Bolivia. Textbook explanations of the Coase Theorem often focus on Coase's examples of low transactions costs where the initial allocation of property rights does not influence the efficiency of the outcome. For water resources, however, transactions costs can often be high. Where transactions costs are high, Coase argues that 'the initial delimitation of legal rights does have an effect on the efficiency with which the economic system operates' (ibid.:16). A human right to a limited quantity of water for essential domestic uses is not incompatible with pricing water in the majority of uses. Indeed, pricing water to prevent it being wasted in low-value uses today may be essential to ensure its availability for higher-value uses in the future.

One consequence of the perceived abundance of water is that water is often treated as a free good, with charges being made only for the infrastructure, energy and other operational costs of treating and transporting it, often with energy costs also subsidised. Clearly defining property rights will raise the price of water in ways that reflect its value as a scarce resource. Pricing water serves to generate information on the value of water in alternative uses, providing information on the cost of replacing one use of water with another. It also gives current holders of rights to use water an incentive to conserve and transfer their rights, increasing transparency while potentially reducing resistance and conflict. Recognizing the role of transactions costs means that it is not only important to determine property rights but also to think about how these rights are assigned. This makes the problem 'one of choosing the appropriate social arrangements for dealing with the harmful effects' that will likely differ across countries or watersheds (ibid.: 18). The appropriate social arrangement should be the one that operates at lowest cost when all costs are taken into account. What works as an appropriate social arrangement at one period of time with a given population and technology may not be appropriate at a later date with a larger population, living more densely in urban areas, higher standards of living and new technologies.

Integrated water resources management

Water resource institutions are facing a time of change. Internationally, there has been a move towards integrated water resources management (IWRM) as recommended by the Dublin Statement of the 1992 International Conference on Water and the Environment. IWRM focuses on managing water resources in ways that are economically, socially and environmentally sustainable. Importantly for water markets, the Dublin Statement explicitly recognised water as an economic good in all its uses. This approach fits with Coase's emphasis on total social benefits: where overlapping legal jurisdictions draw water from the same basin, IWRM focuses on water basin benefits rather than individual user, community or even country benefits (Sadoff et al.: 26–27).

The Dublin Statement recognising water as an economic good noted that 'access to clean water is a basic right of all human beings', highlighting the positive connection between treating water as an economic good and improving access to clean water for the poor. Whatever their income level, people are willing to pay relatively high prices for the first litres of water they consume. In most places today, marginal user values for water are much higher for municipal and industrial uses than for agriculture. While many water trades take place between those with similar uses, for instance between two farmers, the fact that water is currently used for low-value agriculture while high-value domestic uses are not satisfied means that more extensive water markets are likely to see water move away from agriculture to domestic, industrial and instream uses.

A number of countries have already adopted IWRM, including developing markets for water trading to various degrees. A recent study (Grafton et al. 2011) compares the performance of water markets in five countries: Australia, Chile, South Africa, the US and China. These are all places sharing the following characteristics to varying degrees: (1) they are semi-arid regions either experiencing or facing the threat of water shortages; (2) water has different values across uses; and (3) there is sufficiently strong institutional governance and legal capacity allowing for broadly accepted reform. As the authors argue, none of these countries score equally well on measures of efficiency, equity and environmental sustainability and all have room for improvement. However, they each do some things well and can provide guides, if not models, for policy makers elsewhere.

Australia

Australia provides a model of a country that has embraced full-cost water pricing comprehensively, while recognising that institutional details will need to adjust over time. In June 2004, the Council of Australian Governments (COAG) signed the Intergovernmental Agreement on a National Water Initiative (NWI) and established a National Water Commission. With a goal to 'improve the management of the nation's water resources and provide greater certainty for future investment', the NWI built on the prior experience of water rights trading within the Murray-Darling Basin and explicitly embraced water rights, water trading and improved water pricing. Under the NWI, each state or territory is required to clarify and improve the certainty of water rights and to maintain a registry of water titles recording access entitlements, ownership and transfers. On the 10th anniversary of the NWI, Australia's National Water Commission stated that 'although the full extent of the National Water Initiative's aspirations is yet to be realised, we have a framework that 10 years on, is proven and robust.'[4] This assessment is reflected in the relatively high scores that Australia receives in Grafton et al.'s integrated assessment (Grafton et al. 2011: 222, 229, 232).

The need for institutional reform in the management of water resources was first acknowledged within the Murray-Darling Basin in the 1980s through an embargo on new licences and projects to replace open channels with pipelines for the delivery of irrigation water. As a result of this early start, water markets are well-established within the Murray-Darling Basin. Entitlements to water from the

---

4 http://www.nwc.gov.au/nwi/nwi-10-year-anniversary (accessed 3 July 2015).

basin may be either high reliability, where rights holders can expect to receive their full allocation each year, or low reliability with the possibility of no allocation in dry years. Trades may take one of two forms: permanent transfer of the water right or transfer of a single year's water allocation. The Murray-Darling Basin has experienced substantial trading, with about 20% of water rights traded at a value of $1.8 billion in 2009 (ibid.: 229–30). A number of brokers operate in the market to reduce transactions costs.[5] New trading rules introduced on 1 July 2014 aimed to reduce uncertainty by requiring the reporting of all trade prices and limiting restrictions on trade to four clearly stated circumstances, including impacts on third parties.[6]

Australia's NWI has struck an appropriate balance between security of water rights and adaptability to changing circumstances. As statutory rights, water rights can be modified by state governments without compensation. In practice, governments have purchased water rights to increase environmental flows. Such commitments to compensate rights holders are clearly stated in the recent Intergovernmental Agreement and National Partnership Agreement for the Murray-Darling Basin agreed between Commonwealth and New South Wales in February 2014. These agreements state the need for an additional 2,750

---

5   The government of New South Wales provides a list of brokers on its website, explicitly noting that use of a broker may reduce transaction costs.

6   Murray-Darling Basin Authority Fact Sheet: New Basin Plan water trading rules start 1 July 2014. Available at http://www.mdba.gov.au/media-pubs/publications/new-bp-water-trading-rules-start-1st-july-2014 (accessed 3 July 2015).

gigalitres of water to remain in the Basin annually for eco-system protection; they agree that the additional instream flow will be achieved through a combination of infrastruc-ture and environmental works aimed at water recovery plus the purchase of water rights up to a maximum of 1,500 gigalitres.[7] The state's strategy has been to purchase permanent water rights to protect instream flows when necessary but to sell temporary use rights when water is surplus to environmental needs.

United States

California's three-year drought, ongoing in 2015, renewed criticism of the system of rights based on seniority rather than highest value. While failure of the existing system of water rights is recognised and water trading is well estab-lished in some places (resulting in market transactions with a value of over $3 billion between 1987 and 2007), in other parts of the state there is strong resistance to mov-ing to full-cost water pricing and transferable water rights (Anderson et al. 2012: 24). Rather than seeing this as an opportunity to transfer water to its highest-valued uses, those who currently hold senior water rights fear that institutional change will result in a loss of rights to water without compensation. Clarifying water rights requires information on how much water is actually used by rights holders. In California's Central Valley, where over half the

---

7   http://www.water.nsw.gov.au/Water-management/Law-and-policy/
      National-reforms/Basin-Plan/murray-darling-basin-plan (accessed
      9 July 2014).

irrigation water comes from wells, some farmers explicitly resist water metering from a fear that this will allow the state to restrict the amount of water they pump, again without compensation.

New housing estates increase water demand. Recognising that Utah's water was over-appropriated, possibly by as much as 45%, Jerry Olds, the state's engineer from 2002 to 2008, stopped issuing new permits for some basins in the state. He also defined property rights more precisely, to allow transfer and sale of water rights, and to tie development approval to water rights (Glennon 2009: 234). New users, particularly developers, are now required to obtain water rights from those with existing claims. These constraints have not caused Utah to stop development but have required developers to 'purchase and retire some other water user's right' showing that the development is a higher-valued use (ibid.: 237). Although rights transfers can involve significant transaction costs when individual developers are required to seek bilateral deals, because of search costs and uncertainties in the approval process, brokers and an exchange have arisen to lower these costs. This would not have surprised Coase, who encouraged economists to 'study the work of the broker in bringing the parties together' (Coase 1960: 18).

The New Mexico city of Santa Fe followed a similar policy requiring developers to acquire water rights from a willing seller before requesting a building permit. In response to developers' concerns that they would pay for water rights but then might not receive the permit to build for other reasons, the city of Santa Fe established a water bank that allows developers to deposit water rights for future projects (Glennon 2009: 240).

While the western US is making some progress towards integrated water markets the assessment by Grafton and colleagues shows that much remains to be done. In the fast-growing southeast, the need for institutional change has, for the most part, been ignored. Residents of coastal Georgia and South Carolina draw groundwater from the Upper Floridan Aquifer. Heavy pumping in Savannah, Georgia, has reversed the flow of groundwater resulting in salt water contamination of domestic water supply. The state's Environmental Protection Agency responded with regulations in 2006, 2008 and 2013 to reduce withdrawals by existing permit holders and place a moratorium on additional permits, but did not move towards tradable water rights.

Further south, Florida, Alabama and Georgia have been fighting over water from Lake Lanier since 1990 in what has become known as the tristate water war. Property rights to water from Lake Lanier are ill-defined, giving the city of Atlanta no economic incentive to limit extractions. Even though the water is crucial for 'sustaining Florida's $134 million commercial oyster industry', Florida fishermen have no way to compensate Atlanta for allowing water to continue into the Cattahoochee River from Lake Lanier (ibid.: 29).

Critics of water trading argue that the environment will be the loser as the rich will pay to take water for wasteful purposes. Terry Anderson of Montana's Political Economy Research Center (PERC) shows that this is not the case even when instream flows are not explicitly protected as they are for the Murray-Darling Basin. Water rights trading allows environmental groups to purchase water rights to protect or enhance instream flows.[8] For example, in 2006 the Oregon Water Trust kept water in the John Day River to protect Chinook and steelhead salmon by purchasing water rights from a local ranching family (Anderson et al. 2012: 11). By contrast, the regulatory approach creates uncertainty for both rights holders and those wishing to protect fish habitats. In 2014 California's Water Resources Control Board implemented regulations limiting water use during the summer months to ensure sufficient instream flows for fish in the Sacramento River, curtailing farmers' rights to water and generating threats of lawsuits against the Board.

PERC's research highlights the role of 'enviropreneurs' – Coase's brokers – in identifying environmentally beneficial gains from trade and bringing together buyers and sellers. As the value of maintaining instream flows increases, farmers who hold transferable water rights will be encouraged to conserve water to sell some of their allocation and, in some cases, may no longer farm their land (Coase 1960: 4). In Arizona, the Yuma Desalting Plant was completed in 1992 to treat agricultural return flows and reduce the salinity of water in the Colorado River flowing into Mexico. Rather than operate the plant, however, it was cheaper to divert the saline water and obtain flows

8   See 'Thank you, Ronald Coase' at http://www.perc.org/articles/thank-you -ronald-coase (accessed 3 July 2015).

for the Colorado by paying farmers to fallow unproductive fields (Glennon 2009: 149). Water banking offers another way to realise these gains from trade: senior rights holders can 'bank' water that would have been applied to low-value uses, allowing it to be purchased by environmental organizations for higher-valued instream use (Anderson et al. 2012: 8).

South Africa

Before 1998, water rights in South Africa were not clearly defined but were generally connected to land as riparian rights or rights to drill wells. The National Water Act 1998 (NWA) introduced a system of public trusteeship combined with private use rights allocated through licences. South Africa's water policy is best known for its formal recognition of a right to sufficient water for domestic purposes, a right included in sections 2 and 4 of the NWA.[9] While this right to clean water for basic needs has not been achieved for all citizens, there has been significant improvement following the reform of water institutions. According to the World Bank's World Development Indicators, the percentage of the rural population with access to improved water sources increased from 65% in 1995 to 88% in 2012.

In introducing a radical redefinition of water rights, South Africa recognised that the transition to new institutions can impose losses on some individuals despite an

---

9 Water supply sufficient for domestic purposes is defined as '25 litres per person per day accessible within 200 metres' (Pienaar and van der Schyff 2007: 185).

overall social gain. With the state now formally custodian of the country's water resources it has the power to award water use rights, but built into the NWA is the requirement that the state cannot take away water rights without due process and cause. To ease the institutional transition, the NWA included a right to compensation for prior owners of water rights who were negatively affected by the change (Pienaar and van der Schyff 2017: 187).

Based on an integrated water resources management approach, South Africa's NWA requires that water leases take into account environmental protection. While the NWA was understood to allow for the trading of water leases there is significant uncertainty about the legality of individuals selling or otherwise transferring rights to water. For example, a North Gauteng high court ruling in August 2011 approved the transfer of water rights between farmers but the transfer had been denied by the Minister of Water and Environmental Affairs with subsequent appeal to the Water Tribunal delayed due to the tribunal's suspension. Such uncertainty over the legality of transferring water rights means that trades have been few, particularly those transferring water between uses (Grafton et al. 2011: 229).

Chile, China and India

Institutional reform of water markets is being undertaken to various degrees elsewhere. Chile has the longest experience of water rights and is often used as a model for water market reform. Strong private property rights in water were established with Chile's 1981 Water Code and updated with the 2005 Water Code Reforms. Chile's reform was undertaken before and outside of an IWRM approach. This has resulted in property rights to water that have fewer restrictions on use and transfer than in other countries, generating a fairly substantial market for water rights but less consideration of third-party effects (ibid.: 229, 232). Water rights in Chile have allowed water to move to some higher-valued uses, particularly mining, but concerns remain that water is not going to its most valued uses now that Chile's five-year drought has reduced overall water availability. Recent calls for reform within the country remind us that in making changes 'the total effect of these arrangements in all spheres of life should be taken into account' (Coase 1960: 43).

China has made moves towards allowing trade in water rights in its Water Law of 2002, focusing on trades between municipalities.[10] Trades have taken place at directly negotiated prices rather than prices set by market transactions. The Yellow River Conservancy Commission has had the most success in implementing reforms to limit water withdrawals, largely due to an improved monitoring system. Even here, municipalities often violate their limits or withdraw water from tributaries before it reaches the Yellow River rather than purchase rights from other municipalities.

---

10 'Issue brief: water resource issues, policy and politics in China', The Brookings Institution, February 2013. Available at http://www.brookings.edu/research/papers/2013/02/water-politics-china-moore (accessed 27 June 2014).

India's increasingly severe water shortages, considered a crisis by the national government, is driving a review of water institutions (Water Governance Facility 2013: 11). The Supreme Court's recent interpretation of the public trust doctrine identifies the state as responsible for water as a natural resource, despite the common law tradition that landowners have unlimited rights to extract groundwater from beneath their property. In India, water regulation is the responsibility of states, so the central government issues Model Bills as guidelines. The latest 2011 Model Bill includes a right to water of acceptable quality, specifying 70 litres per capita per day as a minimum, and recommends a separation of land and groundwater rights. The federal government's 2012 National Water Policy and 2013 draft Framework Law on Water provided further nudges to reform. Despite central government encouragement, however, few states have taken steps towards water markets and IWRM. The state of Karnataka introduced a Ground Water Act in 2011 requiring the registration of existing wells and prior permission for all new wells but a perceived lack of legitimacy has resulted in low levels of compliance. The act was modelled on prior Model Bills so did not include aspects of IWRM included in the 2011 Model Bill. This may partly be due to uncertainty created by the Model Bill itself: the bill has existing water rights expiring after one year but without compensation for lost rights, creating uncertainty that will generate resistance within states considering adopting such regulation. It also fails to make clear whether the trading of water rights is allowable.

Conclusion

The move to IWRM and an acceptance of more clearly defined property rights, water pricing and water markets is happening slowly but the idea has gained a foothold. The countries discussed above are not the only examples; within Europe, Spain's 1999 Water Law Reform opened the door to water rights trading. The institutional details necessarily differ across countries. This is beneficial because countries differ in terms of water resources, existing institutions and in many other ways that will require different social arrangements to achieve the largest social product. It is also beneficial because competition between, or at least a comparison of, different institutional details provide the information that makes innovation and learning possible.

In the introduction to this book, Veljanovski notes that it took 67 years from Coase's work for the United States FCC to adopt a spectrum market. Spectrum markets now have broad acceptance although, as expected, the institutional details differ across countries. Applying Coase's insights and using markets for water resource management faces even stiffer political challenges, but it has the potential to deliver crucial social and environmental benefits.

7 THE COASE RESEARCH AGENDA: PUBLIC GOODS, TRANSACTION COSTS AND THE ROLE OF COLLECTIVE ACTION

Stephen Davies

Introduction

Throughout his long career Ronald Coase was an independently minded and questioning economist who was never prepared to accept an orthodoxy simply because it was the consensus position of his colleagues. Instead he constantly put difficult questions to that consensus and challenged it. In part this took the form of empirical research, of looking at the ways in which things worked out in the real, historical world rather than in pure models. The other side to this was applying his distinctive insights to questions of theory so as to redefine definitions and challenge commonly accepted arguments. The most important of these was the concept of transaction costs and the way in which these determined and limited the possibilities of collective action on a voluntary basis.

Was the lighthouse a public good?

One famous example Coase's approach was his work on the subject of public goods. The main publication here was his 'The lighthouse in economics' (Coase 1974b) although his even more famous paper 'The problem of social cost' (Coase 1960) is also relevant. The intellectual context for Coase's work was the definitive modern formulation of the notion of public goods by Paul Samuelson (1954, 1955). Samuelson gave what is now the classic theoretical definition of a public good as one that has the two qualities of non-rivalrous consumption and non-excludability. In other words they are collective goods that cannot according to the model be provided optimally by private action because of the 'free rider' problem created by the quality of non-excludability. This effectively replaced the older, and in many ways more subtle, definition that we can trace back to Adam Smith in 1776, according to which public goods are ones where the bulk of the benefit created accrues to society as a whole (it takes the form of positive externalities) so that individual providers do not have enough of an incentive to provide the good at a level that will maximize the social benefit.

There had already been significant reaction to Samuelson's model before Coase's 1974 paper, most notably the classic paper by Buchanan (1965) that formulated the category of club goods (collective goods that are, however, excludable). What Coase did was to take the argument further and look at an example of the successful supply of a good that qualified as a pure public good in the Samuelson model, by an agency other than the government and using a funding model based around the use of fees rather than taxes or compulsory charges. Lighthouses had been thought of as a quintessential public good precisely because they fitted Samuelson's two criteria so exactly – one ship's use of the light did not reduce the value of it to any other user and there was no practical way of excluding non-paying ship owners from the benefit. Coase showed that in the British case lighthouses were provided by a quasi-private body (the Brethren of Trinity House) and more importantly that they were funded by fees collected from ship owners, i.e. the users of the lights. The key factor here is not so much that the government did not provide the good directly, given the mixed private and public nature of the lighthouse authorities but rather the funding method.[1]

What this showed was that the public goods problem identified by Samuelson was real but not necessarily insurmountable by private action, particularly voluntary collective action. The key factor in this case was the way in which pure Samuelsonian public goods could be bundled up with or linked to private goods that were both rivalrous and excludable so that in order to get the private good you had to contribute towards the public one. In this specific case ports charged a lighthouse fee to shippers who used their facilities and so the good of lighthouses was bundled up with the purely private good of port facilities. In other cases the good is transformed into a club good and provided via a club mechanism of one kind or another.

---

1   For critical and supportive comment on Coase's piece, see Barnett and Block (2007), Bertrand (2006) and Van Zandt (1993).

Conditions for private provision

This did not mean of course that public goods could always be provided in these ways, and Coase did not claim this. There are in the real and historical world a number of factors that will determine whether or not a public good is privately provided and if so for how long. One factor is the basic one of whether there is in practice a private good that can be successfully bundled up with the public one at all. If this is not the case then Samuelson's analysis does apply. Even if there is, however, this is not the end of the story. There is then the vital question of whether this bundling can be done at a cost level that makes it worth doing. In other words there is an incentive issue – do private actors have enough of an incentive to do what is needed or do they have a stronger incentive to pass this over to the agency of government, even if this is less efficient from the standpoint of general social welfare? As always with Coase, there is also the problem of transaction costs. If these are sufficiently high then the kind of voluntary collective action that will be needed to supply many goods on a club basis or others on a bundled basis may not be possible.

What this means is that the problem of public goods as reformulated by Coase (and also Buchanan) should not be seen as a static one with fixed incentives facing individual actors. Instead it is a dynamic and above all a historical one, in which things that are possible in some times and places are not feasible in others. This reflects factors such as population density, technology, and social and political institutions, all of which can affect the levels of transactions costs, the incentives facing actors and the degree to which private and voluntary collective action to resolve the public goods problem is feasible or cost effective. The same considerations also apply to government action of course – it may well be that some public goods problems are simply not capable of resolution by any feasible method.

Coase's research agenda

What Coase did then in his essay was to generate an extensive research agenda for empirical economic and economic history research. The central element of this is investigations into the ways in which both public goods and club goods have been provided by private action in the past. This kind of empirical study can help us to answer the question of how and why public goods problems have been resolved without recourse to government action or funding through taxation. We can then also look at the more demanding question of why this has not proved possible in other cases and how the boundaries of what is possible in this regard have shifted or changed over time. There is also the matter of looking at how in theory certain classic public goods might by supplied by private action even if this has not actually happened (although in some of the best known cases you will realise that they have been if you dig deep enough into the historical record, and this is again a case where historical research can inform and amend theory).

On examination, the examples that we can discover from historical research (and indeed research in the contemporary world) can be put into several categories. In the first place are a range of goods that have the quality of excludability and are therefore better thought of as club goods. The crucial thing here is action that transforms a good from one funded by the general taxpayer and provided largely or totally free of charge at the point of use to one that is provided by some kind of club mechanism and is funded primarily by charges for the service. One obvious example of this is education, where before the Forster Act of 1870 most education was provided by organisations such as the Society for the Promotion of Christian Knowledge, or Mechanics Institutes and Lyceums. There was also the enormous and barely studied world of voluntary learned societies and working-class autodidacticism (Rose 2006). All of this saw the delivery of education as a club good – although it is worth pointing out that there were none of the supposed monopolistic features of club supply, quite the contrary in fact.

Turnpike roads

However, perhaps the most striking example of this kind of private supply of good commonly thought to be in the category of public goods was highways, and the transformation of the UK's road system between 1740 and 1850 by turnpike trusts. Before the early eighteenth century, English and Scottish highways were the responsibility of the parishes through which they ran, with an obligation to maintain them by labour enforced by the County Committee of JPs (there were similar systems elsewhere in Europe, notably in France with the system of corvée, a kind of forced labour 'tax' used to maintain the road system). The results were, to put it mildly, underwhelming, with roads that were poorly maintained and often impassable between late October and March. This obviously imposed serious costs on trade and made the development of a national market almost impossible.

The solution was to turn the public good of roads, funded out of local taxation and provided free of charge, into an excludable good supplied by a club mechanism. The means in this case was the turnpike trust. These were statutory bodies, created by a Private Act of parliament and given responsibility for a designated stretch of existing highway or, in some cases, a brand new road. The procedure was that people in a locality would announce a public meeting and get together to form a trust. They would then apply to parliament by petition for the necessary Private Act. This was needed because the trust, having taken over responsibility for a stretch of road, would then charge tolls for the use of the road and use the income from the tolls to maintain it. This meant that a public right of way was converted into a private toll road, something that required the sovereign power of parliament. It was very important to buy off potential objectors before the petition was lodged as an objection or even worse a counter-petition would make what was already a costly procedure prohibitively expensive.

Once it was formed, the trust would typically issue debt to fund the initial improvements to the road and to pay for the erection of toll gates and lodges. The debt was serviced out of the tolls and turnpike paper was a solid investment yielding a return slightly better than that of government debt. Some of the toll income, however, was used for continuous maintenance rather than capital improvement. The first trust was set up in 1707 but thereafter they were set up steadily with surges in formation after 1750 and 1770. There were 150 trusts by 1750, rising to 550 by 1772. By 1800 there were over 700 of them. By 1825 just over 1,000 trusts administered about 18,000 miles of road and by the 1830s they ran over 30,000 miles of highway (Albert 1972; Wright 1992). The effects were dramatic with significant improvement in the quality of roads. Pawson's study measures this by looking at reductions in the cost of travel and the time taken to travel certain routes. In the first instance the cost of moving goods was more than halved while the time taken to travel long distances – such as London to Bath or Holyhead – was also reduced by a similar margin (Pawson 1977).

All of this meant a large increase in trade and also innovations in transport, most notably the rise of the stagecoach as a means of long-distance travel with all of the associated infrastructure such as coaching inns. Even more important was the way in which as time went on the trusts invested in important developments in road building technology, most notably macadamisation, invented by John Loudon Macadam, who worked for a number of trusts in the north of England and Scotland. One of the reasons for this spate of innovation was the sheer number of trusts which meant that there was more scope for experimentation but even more importantly meant that these were not in any meaningful sense monopolies, even at the local level. The density of turnpiked routes meant that in most parts of the UK there were alternatives to any particular route and this both held down prices and encouraged the search for improvements. (The major exception was rural Wales, where a combination of a low density of population and mountainous terrain meant that there were only a few routes. Not surprisingly this was the area that saw significant popular resistance to turnpikes with the 'Rebecca Riots' of the early 1840s.)

If we look at the chronological maps in Albert and Pawson, what we can see is the emergence over the century between 1750 and 1850 of a dense network of turnpikes that came to form a national road system. However, because the trusts were small and formed in response to local needs, the system emerged in a bottom-up fashion with major trunk roads being turnpiked but with also a great deal of infilling through local initiative. In their history of local government the Webbs bemoaned the lack of a national plan but what the turnpike system in fact led to was a dense national system that reflected local needs and knowledge far more than a hypothetical one created by a national authority that would have faced insurmountable knowledge problems in trying to work out where to improve highways and which sections to prioritise (Copeland 1968; Broderick 2002). The example of France (where major trunk mail roads were built by the French state at the same time that the turnpike system was unfolding in Britain) shows what the likely outcome would have been, a system built to address the needs of a national government rather than local communities.

The turnpike system, although an example of providing a service (highways) as a club good rather than a pure public good, also shows several of the things the Coasian research agenda should lead us to look for. There were proposals for moving to a system of this kind from the early seventeenth century but it was a hundred years before these came to anything. One reason for this was the very high transaction costs faced by potential local groups in the earlier period – simply making contact with people over a sufficiently wide area was very difficult. By contrast, the rise of local newspapers and advertising throughout the eighteenth century made these costs much less. There was also a shift in the balance of costs and benefits that brought about a change in the incentives faced by local actors as the steady growth of internal trade (i.e. by land rather than water) made the costs of the inadequate road system ever more pressing and the potential gains from improvement all the greater. Interestingly, the trustees of the turnpike trusts were unpaid (as opposed to their salaried staff) and this was indeed a case where the bulk of the gain accrued to the local community in general through increased trade and economic activity.

However, while Adam Smith may have been correct to say in 1776 that no single person would gain enough from road improvement to be motivated to engage in it, the social and technological changes of the period meant that collective action by local groups who collectively did have enough to gain to make it worthwhile became possible – without having to resort to coercive collective action through the tax system. Finally, the institution of the Private Act of parliament, an undoubted act of state power but one that was made in response to requests and petitions from local voluntary associations, provided a means of dealing with what would otherwise have been very difficult holdout problems and cumulative transactions costs. Imagine how difficult the process of creating a turnpike would have been if every person affected had to be negotiated with individually rather than through the collective processes of a public meeting and canvassing followed by the circulation of a petition and its submission to parliament after objections were addressed.

Bundling private with public goods

Urban planning and infrastructure

When we look beyond clear uses of the club mechanism we can also discover several cases that exemplify the Coasian lighthouse model of bundling together public and private goods. One of the most significant but least studied was the way that urban development and planning was handled in the UK up until just before World War I. The outstanding work of Christopher Chalklin is the only real exception to what is otherwise a profoundly 'presentist' historiography in which the history of urban development is seen as being a dark age of random and chaotic private development finally replaced by rational public planning, culminating in the Promised Land of the Town and Country Planning Act of 1947 – arguably one of the most damaging pieces of legislation ever passed by a British parliament (Chalklin 1974, 2001).

What we can see if we look at the way urban development took place in Britain before 1914 is a classic case of the bundling of public and private goods. The public goods in question were things such as urban infrastructure (streets and pavements), services such as sanitation and street lighting, and the general urban environment. The private goods were building for profit and property development. What tied these together was two things. The first was the way in which large landowners and (less frequently) urban developers put together or inherited large parcels of land that were then developed as entire neighbourhoods or even complete towns. Major examples of the latter included Bath, Ashton-under-Lyne, Eastbourne and Southport. Every major city in the UK has examples of the former from the many London estates such as Russell, Cadogan, Grosvenor and Portland, to the entire West End of Glasgow or most of south Manchester, via other provincial developments such as the Calthorpe estate in Birmingham (Edgbaston) and the historic centre of Newcastle developed by Richard Grainger. In these cases the original owner would lay out streets and other infrastructure and then let or sell plots to developers and speculative builders who would then put up the actual buildings. Sometimes the original developer would do the entire job themselves but this was less common. The original landowner or developer would profit in two ways, through selling off the land or by capturing the increased land value if it was only leased rather than being sold. The developers not only provided basic infrastructure such as streets and lighting, however. They also typically stipulated the construction not just of housing but an entire range of other kinds of facilities such as shops, workshops and public buildings.

The detailed building was usually done piecemeal but typically in a harmonious and planned style, as we can still see in places like Belgravia, Bath or Bloomsbury. This was brought about by the second mechanism that bundled together private and public goods in a Coasian fashion. This was the extensive use of covenants, binding and perpetual clauses in the original leases or sales that stipulated often precise details of matters such as height, external appearance, the number and size of rooms, and the kinds of activity that could be carried on in the completed building (Chalklin 2001; Beito et al. 2006). Generally, the more exact and elaborate the covenants the higher the cost of the finished building; and so covenants were market institutions that responded to the demand for which the developer was catering. If it was for low-cost housing for the less well off, they would be limited and basic, if for the better off more elaborate.

This all meant that, through these two mechanisms, public goods such as urban planning and infrastructure were delivered very successfully by private actors, by tying these public goods to private profit. Again we can see the institutions and social realities that made this possible. One was the concentration of land in the hands of landowners who could develop a large area without needing to go through the often slow process of acquiring a whole number of discrete parcels. Having said that, cases such as Newcastle and Bath show that simple and straightforward ways of transferring clear title to land meant that it was not impossible for private entrepreneurs to put together blocks of land through a series of purchases. The detailed planning of much of the development was made possible by the legal institution of the covenant and the way in which it was upheld and understood by the British legal systems. Finally, but not least, the growth of population and wealth created strong incentives for landowners and developers and gave them a very powerful incentive to find ways of resolving public goods problems because that made their developments more attractive and hence more profitable.

These conditions, however, did not apply during the interwar years. Social changes such as the decline of the aristocracy after World War I and the shifts in the land planning regime in 1910 meant that the eighteenth- and nineteenth-century pattern of integrated development combining public and private goods no longer happened. Instead there was a purely private goods model of development, with purely residential housing developments built alongside radial railway and road links, leading to the infamous pattern of 'ribbon development'. It was this that led to the movement that culminated in the Town and Country Planning Act in 1947.

Policing

Another important example of the historical provision of a public good via the bundling mechanism that Coase identified was in the area of policing. The service of policing has always had two foundational aspects, which are recognised through their separation into distinct forces in most of Europe though not in the UK. The first is the service of investigating reported crimes and if necessary prosecuting them in the courts, while the second is the general maintenance of public order, particularly in public places. The first is an excludable good while the second is not and approaches much more closely to the classic model of a public good.

These two kinds of policing were combined through the institution of prosecution associations or Associations for the Prosecution of Felons to give them their full title (King 2003; Beito et al. 2006). These were simply club organisations that formed by free association to defray the costs of criminal prosecutions, which were considerable under the system that existed before the mid-nineteenth century, whereby the great majority of criminal prosecutions were brought privately. As well as covering the costs of prosecutions, the associations would also cover out of their funds such costs as the placing of newspaper advertisements to help apprehend malefactors, the payment of private detectives to investigate crimes, and compensation for losses from crimes such as theft and burglary. All of these are excludable goods but these essentially private goods came to be rolled up with the public good of maintaining order in public places and punishing or preventing disorderly conduct. What happened was that the larger prosecution associations that had emerged by the 1820s, such as the famous Barnet association, would run regular watches and foot patrols as well as providing the risk pooling and insurance services described earlier. These were clearly a public good since they provided protection against theft and criminal damage to all of the inhabitants of an area regardless of whether they were paid-up members of an association. Thomas Dimsdale, the secretary of the Barnet Association, explicitly acknowledged this fact in testimony to a parliamentary select committee in 1828.

Fire protection

Another example of the tying together of public and private goods was that of general fire protection. Insurance against damage to goods and buildings by fire was provided by insurance companies from the later seventeenth century onwards. The insurance companies were soon issuing policies in enormous quantities – the Sun Fire Office, formed in 1710, had issued over a million policies by the 1730s. The insurance companies had a clear interest in minimising their losses from fires by putting out fires in buildings they insured and helping to recover property from them. A system grew up whereby in large towns, above all in London, the insurance companies would each have their own fire brigade with an engine and other equipment for extinguishing and controlling fires. Policy holders were given a plaque or 'fire mark' to fix to the front of their property so that it could be identified. Initially, company fire brigades would only put out fires in properties insured by their company, but in a short time a system was set up whereby the fire brigade of one company would put out fires in buildings insured by any other with a fee being collected after the event from the other insurance company according to an agreed standard scale. In

London the cooperation between the companies led to the formation of a unified service, the London Fire Engine Establishment, in 1833. This was a substantial establishment with 80 firefighters and 13 stations, which combined all of the previously distinct company fire brigades.

By this time the fire insurance companies had clearly taken on the function of supplying a classic public good, that of general protection against fire in urban areas. Initially, both the insurance and the fire brigade were simple excludable private goods, as the use of the identifying fire mark indicated. However, the insurance companies clearly had an interest in putting out fires in uninsured buildings because of the danger that these would spread to insured buildings and premises. Consequently, the London Fire Engine Establishment, funded entirely by the companies, would intervene and put out fires in uninsured buildings. Here the public good of general fire protection was bundled up with the private good of insurance against loss from fire damage. People who were uninsured would indeed be able to free ride on the supply of the public good of fire protection but would not be able to get recompense for any losses they suffered from fire, in the same way that people who did not join a large prosecution association would benefit from the foot patrols while not getting the insurance benefits or payment of prosecution costs that members enjoyed.

Historical lessons

Here the balance of incentives was enough that private actors would cooperate to provide the public good that was bundled up with the private one. However, two other points become clear when we look at the history of these two apparently successful attempts privately to supply a public good. The first is that in the case of the fire insurance companies, while they had an incentive to provide collectively what was both a public service and a private benefit, they had an even stronger incentive to try to pass off this cost (as it was for them) on to the public authority. After lobbying by the companies the private service was taken over by the state in 1865 through the Metropolitan Fire Brigade Act. Here we can see how the pattern of incentives changed over time so that what had been a case of private supply ceased to be so but without there being any technological change or shift in the nature of the actual service or good.

In the case of the prosecution associations, what is clear from the testimony of Dimsdale and others is that the members of the associations resented being (as they saw it) taken advantage of by non-contributors. Antony De Jasay identifies this as the sucker problem in the private supply of public goods in which people so resent being 'suckers' that they support the state taking over functions that they are providing even though they themselves are made no better off by this or even in some ways worse off. Only if the loss from the state taking over is sufficiently large will they swallow their resentment and put up with it, De Jasay argues (De Jasay 2012). What all of this means is that the research agenda created by Coase's pioneering work also has to look at things such as the attitudes and ideology of social actors, given that these formed subjective perceptions of costs and benefits on their part that in turn influenced the way they responded to what might seem to be a simple objective matter of costs and benefits. So there is a social and cultural aspect to this research agenda as well.

What empirical historical research can do, then, is to uncover many real-life examples of the supply of both club goods and pure public goods by private means, whether through voluntary cooperation or by profit-seeking enterprises. The studies can cast light on the mechanisms by which the undoubtedly real public goods problem was addressed in certain cases, but also suggest why this did not happen in others or went from being successfully handled by private action to being taken over by government or even reverting to a clear market failure and undersupply. Coase's work suggests that the key questions to explore are those of the transaction costs faced by people trying to cooperate and the patterns of incentives that they faced as well as the institutions, social and legal, that were available to them and the mental and cultural world that they inhabited. So, for example, in the case of the private fire brigades, having a simple and cost-effective means of recovering costs from uninsured people who had fires put out in their property would have radically shifted the incentives facing the companies. There was such a mechanism but it was neither simple nor cost effective.

The research agenda that Coase's work generates also leads in other directions. One is to look at contemporary phenomena to see how far the public goods problem can be or is being addressed in today's world. One example of this is the private supply of security by firms such as ADT, Securicor and many others. There are now 2 million workers in this sector in the US alone and the industry there is worth over \$200 billion. This is such a widespread phenomenon that it does not attract much attention but when looked at from the standpoint of Coase's article it becomes very interesting. What examination reveals is that many of the services provided by such firms are clearly private goods, so their supply by profit-seeking firms is not surprising. However, increasingly they also supply the public good of maintaining order in public spaces. This is done by bundling that good up with private goods such as the provision of retail facilities and infrastructure (such as shopping malls) or suburban and urban development. This is much more prevalent in some parts of the world than in others simply because the way that the built environment is constructed varies from one place to another. Where self-contained 'gated communities' and shopping complexes are common, the private supply of the public good of order in common space becomes much easier than in places where the physical structure is more open. Arguably what has happened here is that the concept of 'public space' has been radically redefined and this again is an interesting question for the research agenda. In some places such as South Africa we can also see how the balance of incentives affects actions – in this case you have a serious failure by government to provide a core public good (public safety and property protection), leading to strong incentives to supply the good privately, as is happening.

All of this is part of a related phenomenon that has been looked at by a number of scholars, most notably Robert Nelson. This is the way in which most of the urban development taking place in the US since the early 1980s has taken the form of Home Owner Association property. In this model a self-contained 'gated' community is owned and administered once completed by a corporate body made up of all of the residential owners, a Home Owners Association or HOA (Nelson 2005). These bodies have elaborate constitutions and bylaws and have, according to Nelson and other scholars, increasingly taken on the functions traditionally performed by local government at the city or even county level. These include the management of collective space and regulation of all kinds. Indeed the regulation is often more extensive and explicit than would ever be found in traditional local government because it is based on explicit consent, since the buyer has to sign up to the HOA constitution and all of the rules when purchasing a property. Charges are levied to pay for collective goods, which again are being provided in this case by a club mechanism. In this case there is a monopoly, but one that is highly localised and easy to exit. According to the industry's own body, HOAs governed 24.8 million American homes and 62 million residents in 2010.[2] Similar developments are increasingly common in the UK.

National defence

Policing and security may seem to most a core function of government, but virtually everyone agrees that the central

2   http://www.caionline.org/info/research/Pages/default.aspx (accessed 3 July 2015).

state function and the classic public good of the Samuelsonian type is national defence. Indeed having a monopoly of this kind of activity (large-scale organised deadly force, to be blunt) is seen by most political scientists as being the defining feature of the state. However, alongside private security firms, which provide policing functions, is an entire industry of private contractors who increasingly supply military services (Avant 2005; Mandel 2002; Singer 2003). For medieval and early modern historians this is not as surprising as it might be to other people. The feudal system was essentially a social order where this function of government was privatised or subcontracted by tying the public good of defence of a territory to the private good of land ownership via the institution of the knights' fee. The later Middle Ages and Renaissance saw the appearance of professional military contractors, usually known by their Italian name of Condottieri (literally meaning 'contractors').

What we now see is a revival of this kind of industry with military professional companies such as Academi providing the kinds of service that actual states are increasingly unable to supply. There is an international convention that outlaws such services but it is fair to say that this is very much more honoured in the breach than the observance. This should lead us, when looking at these questions from a Coasian standpoint, to doubt that there is anything automatic or natural about military force being supplied on a monopoly basis by territorial states. Instead we should be looking at the kinds of factors that make it easy to provide this kind of service privately at some times but not at others. These would include technology and the nature of military organisation, but also once again the level of transaction costs and the ability to tie a public good to private ones through institutional arrangements.

Coase's way

When he published his article on public goods and the example of the lighthouse all those years ago, Ronald Coase did what all good social scientists should do. He refused to take for granted and assume without question something that seemed self-evidently correct to most of his colleagues. Instead he looked at the empirical evidence of history and asked pointed and important theoretical questions – in this case granting that there was a public goods problem, why assume that the only way to address it was through government? This generates a very rich and fruitful research agenda, and investigating these matters reveals things such as the contemporary growth of private governance and the plethora of historical private means of solving public goods challenges. We may actually come to very radical conclusions such as that most so-called public goods are actually club goods and that the very need for government is contingent and historically specific rather than essential. All this comes from simply asking questions.

8   STOCK EXCHANGES AS LIGHTHOUSES[1]

Philip Booth

Before 1986, securities and investment markets in Britain were regulated by a combination of private structures and some ad hoc bodies established for tightly defined purposes.[2] There was no overarching system of state financial regulation that sought to control and regulate the markets. These informal organisations and non-state bodies had characteristics that Ronald Coase might well have admired. They were then replaced by statutory bodies that use the theoretical economics of the textbook – in Coase's words, 'blackboard economics' – to determine rules and regulations.

This chapter will begin by describing the story of the lighthouse and how Coase discovered that lighthouses were adequately provided in England despite relatively minimal government intervention. The regulatory structures in relevant parts of the financial markets before 1986 will then be discussed and related to the lighthouse story.

---

1   This chapter was previously published in *Journal of Man and the Economy* 1(2), 171–87, reproduced by permission.

2   For example, the Takeover Panel, which was a quasi-statutory body.

This will be followed by a discussion of the changes in regulation that took place from 1986. Finally, there will be a brief discussion of how a central bank can be organised pragmatically as a broadly private institution in a way that could restrain the development of arbitrary and intrusive bureaucratic regulation of the banking sector.

There are four insights in this chapter. The first is that, just as in the case of lighthouses, regulation can develop in financial markets without state bodies being established. Secondly, there may be some circumstances in which private forms of financial regulation are facilitated by legal privileges or exemptions from laws which are applied to other sectors of the economy. Thirdly, in the case of both lighthouses and financial regulation, incentives are more appropriately aligned if the functions are undertaken privately. Finally, there may be problems with centres of market power developing when private bodies provide regulation just as may also be the case with lighthouses.

In the spirit of Coase, we conclude that economists should make judgements about whether private or state institutions better perform the desired functions; in other words, they should ask 'what are the best institutional arrangements?'[3] This is preferable to simply assuming away the possibility of private bodies operating in these fields and developing state regulatory bureaus that try to perfect the market using blackboard economics. Indeed, the

---

3   Dowd and Hutchinson (2014) ask exactly this question in relation to the supervision and provision of support to the US banking system before the development of the Federal Reserve.

historical evidence suggests that we have gone far too far with the development of detailed statutory financial regulation that attempts to deal with alleged 'market failure', and that we should allow market institutions once more to arise to regulate financial markets. In fact, such institutions still do exist in some areas of financial market activity (for example, the London Stock Exchange does still have a rule book) but they are surrounded by, and stifled by, overarching statutory regulatory bodies.

Lighthouses – what does not work 'in theory' works in practice

At the beginning of his paper 'The lighthouse in economics' Coase (1974b) mentions a number of leading economists who had proposed that the state should provide lighthouses. Mill, for example, held this view on the basis that, without state help, navigation aids would not be provided because enforcing payment and excluding those who did not pay would be impossible. Pigou made a similar point. Samuelson took the argument further. He argued that, even if payment for lighthouse services could be enforced, it should not be required. The light from the lighthouse had zero marginal cost and, as such, excluding a ship from the services of lighthouses would be inefficient if the benefit to that ship were greater than zero. In effect, Samuelson was arguing that lighthouses were a pure public good.

As Stephen Davies pointed out in the previous chapter, Coase investigated the historical provision of lighthouses in England and demonstrated that they were, in fact, provided and that lighthouse fees were actually charged. Furthermore, Coase found that, in practice, the charges were levied in such a way that few ships would have been deterred by the charges at the margin, quite contrary to Samuelson's prior view. In addition, few ships would have benefited from the services of the lighthouse from which a charge was not collected, but from which it would have been feasible to collect a charge, even if the government had been directly responsible for doing so.

Thus, the institutional mechanism that existed in practice for the construction and funding of lighthouses solved the problems identified by economists in a reasonable and practical way. Those economists who said that lighthouses should be provided by the government according to blackboard economics should first have investigated the historical facts. There was no evidence that the provision of lighthouses was more effective in those countries where the government was responsible. In short, lighthouses in England seem to have had the characteristics of club goods rather than of public goods. Lighthouses were not obviously under-provided and mechanisms that economists believed could not work in theory did work in practice.

Financial regulation – what does not work 'in theory' works in practice

Economists have argued in favour of state regulation of financial markets just as they have argued in favour of state provision of lighthouses, though with some differences between the reasoning in the two cases. For example, it is often argued that financial markets need government regulation because of pervasive information asymmetries; because 'market confidence' has externality effects; because of the problem of 'moral hazard'; and because of systemic risk that can lead the financial system to fail if an individual financial institution fails (see, for example, Llewellyn 1999).

Akerlof (1970), in particular, highlighted the problem of information asymmetries in markets. However, it is worth noting that Akerlof's normative conclusions were rather tentative. He concluded that information asymmetries may lead to a situation where government intervention could improve matters, but he also pointed out that private institutions could arise to deal with the problems he identified, while mentioning that such institutions may themselves give rise to problems such as concentrations of power. This view is reasoned and rational and, as we shall see, leads in a Coasian direction that requires economists to evaluate which is the best of alternative institutional arrangements. This view can be contrasted with the rationale put forward by financial regulators for state regulation of financial markets. In one publication (FSA 2003) by the UK financial regulator, the Financial Services Authority, it was stated that:

> In meeting our objectives in a manner consistent with the principles of good regulation, we have adopted a regulatory approach based on correcting market failure ... There are, however, numerous cases where unregulated

financial markets will not achieve the best outcome due to some form of market failure, making action on our part necessary.

Starting from this perspective, there is no effective limit on the amount of financial regulation that can be justified, because a market can never be perfected and is always subject to what some economists describe as 'market failure'.

It would be instructive for 'blackboard economists' in this field to examine the forms of regulation that actually developed historically within financial markets. Institutions important in creating a stable order in financial markets included independent professions (see, for example, Booth 2007; Bellis 2000)[4]; the development of intermediaries and trustee bodies to deal with information asymmetries; special corporate governance arrangements (such as customer-owned firms and banks with double or unlimited liability for shareholders) to address conflicts of interest; and the use of 'reputation' to distinguish between good and bad firms (Macey 2013).

In addition to the above institutions that regulate behaviour in finance, markets can develop their own comprehensive regulatory institutions. Though it is the

---

4 With regard to professions, some of these were effectively products of the market and entirely independent of government, others had government protection. It is because of the prominence of the latter in so many areas that professions have tended not to get praise from supporters of a market economy (see, for example, Friedman 1962). As we shall see, this issue of government protection and market power is important in the debate about the lighthouse.

intention of this chapter to examine what happened in practice rather than tie the issues in to a body of theory, it is worth noting that these regulatory institutions operated on a club-like basis.[5] They developed rules to which their members had to adhere. Adherence to the rules came with a cost because the rules involved the prohibition of certain practices that may have been remunerative to individual members of the club. However, the rules also had a benefit because, if they were obeyed by all members of the club, adherence would enhance the reputation of all the members. In other words, market confidence and trustworthiness can be thought of as a club good and the price of obtaining that good is adherence to the rules (in addition to any membership fees). It is important that free riders cannot operate under the protection of the private regulatory body without obeying the rules: that is, it must be possible to exclude rule breakers.

Below we will examine two such mechanisms in financial markets: stock exchanges and central banks.

Private regulation and stock exchanges

In Britain, modern stock exchanges first developed in coffee shops, such as Jonathan's Coffee House in Change Alley, where a group of 150 brokers and jobbers formed a club in 1761 superseding more informal arrangements that had existed since 1698. This club developed into the first formally (though privately) regulated exchange in

---

5   See Buchanan (1965) for the theory of the club good.

1801 and, the following year, the exchange moved to Capel Court. The characteristics of the stock exchange included restrictions on membership, the publication of prices and lists of stocks that were traded, and the potential for the development of a rule book.

In the early years, the exchange was regulated by convention, reputation and informal rules. For example, when delayed settlement was introduced to increase liquidity, those who did not settle their accounts would be labelled 'lame duck' on a board and could be prevented from acting as brokers. It is also worth noting that, in common with other exchanges at various times, the London exchange succeeded in the 1730s in enforcing orderly transactions that were unenforceable in a court of law (Kynaston 2012: 14). This was also the case in Amsterdam, where the exchange facilitated the trading of forward contracts and short sales that were prohibited by government and therefore unenforceable in law (Stringham 2003). There were unlicensed brokers in Amsterdam, as elsewhere, that provided competition, but reputation was important in governing business on the market (Stringham and Boettke 2004).

As Stringham writes in criticising the belief that regulation has to come from the government (Stringham 2015: 48, 50):

> But the Amsterdam traders were cleverer than the blackboard theorists ... who assert that financial markets emerged because of government. We can see how markets actually worked by analyzing some firsthand accounts,

the best of which was published in 1688 by stockbroker, Joseph Penso de la Vega. Written in his native Spanish in the form of a dialogue, *Confusion de Confusiones* is a sort of seventeenth century frequently asked questions, most likely for people looking to get into the stock market. In the book de la Vega describes numerous transactions including short sales, forward contracts, option contracts, and other transactions that occurred even though they were unenforceable in courts of law.

Regulation by reputation is commonplace in markets. What was different about stock exchanges, however, was their ability to develop codified rules. This happened in two ways. Firstly, there were rules governing behaviour of members and the quotation of stock prices. Secondly, there were rules for companies listed on the exchange. The latter type of regulation developed rather later. These are precisely the forms of financial market regulation that is commonly thought necessary for the state to provide and which the state now does provide.

The first codified rule book covering topics such as default and settlement was developed by the London exchange in 1812. This rule book included provisions for settlement, arbitration and dealing with bad debts. There were also rules about general behaviour designed to increase transparency (for example, partnerships among members had to be listed publicly) and about the quotation of prices. Davis et al. (2004: 12) report how the exchange collectively absorbed losses from an event of market manipulation and the inappropriate use of insider information in 1814, while ensuring that those who attempted to profit did not gain.[6] These are now matters that are entirely handled by government regulation.

In 1844 it became a requirement for securities to be sanctioned by the stock exchange committee before being listed on the exchange (ibid.). In effect, this was the introduction of the other important aspect of regulation provided by exchanges – rules for the quotation of a company's shares. Indeed, rules for the quotation of a company's shares complement rules in relation to the behaviour of members. Without an orderly market, companies will not seek a listing, and, without reasonable listing rules, investors will be discouraged from trading on the market. At the turn of the twentieth century, these listing requirements then became more onerous.

Until all-encompassing regulation was developed by bodies reporting to the UK government under the 1986 Financial Services Act, regulation remained entirely a private matter. After World War I, various Companies Acts were passed which mandated information provision by companies, but, even then, the stock exchange imposed additional requirements on companies quoted on the exchange such as the requirement for interim reports (see Goff 1982).

The ability of the exchange to determine its own membership and to set the rules by which members work was crucial. The members incurred the costs and reaped the

---

6   Those gaining from the activity were fined their profits, which had to be paid to charity.

benefits of a well-functioning rule book because it helped to create an orderly market and enhanced the reputation of the exchange. The companies quoted on the exchange also reaped the benefit of an orderly market through, for example, a lower cost of capital and, in later years, companies had to pay for the benefit of being listed. The benefits of those rules were excludable in that the benefits would not be obtained by companies not quoted on the exchange or by those involved in exchanging stocks and shares who were not members of an exchange with a good reputation. Similarly, the costs of the rules would be borne by those trading in the form of membership fees and in the form of the non-pecuniary costs of self-restraint. The costs of self-restraint could be considerable. For example, from 1909, members were prohibited from performing broking functions if they also traded on their own book[7] – something which reduced the likelihood of conflicts of interest.

A Royal Commission enquiry in 1877–78 illustrates two features that seem to be important in the regulation of securities business. The first is the influence of a small number of important players on the rules that were developed (Kynaston 2012: 91). The second is confirmation of the club-like nature of the exchange. In reporting the outcome of the Commission, Kynaston comments (ibid.: 92):

---

7   The rules surrounding this issue evolved but were clarified and made explicit in 1909 (see Burn (1909), and the article reproduced therein from *The Times*, pages 134–36). This rule involved considerable restraint on behalf of some members, as was made clear in *The Times*'s article, but it was considered that it benefited the reputation of the exchange.

> Pre-allotment dealings remained the norm; settlement and quotation remained wholly within the Committee's jurisdiction; the Stock Exchange remained a self-regulating decidedly unincorporated body; and would-be public spectators remained excluded for another three-quarters of a century. The club, in short, preferred to stay just that[...]

The Royal Commission noted that the exchange's rules 'had been salutary to the interests of the public' and that the exchange had acted 'uprightly, honestly, and with a desire to do justice'.[8] It further commented that the exchange's rules were 'capable of affording relief and exercising restraint far more prompt and often satisfactory than any within the read of the courts of law.'

Not only were the benefits of the club rules excludable, it was possible for non-members to form a competing exchange with different rules. In practice, however, competition was limited. Developments in technology from the beginning of the 1980s, however, changed this and there is now considerable competition between exchanges on an international level. Competition also came from other markets that were effective in providing capital to companies. For example, before the stock exchange 'club' was broken up in 1986, the euro bond markets had developed without any centralised exchange or regulatory body, whether private or state,

---

8   Royal Commission on the London Stock Exchange (1878: 5), quoted in Stringham (2015).

and the euro bond markets were an important alternative source of capital to local equity markets for large companies (see Kynaston 2012).

The state regulation of UK securities markets began in 1986. The state regulation of the US stock exchange occurred well before that of the UK. However, Paul Mahoney, mainly describing the development of the New York Stock exchange but referring also to others, has said (Mahoney 1997: 1462):

> [I]n summary, many stock exchange rules in the era before governmental regulation were premised on the idea that to attract investors, the exchange had to provide elementary protection against defaults, forgeries, fraud, manipulation and other avoidable risks. Thus stock exchange rules dealt with most of the broad categories of issues with which modern securities regulations are concerned.

Indeed, the reputation for trustworthiness on the London exchange was such that, in 1923, when it received its coat of arms, its motto was: 'my word is my bond'.

'Big bang' and 'deregulation'

In 1986, the stock exchange system of private rule-making was broken open and the London exchange opened to foreign banks. At the same time, the separation of broking and dealing functions was ended. This was known as 'big bang'.

The motivation for reform was a belief that the restrictive practices on the stock exchange were causing it to lag behind other international exchanges (Creaven 1992). The sweeping away of the various restrictive practices (limitations on entry to the market, fixed commissions and the separation of trading and broking) followed an agreement with the government that led to the suspension of a six-year-long enquiry by the Office of Fair Trading, which had previously had its powers extended to include service industries.

Big bang is widely regarded as a process of 'deregulation'. That the so-called deregulation of the City of London arose as a result of challenges to the existing structures from the competition authorities is significant. Whether this action was right or wrong, Akerlof can be thought of as being rather perceptive in identifying the issue of market power as a potential problem in privately provided systems designed to deal with information asymmetries in markets. Essentially, in 1986, the competition authorities removed from the private institutions that regulated the market their ability to exclude members and their ability to set rules (such as commission levels, separation of trading and broking, etc.). This breaking up of private regulation was followed by the development of government regulatory agencies which had arbitrary and more-or-less unlimited powers to regulate to correct what many perceived to be market failures.

There are many similarities between the regulatory situation in securities markets in 1986 and Coase's observations regarding lighthouses. Two are perhaps especially noteworthy. Firstly, it is widely thought among economists that state regulation of securities markets is necessary – in other words that the market cannot provide regulation through institutions that arise from within the market. The assertion that state regulation is necessary tends to be justified through the application of blackboard economics in exactly the same way as it was argued that lighthouses were a public good according to economic theory. Secondly, there seems to be a lack of curiosity among mainstream economists about the history and economic nature of regulation in financial markets. In the same way that Coase's paper on lighthouses described the situation that actually existed in practice after other authors had said that lighthouses could not be financed privately in theory, there seems to be general denial of the most basic facts regarding financial regulation in the UK up to 1986. What is often described as a process of 'deregulation' to promote free markets in 1986 was, in fact, a process of prohibition of private regulation and its replacement by state regulation.

Even though the state has taken over regulatory oversight in all developed countries, exchanges still do exist to provide different and competing regulatory environments for listing and trading though all have to enforce state regulation. Especially in the field of listing requirements for companies, there is still some discretion for exchanges to develop their own requirements. For example, the Alternative Investment Market (AIM) is a relatively lightly regulated market in the UK, and there are markets that perform similar functions in the US such as NASDAQ.

Indeed, a number of companies that are quoted on AIM are small enough for statutory regulatory requirements not to apply to them. And yet, as Stringham (2012) demonstrates, AIM is successful as a regulatory environment. At the same time, there are markets which have much more detailed and onerous rulebooks for quoted companies (in addition to the requirements of statutory regulators) such as the main market of the London Stock Exchange.

The further development of statutory regulation

Soon after big bang in 1986, there was a huge extension of the regulation of securities markets as a result of the Financial Services Act 1986, which came into operation in 1988. Goodhart (1988) suggested that just one rule book, developed as a result of the 1986 Act on one aspect of regulation, weighed around two kilograms. The Act itself is reproduced in 230 pages (not including the associated regulations) in the standard textbook by Wedgwood et al. (1986).

The Financial Services Act 1986 established that the Securities and Investment Board (SIB) would be responsible to the Secretary of State. The act followed the Gower Report, Review of Investor Protection, published in 1984. The SIB's powers were very wide-ranging. It authorised businesses, intermediaries and individuals and gave recognised status to professional bodies whose members could carry on limited de minimis regulated activities under the supervision of their professional body. Matters which were previously governed by common sense, ethical codes, private stock exchanges or professional bodies became regulated activities under the Financial Services Act.

In describing the transition Sir Kenneth Berrill, first chairman of the SIB said that the City was no longer a place 'where you look after yourself according to a code of honour of conduct. It is a tough regulatory system' (Hilton 1987: 48). Lomax (1987) stated: 'There is a substantial risk, in fact, that we now have massive overkill of the supervisory structure in the financial industry' (Chapter 3, Section 9).

The market moved from polycentric and largely private systems of regulation, to a system of regulation that allowed rules to be spurned with little accountability. Goodhart (ibid.), commenting soon after the Financial Services Act, felt that standards could have continued to have been maintained in most areas through the use of 'clubs' with perhaps some small role for the state in regulating entry standards where this was not effectively done.

Since 1986, financial regulation has become even more centralised and, arguably, the powers of the regulator have become more arbitrary. In 2001, the Financial Services Authority was given power to regulate the whole UK financial sector and it is impossible to perform any function in securities markets without being regulated by that body.[9] There are probably millions of paragraphs[10]

---

9   Regulatory functions were reorganised in 2013.

10 It has been calculated that there are 4,000,000 words from one of the bodies alone that succeeded the FSA. See http://www.conservativehome.com/thecolumnists/2014/10/lord-flight-regulation-the-collectivist-wolf-in-sheeps-clothing.html (accessed 3 July 2015).

of financial regulation and in the last year of its operation (before the regulatory functions were divided between different statutory bodies) the FSA had a budget of £547m.[11] By 2013, the body had accrued powers to regulate areas of financial activity, such as mortgages and non-life insurance, that had been entirely free of regulation in the past and in relation to which there had been no clear problem that required statutory regulation. Bank of England Chief Economist Andrew Haldane noted: 'In 1980, there was one UK regulator for roughly every 11,000 people employed in the UK financial sector. By 2011, there was one regulator for every 300 people employed in finance' (Haldane 2012). There has been a similar trend in the US, where it is commonly suggested that the regulations arising from the Dodd–Frank Act enacted following the financial crash will run to around 30,000 pages (see, for example, Dowd and Hutchinson 2014).

As noted above, the FSA justified its approach according to the blackboard economics concept of 'market failure'. However, statutory regulation effectively displaced the evolution of institutions within the market that could have improved the workings of markets, perhaps in a more satisfactory way. We know from the historical evidence that institutions of regulation can evolve within securities markets. One interesting issue, in the wake of the financial crisis, is whether the same could happen with regard to the regulation of banks. In the next section we look briefly at this.

---

11 See Annual Report and Accounts: http://www.fca.org.uk/static/documents/annual-report/fsa-annual-report-12-13.pdf (accessed 9 July 2015).

Could bank regulation be provided by market institutions?

As Coase taught us in 'The economics of lighthouse', it is important to look at the past in order to discover what actually happened, rather than rely on our textbooks to tell us about what can only happen in theory. It is also important to consider conceptually how we might apply our economic knowledge to solve new problems. In this section we consider briefly the possibility of understanding central banking and banking regulation as a club good.

Different schools of thought attribute the development of central banking to different origins. On the one hand, it is often suggested that central banks arose from the desire of the state to monopolise the money supply. On the other hand, it has been suggested that they were a natural evolution of a monetary system that needed a 'banks' bank' (Congdon 2009). This chapter does not make a judgement on this debate, though it should be noted that central banks are certainly not a purely private phenomenon, even when they are privately owned and governed – they are given certain statutory powers and monopolies by government. However, in making a comparison with the case of lighthouses in Britain, it should also be noted that lighthouses were also not provided only by a purely private club: Trinity House had certain privileges granted to it by the state.

Central banks have, at some points in history in some countries, had club-like characteristics in their relationship with clearing banks. This was certainly so in Britain in the nineteenth century.[12] Congdon argues that such club-like characteristics could be enhanced by simple reforms which could make both the regulatory system for banks more independent of government, make it more responsive to the needs of participants and also make it more effective. The Bank of England will be used as the example in this section – other central banks have different origins, history and modus operandi.

In 1844, the Bank Charter Act gave the Bank of England a quasi-monopoly of the note issue even though, importantly for our argument, it was privately owned. The Act also restricted the note issue to a fixed amount plus an additional sum that had to be backed by gold. This gave the Bank of England a privileged position (in the literal sense of the word 'privileged') and enabled it to lend against collateral to other banks when they could obtain no other source of finance. The ability to lend in this way was enhanced because, in a crisis, the Bank Charter Act was often suspended (for example in 1847, 1857 and 1866) allowing the Bank of England to extend its note issue.

In effect, the Bank of England became the head of a club of financial institutions. If a member of that club was illiquid but solvent, the Bank of England could come to its rescue by lending against collateral. If the Bank of England

---

12 Dowd and Hutchinson (2014) describe a purely private system of support for banks in the US before the development of the Federal Reserve, which was not dependent on a central bank at all. Given that the story of the lighthouse did not involve purely private provision with no state involvement, the analogy with the Bank of England in nineteenth-century Britain and how it could be reformed today is adequate for our purposes.

considered the behaviour of the club member seeking help to be inappropriate or if it thought that the solvency of the member was in danger then help could be refused. Indeed, that is precisely what happened in the case of Overend Gurney in 1866. Describing this incident, Kynaston (2012: 83) writes:

> Should the Bank have stepped in? Once it became clear that Overend Gurney required assistance to survive, it appointed a committee ... to scrutinise the books. The three wise men determined that the business was rotten beyond redemption and no helping hand was held out.

Then, relating the refusal of the Bank of England to assist with Overend Gurney's earlier decisions not to play by the implicit rules of the club, Kynaston continues: 'Overend Gurney had once very much been members of the club ... but it was a club that would never condone such barefaced tactics directed against its ex officio chairman[13]'.

This emphasises what we have noted already in the case of exchanges. There were significant concentrations of market power in this system. In effect, the Bank of England could determine whether a given firm should survive or fail.

The Bank of England was nationalised in 1946 and its role has changed. Indeed, in 1997 it was stripped of its power in relation to the regulation of banks and the issue of government debt, though it has since regained the former. Congdon (2009) proposes not just a return to the principles

---

13 The governor of the Bank of England.

by which the Bank of England operated before 1946 but an extension and formalisation of that role.

He suggests that the Bank of England should have its capital provided by the clearing banks it regulates.[14] There is thus a formal club of banks with the Bank of England regulating its members for their mutual benefit.[15] In return for the banks following the regulation set by the central bank, the central bank would provide lender of last resort facilities on an explicit contractual basis to those banks which became illiquid but were solvent. This would operate entirely privately.[16] The members of the club would own the central bank that sets the rules; the banks would have to follow the rules for the benefit of the whole club to ensure the safety of the banking system; but the members of the club that were short of liquidity would receive support through lender of last resort facilities if they kept to the rules. It should also be noted that Congdon argues that those banks that do not wish to submit themselves to the regulation of the Bank of England could choose not to do so and would not receive lender of last resort support. Any counterparty dealing with such banks would be aware of this.

Essentially, Congdon proposes a system that would take a 'market failure' problem identified by blackboard

---

14 What follows is my interpretation of Congdon expressed in the language used elsewhere in this chapter.

15 To protect the payments system – classically, the most important reason for regulating banks.

16 Though it should be noted that the ability of the central bank to play this role depends on its legal privilege as a central bank that can print money.

economics (externalities arising from the risk to the whole banking system of an individual bank failure) and proposes a solution that involves all parties agreeing to an institutional arrangement that would internalise the externality (to use the jargon of modern economics). This is not, itself, a blackboard economics solution dreamed up by Congdon, but a proposed evolution of arrangements that arose in the market in the nineteenth century, albeit encouraged by the legal privilege given to the Bank of England. It would, it should be noted, give substantial market power to the Bank of England, though in principle it would be constrained by the club members who provided the capital and determined the governance of the organisation as well as by the competitive threat from banks who chose not to join the club. As we shall see in the conclusion, there are several analogies with the lighthouse here.

Conclusion

In the story of the lighthouse, Coase showed that a system that blackboard economists believed not to be possible in theory actually developed in practice. There is a similar, though not identical, situation in financial markets. It is widely believed by economists who use a blackboard, market-failure-type approach that financial markets require state regulation. However, if we look at the historical practice, we find that financial markets regulated themselves. Furthermore, it is possible that banking regulation could be provided by an independent, privately owned central bank without direction from the state. It is worth noting that there are still several examples of club-based financial regulation operating internationally (for example, the International Swaps and Derivatives Association) and also examples of private regulation – though very much under state supervision – such as the UK's Alternative Investment Market.

There are several further interesting parallels between the examples found from financial markets and the study of lighthouses.

In the case of both lighthouses and the central bank in Britain, legal privileges were given to key players and this might have been necessary for the system to work effectively. [17]

In the case of lighthouses, Coase notes that, if lighthouses were financed by direct taxation, their building, administration and operation would not necessarily be carried out in the interests of lighthouse users. Congdon makes an exactly analogous point in justifying the provision of capital to the central bank by the banking sector that the central bank regulates.

In all three cases – lighthouses, central banks and exchanges – issues of market power arise. It is interesting to note that, as early as 1801, those brokers who were excluded from the stock exchange petitioned parliament to ask the government to force the exchange to be opened to all members of the public (Stringham 2002). However, the opponents of a bill that was drafted to that effect argued

---

17 Bertrand (2006) argues that the system Coase identifies as being successful relied on special privileges granted by the state. It should be noted there were no privileges granted by the state in relation to stock exchanges.

that private rules had to be enforced if the institution was to thrive. In this context, it is also important to note, as is discussed in Burn (1909), that it was possible to deal in stocks through non-members of an exchange – there was no monopoly, though only member brokers and dealers (jobbers) were considered as being beyond reproach. Indeed, it was a competition enquiry which ended the stock exchange's role in financial regulation in 1986. Also, when the Bank of England acted as a banker to the club of banks it was in a position where it could use its power to decide whether to allow a bank to fail (or otherwise). It is also the case that the provision of lighthouses became gradually more centralised under the jurisdiction of Trinity House. In this context, it is worth highlighting again the concern of Akerlof (1970) that institutions that develop within the market to deal with problems such as information asymmetry might accrue significant market power to which there might be objections.

Indeed, this point is perhaps the key issue for discussion. The debates surrounding financial regulation have tended to assume that markets cannot develop their own regulatory institutions. We should not be debating this question because history demonstrates that they can. It is, however, worth debating two different questions. Firstly, the empirical matter as to whether private financial regulation is better than state regulation. Secondly, there is the question of whether private regulation, in certain circumstances, gives rise to an undesirable concentration of power in private markets. This is precisely the point that Akerlof makes.

As it happens, in financial markets the concentrations of power were in the process of being dispersed at the very moment the state stepped in after nearly 300 years of private regulation (Kynaston 2012: 567–68). Furthermore, since the power to regulate financial markets moved from the clubs to the state, the regulator has accrued power with few checks, grown its budget and grown the number of employees at a rate that few would have anticipated in 1986. At best, concentrations of power within the private sector have been replaced by concentrations of power in state bureaucracies.

Nevertheless, there is a debate about which of the alternative institutional mechanisms is desirable. This is a debate which Coase would have believed it important to conduct. What economists should not do is assume that what clearly has happened cannot happen – whether this be in the City or the sea.

Coda[18]

As far as the future is concerned, a start could be made by removing statutory regulation of financial markets from those areas on which it has most recently been imposed without any clear cause (mortgages, non-life insurance and so on). Secondly, in some areas, businesses should be able to opt out of the statutory regulatory system as long as it is very clear that they are doing so. This would at

---

18 This coda has been added to the article to bring out its relevance to the theme of the book.

least create competition between firms that were clearly regulated and those that were clearly not. Furthermore, the new forms of finance that are developing (for example, peer-to-peer lending, crowd funding and crypto currencies) should be left entirely unregulated. It would be clear to all who used them that they would be so. And, of course, the point of these innovations is that they grow up alongside existing forms of financial services, so that nobody is obliged to use them. The markets would then be allowed to develop their own regulatory mechanisms. In general, they should be subject to basic laws of fraud and so on, but not to prescriptive regulation.

9 COASE AND THE 'SHARING ECONOMY'

Michael Munger[1]

Introduction

In an interview conducted by Richard Epstein in 2002, Ronald Coase recounted his original puzzlement with what seemed to him an obvious question. In the interview, he put it this way (Coase 2002b):

> We were discussing the way that businesses were controlled, and their plans were made, and all that sort of thing. On the other hand, [Professor Arnold] Plant told us all about the 'invisible hand', and how the pricing system worked itself, and you didn't need any plans and so forth. It seems quite natural to me now, though it doesn't seem to have bothered many other people: here you had these two systems operating simultaneously. One, within the firm, a little planned society, and on the other hand

1 The author thanks participants at the 'Think' Conference, 11–12 July 2015, at the Royal Geographic Society in London, England, sponsored by the Institute for Economic Affairs. In addition, very useful comments and corrections were offered on earlier versions of this paper by Philip Booth, Michael Gillespie, Len Shackleton and Cento Veljanovski. The shortcomings that remain are surely the fault of the author alone.

relations between firms conducted through the market. And yet, according to the way people looked at it, the whole thing could have been done through the market.

If markets and prices are so great, why are there firms? On other hand, any theory that answered that question would also have to address the implied corollary: if firms are so great, why isn't there just one big firm?

My own introduction to Coase's answer was memorable, though rather painful. When I was in graduate school at Washington University, Douglass North was on my dissertation committee. At my defence, he asked a question. It seemed like a complicated question, and I went to the board and wrote some equations. Finally (and mercifully), Doug interrupted me. Waving his hand slowly, addressing a not-very-bright child, he said, 'Michael, the answer is just two words ... *transactions costs*!'

And I should have known. For North, it didn't really matter what the question was, the answer, or at least the start of the answer, had to do with transactions costs. He had fully appreciated the Coasian insight that economic (and many political and social) institutions had as their primary function the optimisation of transactions costs. In some cases (e.g. both the price mechanism and organisation by firms), the objective was to reduce transactions costs. In other cases, the objective was to *increase* transactions costs. A celebrated example was the so-called Australian or 'secret' ballot, which makes it impossible to tell if the voter complied with an agreement to vote as bribed, thereby making effective vote buying much harder.

In the case of markets, and firms in particular, Coase's answer is now standard in economics: firms will expand, or shrink, at the margin, until the cost of the last transaction organised internally equals what that transaction would have cost using the price system. In business schools this is presented as the 'make or buy' decision: the firm can acquire or build the capacity to make an additional input or service, or it can buy input or service in the open market. Changes in transactions costs will change where that margin is located, and the size of firms will change, sometimes quite quickly as innovations in informing, transacting and enforcing agreements come on the scene.

In this essay, I take up a question that Coase would likely have thought quite similar to 'make or buy', and the answer would have been equally obvious to him. The question is: should we rent or own? The answer, not surprisingly, depends on transactions costs.

Tomorrow 3.0: rent or own?

We have the good (or bad?) luck to be alive at the beginning of the third great human entrepreneurial revolution, the Transactions Costs revolution. The result will be an economy where the key value proposition won't be selling products, but *selling reductions in transactions costs*. The first revolution, the Neolithic, enabled fixed agriculture and population densities that sustained complex interdependence and the realisation of economies of scale in defence. In other words, cities.

The second revolution, the Industrial, enabled the factory production line and fostered improvements in transportation and other infrastructure, as division of labour pressed markets to become more territorially extensive and to provide more and better goods at lower cost.

The Transactions Costs revolution will be different, because for the first time the disruption will be caused, not by a flood of new goods or services, but by much more intensive use of existing goods and skills of service providers. Many have called this the 'sharing economy' but, while catchy, this is misleading. Sharing would appear to imply communal use, and even communal ownership. The Transactions Costs economy will still involve private ownership, but each of us will probably need to own much less.

Still, the implications and practical effects, like the results of the first two revolutions, will be profoundly disruptive. And as with the first two revolutions, some of the institutions we have come to depend on will be swept away, and attempts to preserve artificially the approaches we have long depended on will cause unnecessary and very costly delays. This third revolution – whose leading edges we have now crossed – will make it possible to rent almost all the durable commodities we now own. Entrepreneurs will create, and capture, value almost exclusively by reducing the transactions costs of sharing existing commodities. Eventually, the remaining shared durable goods that are produced will be made expressly to be shared by the new platforms and new market processes.

The power drill trope: it's about time

It is estimated that there are 80 million power drills in closets, garages and sheds around the US. Many of these have been used for only a few minutes, and people claim (e.g. Friedman 2013) that the median lifetime use of a power drill is less than 20 minutes, total. It seems wasteful to have such replication and excess capacity, since few of these tools are being used at any particular point in time. Others[2] have raised some valid objections, focusing on the transactions cost of avoiding the 'waste' and pointing out (rightly) that if it were really possible, and desirable, to rent rather than own, people would be doing it. So, with existing ways of doing business, the business opportunity apparently presented by the fact that everyone owns a drill but rarely uses it is not real. Fair enough.

But to answer 'rent vs own' *with existing ways of doing business* misses a key distinction. What we seek from a transaction involving a tool is not (necessarily) ownership of the tool but access to the services that the tool can provide. More simply, Jones doesn't need a drill. What Jones needs is a hole in this wall, right here, right now.

The question is how Jones can achieve his object – *a hole in this wall, right here* – at the lowest total cost, including (crucially) transaction costs. Let's define 'transaction costs' as *all the costs of achieving my object in addition to the marginal opportunity cost of the resources required actually to*

---

2   See, for example, 'Why a drill is a bad example for the sharing economy': http://www.credport.org/blog/12-Why-a-Drill-is-a-Bad-Example-for-the-Sharing-Economy (accessed 6 August 2015).

accomplish this object. That's a vague definition, of course, but it's useful analytically. What is required to achieve the 'hole drilled in wall at exact point desired, right now' is the services, in effect the time, of a drill and the effort required to press the drill for a few seconds into the wallboard. Everything else is transactions costs, costs paid so that the required time can be used productively.

It would seem, given the centrality of Coase's transaction costs concept to his work, and to my claims here, that a clear definition of the concept would be useful, perhaps even necessary. But the quest for clear definition is bound to be frustrated, for two reasons. First, Coase himself was reluctant to define transaction costs in any restrictive way. Second, the very nature of transactions make precise definitions difficult, and perhaps misleading.

Goldberg (1989: 21) put it this way:

> Since firms do exist, and do thrive, we must ask how such organizations could be superior to the impersonal markets. The answer – or really the first part of the answer – was that impersonal markets weren't so darn perfect anyway; their imperfection [Coase] called 'transactions costs' ... Coase never bothered to give a precise definition of transactions costs because he didn't take the concept very seriously. It was only the name of whatever it was the economists had been ignoring.

I think it's inaccurate, or at least infelicitous, to say that Coase 'didn't take the concept very seriously'. Instead, it would be more accurate to say that transactions costs cannot be defined precisely, because they are dependent on the particular circumstances of time and place for that commodity and that transaction. It is tempting to define transactions costs as all the costs of completing a transaction other than the costs of producing the good or service being sold, but that would be a mistake. The notion of separating the good itself from the way that it is produced or sold requires ownership. If the nature of entrepreneurship is now focused on providing the services of the good but not the good itself, the notion of 'cost' is confused. In a way, all costs in the new rentership economy are transactions costs.

Consequently, the key to solving the problem is to have a clearer conception of the transaction, and what is being transacted. And that is the heart of the Coasian analysis, in any case. What the consumer wants is access to the ability to make 'a hole in this wall, right here' at future times at the (arbitrary, possibly currently unknown) discretion of the potential consumer. When any commodity, particularly a durable commodity such as a power drill, is *purchased*, what is really being bought is the ability to make a hole in the wall anytime that one desires at very low cost, transactions cost or otherwise. The consumer is looking to acquire access to a stream of services – services that can be cheaply and conveniently employed at the consumer's option – but the 'transaction' has until now been is a purchase for ownership because little is known about the future timing, duration or exact location for the consumer's desire to make holes in walls, or boards, or use the Philips screwdriver head to assemble a table from Ikea or Homebase.

What is missing from the discussion of the power drill, and the rent vs own choice, then, is the idea of time. The power drill is a durable good, but most consumers actually want only relatively small slices, and those intermittently, of the effective life of the drill. Still, if it is cheaper to 'rent' from myself (paying the opportunity rate on the capital costs of the funds tied up in the drill, and storing the drill in a space where it does not get wet, or damaged) by owning, then I will buy the drill rather than rent it.

But what if it isn't cheaper? What if an entrepreneur could sell reductions in the transactions costs of renting, using a combination of delivery services and software platform, such as Uber? The third entrepreneurial revolution will be based on innovations that reduce transactions costs, rather than reducing the costs of the products themselves. An unimaginable number and variety of transactions will be made possible by software innovations that solve three problems: (a) information, (b) transaction-clearing, and (c) trust. The result will be that the quality and durability of the items being used (in effect, rented) will increase, but the quantity of items actually in circulation will plummet.

It is important to distinguish this revolution as qualitatively different from what has gone before. Some observers (see, for example, Cairncross 1999) have focused on the importance of improved communications technologies, and network economies in communications devices. But computers and smart phones are just the platforms on which the actual cost reductions, and the rapid expansion of transaction density, depend. Being able to consummate complex transaction without fear of fraud or robbery is more than a change in 'communications'; it is a reduction in the cost and risk of engaging in a wide variety of economic activities that have never before been possible. Likewise with the out-sourcing of trust: it is not true that information is now being more cheaply transmitted. The software platforms of the future will generate trust-enforcing mechanisms where now no reliable metric exists. Crediting the transactions cost revolution to 'communication' is as misleading as basing credit for innovations in personal computing on 'advances in electricity'.

Entrepreneurs can sell reductions in transactions costs

Entrepreneurs imagine alternative futures, and then try to build them, even if the result is fiercely corrosive to the existing order of things. As Joseph Schumpeter (1934: 132) put it:

> The introduction [of new products] is achieved by founding new businesses, whether for production or for employment or for both. What have the individuals under consideration contributed to this? Only the will and the action; not the concrete goods, for they bought these – either from others or from themselves; not the purchasing power with which they bought, for they borrowed this – from others or, if we also take account of acquisition in earlier periods, from themselves. And what have they done? They have not accumulated any kind of good, they have created no original means of production, but

> have employed existing means of production differently, and more appropriately, more advantageously. They have 'carried out new combinations'. They are entrepreneurs. And their profit, the surplus, to which no liability corresponds, is an entrepreneurial profit.

Elsewhere, Schumpeter famously described entrepreneurs as even more destructive: 'Entrepreneurs are innovators who use a process of shattering the status quo of the existing products and services, to set up new products, new services'. This is something more than arbitrage, or making money by trading – buying low and selling high. Rather than simply 'correcting' errors in the price system, and causing the convergence of prices of a single existing commodity, entrepreneurs imagine alternative futures, new products and possible ways of organising production.

It is difficult to overstate the importance of this distinction. An entrepreneur does not (just) take advantage of errors (i.e. differences) in prices. An entrepreneur is alert to entirely new possibilities, to products and innovations that consumers may well not even be aware that they could have, much less want. Steve Jobs, of Apple, famously observed that entrepreneurs could not rely on static conceptions of 'demand': 'You can't just ask customers what they want and then try to give that to them. By the time you get it built, they'll want something new'.[3]

A decade later, Jobs went further: 'But in the end, for something this complicated, it's really hard to design

---

3   http://www.inc.com/magazine/19890401/5602.html

products by focus groups. A lot of times, people don't know what they want until you show it to them' (*Business Week* 1998). This echoes Henry Ford's famous, though perhaps apocryphal, claim that: 'If I had asked [consumers] what they wanted, they would have said, "Faster horses!"' The point, for present purposes, is that the implications of selling reductions in transactions cost are impossible to foresee. Many things that are now owned can be rented, and this can be done in a way that benefits both owner and renter.

Middlemen as brokers and sellers of connections

We tend not to like middlemen.[4] They seem parasitic, buying products and then reselling them without improvement. If middlemen make profits, surely they don't earn them? 'Eliminate the middleman' is the maxim of many simplistic schemes for increasing profit or reducing costs. Why do middlemen exist?

The answer is, unsurprisingly, transaction costs. Middlemen buy something, transport or store it, and then resell it at a higher price. But what the middleman is actually selling is a reduction in transaction costs. A transaction can only take place if the amount that a potential buyer can offer exceeds the marginal production costs of the seller plus transactions costs. This condition is not sufficient, of course, as the seller may hold out for more, the

4   There is no obvious gender-neutral term.

buyer for less, or something else can block the transaction. But the surplus of *reservation offer to pay* minus *reservation offer to sell* must exceed transactions costs before the transaction is even possible.

And what that means is that the middleman makes possible transactions that otherwise could not take place. Transportation, information, assurance of quality through brand name, financial clearing services – all of these are means of making possible transactions that otherwise would be blocked by transactions costs.

An example makes this clear. Suppose that A is willing to rent widget W for any price over $40 per day. B wants to use a widget for a day, and will pay any price less than $75. In principle, there is a bargaining space where any rental offer greater than $40 and less than $75 makes both parties better off. And in a welfare economics sense W 'should' be used by B, because he values it more than A.

But A may not know where or even who B is, and it's expensive to go looking. They may be physically distant, meaning that there are transport costs. The medium of exchange may be cumbersome, requiring costs to clear the transaction if it takes place. And they don't trust each other: say the widget is valuable and A is not sure B won't break it. These costs could easily be $50 or more. Assume the transactions costs are split evenly, $25 each. That means that A will require a payment of at least $65 to sell W, and B will pay at most $50. There is now no price where the transaction can take place. And because of this *A and B may not even imagine the idea of renting widgets*. No one has ever made an effort to set up a widget rental company, and no effort has been devoted to developing institutions for reducing the transactions cost. In standard economics we might call this a 'deadweight loss', but only if some entrepreneur has recognised the opportunity.

We are missing the particular kind of entrepreneur called a 'middleman', someone who sells reductions in transactions costs. Companies that specialise in renting complicated commodities, such as cars, have figured out ways to reduce the transactions costs dramatically, both those faced by consumers and those faced by the company. It happens that the author is a 'member' of the Hertz Gold #1 programme, meaning that he can exit an airplane and immediately walk directly to his rental car, which has the keys waiting inside. He was directed to precisely the correct parking spot by a text message, sent by a Hertz computer. All the information about eligibility to drive, background car preferences, and payment are stored in that same computer. The only employee the author sees is a human being who checks for identification at the exit gate. All of the other aspects of the transaction are handled behind the scenes, and essentially instantaneously, by a software platform.

Different car rental companies offer essentially the same prices, and the same cars. Hertz actually charges slightly more for each car per day, but the transactions costs of renting from Hertz are much lower. Consequently, the total costs of renting from Hertz are lower (at least in the US), and Hertz makes greater profits and the author derives more consumer surplus from the rental. Hertz is successful because it sells a bigger reduction in transactions costs than its competitors.

Why sell products when you can sell reductions in transactions costs?

Walk through a neighbourhood in New York City on a weekend in August. Or December. Lots of dark windows, sometimes for a week or more, people paying $1,500 per week or more to store their belongings. At the same time, all the hotels are full, and in any case outrageously expensive. Many visitors stay far out of the city, in New Jersey or Connecticut, spending an hour or more on a crowded train in the morning and evening just to visit the city. If the people who want a place to stay could just find someone who has a place, or a room, a mutually beneficial exchange could be effected. But the transactions costs are prohibitive.

Drive around the Financial District in Boston. If you stop at the corner of Devonshire and Milk Streets, you'll notice that there are at least six enormous parking garages within two blocks. They're full, too, most days, with thousands of cars ... sitting there doing nothing. People pay for the car, and they pay for land to park the car ... to ... do ... nothing. At the end of the day, they drive home with hundreds of thousands of other people doing the same thing. When they arrive home, they park their car on a street that could be used instead for traffic, or in a driveway or garage on land that costs hundreds of thousands of dollars per acre.

I picked these two transactions because they are the most salient successes to date in the sharing economy. The reader will recognize the 'sharing housing' example as the value proposition for AirBnB, and the 'sharing transport' example as the value proposition for Uber or Lyft. These companies claim that they are not in the (respectively) hotel or taxi business, but instead just operate software platforms that reduce the transactions costs of facilitating exchanges that were always possible, and always mutually beneficial, if the transactions costs problems could be solved.

This harkens back to the earlier point, of course, about the power drill. I don't really want a drill, I want a hole in this wall, right here at this point. I don't really want to own a car, I want convenient, safe and reliable transportation services. I don't really want to own a house, I want a comfortable, anodyne and attractive space to spend the night, or maybe a week.

To succeed, a middleman has to reduce three key transactions costs:

- Provide information about options and prices in a way that is searchable, sortable and immediate.
- Outsource trust to assure safety and quality in a way that requires no investigation or effort by the users.
- Consummate the transaction in a way that is reliable, immediate and does not require negotiation or enforcement on the part of the users.

It is tempting to think that the reason that Uber has succeeded is that it avoids the costs of complying with the regulations, taxes and restrictions that affect taxis. And that may be part of the story. But if you call an Uber driver she appears almost immediately; you don't have to wait, or wave at taxis that don't stop. That driver comes looking for you, and because of the software knows where you are. Further, you can see the name and licence information of the driver, and you know the company has the driver's personal and financial information. You don't need to give the driver directions, because you have already provided your destination to the software, which the driver can then use to navigate while you think about something else. And the driver is paid, and tipped, without you having to touch your wallet. Finally, you get to rate the driver and the ride, and Uber pays for background checks. Drivers with less than 4.5/5 score on ratings are dropped.[5]

Most importantly, the reduction in transactions costs may enable transactions that could not even be imagined by consumers. Once a platform is able to sell reductions in transactions costs, the original business model may be adapted to a variety of other activities that were not part of the set of things anyone thought might be rented or sold. An obvious example is Amazon.com. Few remember now that Amazon was originally a bookstore, the bane of bricks-and-mortar bookstores like Barnes and Noble or Borders, which had themselves been decried as causing the death of small, inefficient 'Mom and Pop' bookstores. Amazon provided a way to find almost any book, to pay for it using an existing account, often with 'one-click' selection,

---

5   Some people argue that Uber's (and Lyft's) safety and background checks are insufficient, and that this cheating is how they make money. But Feeney (2015) gives a detailed assessment of ride-sharing safety and driver reliability, and while there are some problems they are likely if anything to be less severe than the problems taxi drivers are likely to cause.

sending it to an address established in advance on that same account. Then the book was transported quickly and cheaply, arriving in just a few days. And then, with Amazon Prime, the item arrived in just two days ... for zero transport costs. A more direct reduction in transactions costs is hard to imagine.

But the software is disruptive, and in fact voracious. Once Amazon was able to sell reductions in transactions costs, it turned out that there was nothing special about books. Amazon quickly expanded to a few, and then many, other products. The advantages of the reduction in transactions costs was so enormous that many sellers flocked to use Amazon's software. That software became so valuable as a means of reducing transactions costs, in fact, that Amazon began selling it directly, under Amazon Web Services (AWS). There is even a dedicated 'Amazon Web Services for Dummies' book (Golden 2013) so that Amazon can reduce the transactions cost of learning how to purchase their software and hosting platform that reduces transactions costs.

To understand the role of middlemen in selling reductions in transactions costs, one needs to recognize that the kind of disruption caused by Amazon is just the beginning. There is nothing special about the transportation of human bodies; the Uber software is a new and extremely dangerous (to other middlemen) way to sell reduced transactions costs. Uber is not a threat to taxi companies. *Uber is a threat to Amazon.* Instead of having to wait two days for the power drill you bought, or the espresso maker, or the bread-maker that you would happily rent but would never buy, you can use Uber. You start the app, scroll through categories, and then select on the touchscreen the item you want to rent. The software already has your rental information, your financial information, and your address.

An Uber driver whom you don't even know will pick up the item at a store you don't know, and then deliver it to a lockable dedicated pod at your apartment. Your phone notifies you the item has been delivered. When you are finished, you return the item to the pod, and the pod itself contacts another Uber driver to pick up the item and return it.

Thus it is important to recognise that the changes we are observing are not simply driven by passive, exogenous changes in transactions costs. Coase (2000) was himself rather scornful of the notion that transactions costs were a definable, measurable variable that should be seen as driving economic change. The key factor is the innovation in software platforms that *reduce the costs of the entire transaction* to the point where that activity is now profitable for the entrepreneur and beneficial for the consumer. The transaction is paid for within the software itself, and both you and the renter (who may just be a private citizen who happened to have a drill) will rate each other. Services like this already exist in many cities for high-quality bicycles, luggage, clothing and appliances. As transactions costs are reduced by software platforms, enormous value is created for consumers and entrepreneurs grow rich.

Coase's insight

There is one more implication to be discussed, perhaps the most radical implication of all, and it comes directly out of

Coase's core insight about the existence of firms and transactions costs. Coase made an observation about the size of the firm, and the dynamics of how optimal firm size would change, in his original 'Nature of the firm' paper (Coase 1937b: 393):

> The approach which has just been sketched would appear to offer an advantage in that it is possible to give a scientific meaning to what is meant by saying that a firm gets larger or smaller ... The question which arises is whether it is possible to give a scientific meaning to what is meant by saying that a firm gets larger or smaller. Why does the entrepreneur not organize one less transaction or one more?

If the reason that firms exist is transactions costs, and if entrepreneurs are finding ever more creative and effective ways to sell reductions in transactions costs, what will happen to firms? It is tempting to think that the answer is obvious based on the theory alone, a conclusion that Coase usually derided. The hallmark of the Coasian approach, as other chapters have noted, was to get out and poke around, and try to figure out what was actually happening, in real markets. Five years from now, when the transactions costs revolution in software and rentership has developed more fully, we might be able to answer the question empirically.

Still, there are two considerations that appear salient even at this early stage. The first is the potentially dramatic reduction in the amount of new stuff that we need to manufacture. If I'm right that we will need 10 million, not 100 million, power drills in the US, then the number of power drills being manufactured will fall by 90%. Some of the difference will be made up by higher quality, more durable drills, and faster wearing out of the drills we have. But it is reasonable to expect a 50% reduction in drill output as a result of the transactions cost revolution. And of course this reduction in manufacturing capacity, and therefore manufacturing jobs, will be multiplied across the economy. If transactions costs fall far enough, we will be able to share almost everything.

The second consideration relates directly to the size of firms, as a variable. As was noted at the outset, the firm can 'make or buy' the things it needs to sell its products. In principle a car maker could purchase all of the components that make up a car from other sellers, and simply assemble the car. Alternatively, a consumer could purchase all the parts and then hire someone to assemble the car, inside the owner's garage. These suggestions seems silly, of course, but only because of transactions costs. The components of the car are already a 'car' in a sense, except for the detail of assembly.

We see the influence of the 'rent vs buy' decision in labour markets. It is much more common for firms to 'rent' workers, hiring temporary workers or teams of workers for 'gigs' forming what some people are calling the 'gig economy'. If this movement continues, the very notion of a 'firm' may start to be eroded. A group of people, each of whom has developed a set of specialized skills and a reputation based on ratings on software such as LinkedIn, would be hired for a project. At the project's completion, the group would break up, only to reform anew in kaleidoscopically different combinations of workers and projects. Hollywood films, for example, were once made by the major studios (corporations) such as Metro-Goldwyn-Mayer or 20th Century Fox. These 'studios' now are distributors, and movies are made by 'gig' workers, hired for the duration of the shooting of the film. After the film is completed, the gig is over.

Obviously, no one 'buys' workers outside of a system of slavery. But a long-term contract of the sort we associate with firms may well become quite rare. Firms may rent capital equipment and labour for very short periods, increasing the productivity of the workers for the period that they are employed and dramatically reducing the fixed costs of the firm. In the limit, firms themselves might simply become individuals or small teams that hire out for specific projects. Workers in this system would be private contractors, not 'employees' in the traditional sense. Unsurprisingly, the counter-revolutionary fervour of those who wish to protect existing power structures of both firms and unions[6] will call for attempts to control the sale of transaction cost reductions.

But that is the wrong way to think about it. There is nothing intentional or planned about the changes that are coming. Neither, however, can they be stopped. And that's the real power of the Coasian insight about transactions

---

6   See, for example, 'Defining "employee" in the gig economy', Editorial, *New York Times*, 18 July 2015: http://www.nytimes.com/2015/07/19/opinion/sunday/defining-employee-in-the-gig-economy.html (accessed 6 August 2015).

costs. The margin at which it becomes profitable to organise more, or fewer, transactions within a firm is entirely dependent on the mechanisms that entrepreneurs can devise for controlling and reducing transactions costs. The firm of the future may operate primarily as a software platform rather than as a physical location.

PUBLICATIONS BY RONALD H. COASE
IN CHRONOLOGICAL ORDER[1]

1935

(a) Bacon production and the pig-cycle in Great Britain. *Economica* 2: 142–67 (with R. H. Fowler).

(b) The pig-cycle: a rejoinder. *Economica* 2: 423–38 (with R. H. Fowler).

(c) The problem of duopoly reconsidered. *Review of Economic Studies* 2: 137–43.

1937

(a) The pig-cycle in Great Britain: an explanation. *Economica* 4: 55–82 (with R. H. Fowler).

(b) The nature of the firm. *Economica* 4: 386–405.

(c) Some notes on monopoly price. *Review of Economic Studies* 5: 17–31.

1938 Ronald H. Coase, business organization and the accountant (a series of 12 articles). *The Accountant* 13 (October–December 1938), 470–72, 505–7, 537–38, 559–60, 607–8, 631–32, 665–66, 705–6, 737–39, 775–77, 814–15, 834–35. Reprinted in *Studies in Costing* (ed. D. Solomons), Sweet and Maxwell, 1952. Shorter

---

1 This is not a comprehensive list of Coase's published work. It excludes conference proceedings, book reviews and other limited circulation writings such as reports and working papers. For a fuller bibliography which includes these see that published by the Coase Institute at https://www.coase.org/coasepublications.htm

version: *LSE Essays on Cost* (ed. J. Buchanan and G. F. Thirlby), London School of Economics and Political Science, 1973.

1939 Rowland Hill and the Penny Post. *Economica* 6: 423–35.

1940 The analysis of producers' expectations. *Economica* 7: 280–92 (with R. H. Fowler).

1946

(a) The marginal cost controversy. *Economica* 13: 169–82.

(b) Monopoly pricing with interrelated costs and demands. *Economica* 13: 278–94.

1947

(a) The marginal cost controversy: some further comments. *Economica* 14: 150–53.

(b) The origin of the monopoly of broadcasting in Great Britain. *Economica* 14: 189–210.

1948 Wire broadcasting in Great Britain. *Economica* 15: 194–220.

1950 *British Broadcasting: A Study in Monopoly.* London: Longmans, Green and Co.

1954 The development of the British television service. *Land Economics* 30: 207–22.

1955 The postal monopoly in Great Britain: an historical survey. In *Economic Essays in Commemoration of the Dundee School of Economics 1931–1955* (ed. J. K. Eastham), Blairgowrie: William Culcross and Sons.

1959 The Federal Communications Commission. *Journal of Law and Economics* 2: 1–40.

1960 The problem of social cost. *Journal of Law and Economics* 3: 1–44.

1961

(a) The British Post Office and the messenger companies. *Journal of Law and Economics* 4: 12–65.

(b) Why not use the price system in the broadcasting industry? *The Freeman* 11: 52–57.

1962 The Interdepartment Radio Advisory Committee. *Journal of Law and Economics* 5: 17–47.

1964 Discussion of 'Direct regulation and market performance in the American economy' by Richard E. Caves, and 'The effectiveness of economic regulation: a legal view' by Roger C. Crampton. *American Economic Review* 54: 194–97.

1965 Evaluation of public policy relating to radio and television broadcasting: social and economic issues. *Land Economics* 41: 161–67.

1966

(a) The economics of broadcasting and government policy. *American Economic Review* 56: 440–47.

(b) The theory of public utility pricing. In *The Economics of Regulation of Public Utilities*, pp. 96–106. Evanston, IL: Northwestern University.

1968

(a) *Educational TV: Who Should Pay?* Washington, DC: American Enterprise Institute (with E. W. Barrett).

(b) Consumer's surplus. In *International Encyclopaedia of the Social Sciences*, pp. 354–58. London: Macmillan.

1970

(a) Social cost and public policy. In *Exploring the Frontiers of Administration* (ed. G. A. Edwards), pp. 33–44. York University.

(b)   The theory of public utility pricing and its application. *Bell Journal of Economics* 1: 113–28.

(c)   The auction system and North Sea gas: a comment. *Journal of Law and Economics* 13: 45–47.

1972

(a)   Industrial organization: a proposal for research. In *Economic Research: Retrospective and Prospect*, vol. 3: *Policy Issues and Research Opportunities in Industrial Organization* (ed. V. R. Fuchs), pp. 59–73. NBER General Series 96. Cambridge.

(b)   Durability and monopoly. *Journal of Law and Economics* 15: 143–49.

1974

(a)   The market for goods and the market for ideas. *American Economic Review* 64: 384–91.

(b)   The lighthouse in economics. *Journal of Law and Economics* 17: 357–76.

(c)   The choice of the institutional framework: a comment. *Journal of Law and Economics* 17: 493–6.

1975

(a)   Economists and public policy. In *Large Corporations in a Changing Society* (ed. J. Fred Weston). New York University Press.

(b)   Marshall on method. *Journal of Law and Economics* 18: 25–31.

1977

(a)   Economics and contiguous disciplines. In *The Organization and Retrieval of Economic Knowledge* (ed. M. Perlman). London: Macmillan.

(b)   The wealth of nations. *Economic Inquiry* 15: 309–25.

(c) Advertising and free speech. *Journal of Legal Studies* 6:1–34.

1978

(a) Economics and contiguous disciplines. *Journal of Legal Studies* 7: 201–11.

(b) Economics and biology: a comment. *American Economic Review* 68: 244.

1979

(a) Payola in radio and television broadcasting. *Journal of Law and Economics* 22: 269–328.

(b) Should the Federal Communications Commission be abolished? In *Regulation, Economics, and the Law* (ed. B. H. Siegan). Idaho Falls: Lexington Books (with N. Johnson).

1981

(a) The Coase Theorem and the empty core: a comment. *Journal of Law and Economics* 24: 183–87.

(b) Duncan Black: a biographical sketch. In *Toward a Science of Politics: Essays in Honor of Duncan Black* (ed. G. Tullock), pp. 1–10. Blacksburg, VA: Virginia Polytechnic Institute and State University.

1982

(a) How should economists choose? G. Warren Nutter Lecture in Political Economy. Washington, DC: The American Enterprise Institute for Public Policy Research.

(b) George J. Stigler: an appreciation. *Regulation* November/December: 21–24.

(c) Economics at LSE in the 1930s: a personal view. *Atlantic Economic Journal* 10: 31–34.

1984

(a) The New Institutional Economics. *Journal of Institutional and Theoretical Economics* 140: 229–31.

(b) Alfred Marshall's mother and father. *History of Political Economy* 16(4): 519–27.

1986 Professor Sir Arnold Plant: his ideas and influence. In *The Unfinished Agenda: Essays on the Political Economy of Government Policy in Honour of Arthur Seldon* (ed. M. J. Anderson), pp. 81–90. London: Institute of Economic Affairs.

1987 Plant, Arnold. In *The New Palgrave Dictionary of Economics*, vol. 3 (ed. J. M. Eatwell, M. Milgate and P. Newman), pp. 891–92. London: Macmillan.

1988

(a) *The Firm, the Market and the Law*. University of Chicago Press.

(b) The nature of the firm: origin. *Journal of Law, Economics, and Organization* 4: 3–17.

(c) The nature of the firm: meaning. *Journal of Law, Economics, and Organization* 4: 19–32.

(d) The nature of the firm: influence. *Journal of Law, Economics, and Organization* 4: 33–47.

(e) The 1987 McCorkle Lecture: Blackmail. *Virginia Law Review* 74: 655–76.

1990

(a) Alfred Marshall's family and ancestry. In *Alfred Marshall in Retrospect* (ed. R. McWilliams Tullberg). Cheltenham: Edward Elgar.

(b) Accounting and the theory of the firm. *Journal of Accounting and Economics* 12: 3–13.

1991

(a) George J. Stigler. In *Remembering the University of Chicago* (ed. E. Shils). University of Chicago Press.

(b) Contracts and the activities of firms. *Journal of Law and Economics* 34: 451–52.

1992 The institutional structure of production: 1991 Alfred Nobel Memorial Prize Lecture in Economic Sciences. *American Economic Review* 82: 713–19.

1993

(a) Coase on Posner on Coase. *Journal of Institutional and Theoretical Economics* 149: 96–98.

(b) Concluding comment. *Journal of Institutional and Theoretical Economics* 149: 360–61.

(c) Law and economics at Chicago. *Journal of Law and Economics* 36: 239–254.

(d) Duncan Black 1908–1991. *Proceedings of the British Academy* 82.

1994 *Essays on Economics and Economists.* University of Chicago Press.

1995 Lives of the Laureates: thirteen Nobel economists: Ronald H. Coase. In *Lives of the Laureates. Thirteen Nobel Economists* (ed. W. Breit and R. W. Spencer), 3rd edn, pp. 227–49. Cambridge, MA: MIT Press.

1996

(a) Law and economics and A. W. Brian Simpson. *Journal of Legal Studies* 25: 103–19.

(b) The problem of social costs: the citations. *Chicago–Kent Law Review* 71: 809–12.

1997

(a) Looking for results. Interview with Thomas W. Hazlett. *Reason* January: 40–46.

(b) Interview with Ronald Coase. Inaugural Conference, International Society for New Institutional Economics, St. Louis, 17 September. http://www.coase.org/coaseinterview.htm (accessed 17 August 2015).

(c) Ronald Coase. In *Nobel Lectures: Economic Sciences 1991–1995* (ed. T. Persson). World Scientific.

1998

(a) The New Institutional Economics. *American Economic Review* 88: 72–74.

(b) Comment on Thomas W. Hazlett: assigning property rights to radio spectrum users: why did FCC licence auctions take 67 years? *Journal of Law and Economics* 41: 577–80.

(c) *The Firm, the Market and the Law*. University of Chicago Press.

(d) Foreword. In *The Theory of Committees and Elections* (ed. D. Black), revised 2nd edn. Alphen aan den Rijn: Kluwer.

(e) Aaron Director. In *The New Palgrave Dictionary of Economics and the Law* (ed. P. Newman). London: Macmillan.

1999 The task of the society. Opening Address to the Annual Conference, International Society of New Institutional Economics. Washington, DC, 17 September. https://www.coase.org/coasespeech.htm (accessed 17 August 2015).

2000 The acquisition of Fisher Body by General Motors. *Journal of Law and Economics* 43: 15–31.

2002
  (a) Remarks at the University of Missouri, 4 April. http:// www.coase.org/coaseremarks 2002.htm (accessed 8 August 2015).
  (b) The intellectual portrait series: a conversation with Ronald H. Coase, Richard Epstein, Interviewer. Indianapolis: Liberty Fund. http://oll.libertyfund.org/ titles/979 (accessed 23 July 2015).

2006 The conduct of economics: the example of Fisher Body and General Motors. *Journal of Economics and Management Strategy* 15: 255–78.

2011 Economy. *Entrepreneurship Research Journal*, Berkeley Electronic Press, vol. 1 (with Ning Wang).

2012
  (a) *How China Became Capitalist*. London: Palgrave (with Ning Wang).
  (b) Saving economics from the economists. *Harvard Business Review*, 20 November.

2013 How China became capitalist. *Cato Policy Report* XXXV, January/February (with Ning Wing).

REFERENCES

Akerlof, G. A. (1970) The market for 'lemons': quality uncertainty and the market mechanism. *Quarterly Journal of Economics* 84: 488–500.

Albert, W. (1972) *The Turnpike Road System in England 1663–1840.* Cambridge University Press.

Alchian, A. A. (1961) Some economics of property rights. Rand Paper 2316.

Alchian, A. A. (1967) *Pricing and Society.* London: Institute of Economic Affairs.

Alchian, A. A. and Allen, W. R. (1977) *Exchange and Production: Competition, Coordination and Control.* Belmont, CA: Wadsworth.

Alchian, A. A. and Demsetz, H. (1972) Production, information costs and economic organization. *American Economic Review* 62: 777–95.

Alchian, A. A. and Demsetz, H. (1973) The property rights paradigm. *Journal of Economic History* 33: 17–27.

Alchian, A. A. and Woodward, S. (1987) Reflections on the theory of the firm. *Journal of Institutional and Theoretical Economics* 143(1): 110–36.

Anderson, E. (1990) The ethical limitations of the market. *Economics and Philosophy* 6: 179–205.

Anderson, T. and Leal, D. (2001) *Free Market Environmentalism.* New York: Palgrave.

Anderson, T. and Libecap, G. (2014) *Environmental Markets*. Cambridge University Press.

Anderson, T. L., Scarborough, B. and Watson, L. R. (2012) *Tapping Water Markets*. Washington, DC: RFF Press.

Armstrong, M. and Sappington, D. (2007) Recent developments in the theory of regulation. In *Handbook of Industrial Organisation* (ed. M. Armstrong and R. Porter), vol. 3. Oxford: Elsevier.

Avant, D. D. (2005) *The Market for Force: The Consequences of Privatizing Security*. George Washington University.

Barnett, W. and Block, W. (2007) Coase and Van Zandt on lighthouses. *Public Finance Review* 35: 710–33.

Barry, J. (1999) *Reinventing Green Politics*. London: Sage.

Bate, R. (2001) *Saving Our Streams*. London: Institute of Economic Affairs.

Beito, D. T., Gordon, P. and Tabarrok, A. (2006) *The Voluntary City: Markets, Communities and Urban Planning*. Independent Institute/Michigan University Press.

Bellis, C. S. (2000) Professions in society. *British Actuarial Journal* 6(II): 317–44.

Bertrand, E. (2006) The Coasean analysis of lighthouse financing: myths and realities. *Cambridge Journal of Economics* 30: 389–402.

Betton, S., Eckbo, B. and Thornburn, K. (2008) Corporate takeovers. In *Handbook of Empirical Corporate Finance* (ed. B. Eckbo), vol. 2. New York: Elsevier.

Booth, P. M. (2007) Freedom with publicity – the actuarial profession and insurance regulation from 1844 to 1945. *Annals of Actuarial Science* 2(1): 115–46.

Breit, W. and Spencer, R. W. (eds) (1995) *Lives of the Laureates. Thirteen Nobel Economists*, 3rd edn. Cambridge, MA: MIT Press.

Broderick, D. (2002) *The First Toll Roads: Ireland's Turnpike Roads 1729–1858*. Collins Press.

Buchanan, J. M. (1965) An economic theory of clubs. *Economica* 32(125): 1–14.

Buchanan, J. and Thirlby, G. F. (eds) (1973) *LSE Essays on Cost*. London School of Economics and Political Science.

Buchanan, J. and Tullock, G. (1962) *The Calculus of Consent*. University of Michigan Press.

Burn, J. (1909) *Stock Exchange Investments in Theory and Practice*. London: Charles and Edwin Layton (for the Institute of Actuaries).

Cairncross, F. (1999) *The Death of Distance: How the Communications Revolution Will Change Our Lives*. Cambridge, MA: Harvard Business Press.

Calabresi, G. (1967) Some thoughts on risk distribution and the law of torts. *Yale Law Journal* 70: 499–553.

Calabresi, G. (1970) *The Costs of Accidents: A Legal and Economic Analysis*. Yale University Press.

Carter, R. and Hodgson, G. M. (2006) The impact of empirical tests of transaction cost economics on the debate on the nature of the firm. *Strategic Management Journal* 27: 461–76.

Casadues-Masanell, R. and Spulber, D. F. (2000) The fable of Fisher Body. *Journal of Law and Economics* 43: 67–104.

Casson, M. (1987) *The Firm and the Market: Studies on Multinational Enterprise and the Scope of the Firm*. Oxford: Basil Blackwell.

Chalklin, C. W. (1974) *The Provincial Towns of Georgian England: A Study of the Building Process, 1740–1820*. Edward Arnold.

Chalklin, C. W. (2001) *The Rise of the English Town, 1650–1850*. Cambridge University Press.

Cheung, S. N. S. (1973) The fable of the bees: an economic investigation. *Journal of Law and Economics* 16: 11–33.

Commons, J. R. (1924) *Legal Foundations of Capitalism*. Macmillan.

Congdon T. (2009) *Central Banking in a Free Society*, Hobart Paper 166. London: Institute of Economic Affairs.

Copeland, J. (1968) *Roads and Their Traffic, 1750–1850*. Newton Abbot: David & Charles.

Creaven, P. M. (1992) Inside outside leave me alone: domestic and EC-motivated reform in the UK securities industry. *Fordham Law Review* 60(6): S286–S318.

Dahlman, C. J. (1979) The problem of externality. *Journal of Law and Economics* 22: 148–62.

Dales, J. (1968) *Pollution, Property and Prices*. University of Toronto Press.

Davis, L., Neal, L. and White, E. N. (2004) The development of the rules and regulations of the London Stock Exchange, 1801–1914. Paper prepared for the Vanderbilt University seminar, 2004. http://www.vanderbilt.edu/econ/sempapers/Neal.pdf.

De Jasay, A. (2012). *Social Contract, Free Ride: A Study of the Public Good Problem*. Liberty Fund.

Demsetz, H. (1966) Some aspects of property rights. *Journal of Law and Economics* 9: 61–70.

Demsetz, H. (1967) Toward a theory of property rights. *American Economic Review* 59: 347–59.

Demsetz, H. (1968) Why regulate utilities? *Journal of Law and Economics* 11(1): 55–65.

Demsetz, H. (1969) Information and efficiency: another viewpoint. *Journal of Law and Economics* 12: 1–6.

Dowd, K. and Hutchinson, M. (2014) How should financial markets be regulated? *Cato Journal* 34(2): 353–88.

Dryzek, J. (1987) Political and ecological communication. *Environmental Politics* 4(4): 13–30.

Dunning, J. H. (1973) The determinants of international production. *Oxford Economic Papers* 25(3): 289–336.

Ergas, H. (2009) An excess of access: an examination of Part IIIA of the Australian Trade Practices Act. *Agenda: A Journal of Policy Reform* 16(4): 37–66.

Feeney, M. (2015) Is ridesharing safe? Cato Policy Analysis, 27 January, no. 767. http://www.cato.org/blog/ridesharing-safe (accessed 9 August 2015).

Freeland, R. (2000) Creating holdup through vertical integration: Fisher Body revisited. *Journal of Law and Economics* 43(1): 33–66.

Friedman, M. (1962) *Capitalism and Freedom*. University of Chicago Press.

Friedman, T. (2013) Welcome to the sharing economy. *New York Times*, 20 July 2013. http://www.nytimes.com/2013/07/21/opinion/sunday/friedman-welcome-to-the-sharing-economy.html?pagewanted=all&_r=0 (accessed 9 August 2015).

FSA (2003) *Reasonable Expectations: Regulation in a Non-Zero Failure World*. London: Financial Services Authority.

Glennon, R. (2009) *Unquenchable: America's Water Crisis and What to Do About It*. Washington, DC: Island Press.

Goff, T. G. (1982) *Theory and Practice of Investment*, 4th edn. London: Heinemann.

Goldberg, V. (1989) Production functions, transactions costs, and the new institutionalism. In *Readings in the Economics of Contract Law* (ed. V. P. Goldberg). New York: Cambridge University Press.

Golden, B. (2013) *Amazon Web Services for Dummies*. New York: For Dummies.

Goodhart, C. A. E. (1988) In *Financial Regulation – Or Over-regulation?* (ed. A. Seldon), Readings 27. London: Institute of Economic Affairs.

Grafton, R. Q., Libecap, G., McGlennon, S., Landry, C. and O'Brien, B. (2001) An integrated assessment of water markets: a cross-country comparison. *Review of Environmental Economics and Policy* 5(2): 219–39.

Graham-Leigh, J. (2000) *London's Water Wars – The Competition for London's Water Supply in the Nineteenth Century*. London: Francis Boutle.

Furubotn, E. and Pejovich, S. (eds) (1974) *The Economics of Property Rights*. Cambridge: Ballinger.

Haldane, A. (2012) The dog and the frisbee. Speech given to Federal Reserve Bank of Kansas City's 36th Economic Policy Symposium, The Changing Policy Landscape, Jackson Hole, WY, US.

Hansmann, H. B. (1980) The role of non-profit enterprise. *Yale Law Journal* 89: 835–901.

Hansmann, H. B. (1996) *The Ownership of Enterprise*. Cambridge, MA: Harvard University Press.

Hart, O. (1995) *Firms, Contracts and Financial Structure*. Clarendon Press.

Hazlett, T. W. (1997) Looking for results – Nobel laureate Ronald Coase on rights, resources, and regulation. *Reason*, January.

Hazlett, T. W. (1998) Assigning property rights to radio spectrum users: why did FCC licence auctions take 67 years? *Journal of Law and Economics* XLI: 529–75.

Helm, D. (2010) Government failure, rent seeking and capture: the design of climate change policy. *Oxford Review of Economic Policy* 26(2): 182–96.

Herzel, L. (1951) Public interest and the market in color television. *University of Chicago Law Review* 18: 802–16.

Hilton, A. (1987) *City within a State: A Portrait of Britain's Financial World.* London: I. B. Tauris.

Hotelling, H. (1938) The general welfare in relation to problems of taxation and of railway and utility rates. *Econometrica* 6: 242–69.

Jensen, C. M. and Meckling, W. H. (1976) Theory of the firm: managerial behavior agency costs and ownership structure. *Journal of Financial Economics* 3(4): 305–60.

Kay, N. M. (1979) *The Innovating Firm: A Behavioural Theory of Corporate R and D.* London: Macmillan.

Kelman, M. (1987) *A Guide to Critical Legal Studies.* Cambridge, MA: Harvard University Press.

King, P. (2003) *Crime, Justice, and Discretion in England 1740–1820.* Oxford University Press.

Klein, B. (1988) Vertical integration as organizational ownership: the Fisher Body–General Motors relationship revisited. *Journal of Law, Economics, and Organization* 4: 199–213.

Klein, B. (2000) Fisher–General Motors and the nature of the firm. *Journal of Law and Economics* 43: 105–41.

Klein, B., Crawford, R. G. and Alchian, A. A. (1978) Vertical integration, appropriable rents, and competitive contracting process. *Journal of Law and Economics* 21(2): 297–326.

Knight, F. H. (1921) *Risk, Uncertainty and Profit.* Boston, MA: Houghton Mifflin.

Kynaston, D. (2012) *City of London – The History.* London: Vintage.

Laffont, J. and Tirole, J. (2001) *Competition in Telecommunications*. Cambridge, MA: MIT Press.

Landes, W. M. (1983) The fire of truth: a remembrance of law and economics at Chicago. *Journal of Law and Economics* 26: 163–234.

Landes, W. M. and Lahr-Pastor, S. (2011) Measuring Coase's influence. *Journal of Law and Economics* 54: 382–401.

Landes, W. M. and Posner, R. A. (1988) *The Economic Structure of Tort Law*. Harvard University Press.

Landes, W. M. and Posner, R. A. (1993) The influence of economics of law: a quantitative study. *Journal of Law and Economics* 36: 385–424.

Landes, W., Carlton, D. and Easterbrook, F. (1983) On the resignation of Ronald H. Coase. *Journal of Law and Economics* 26(1): iii–vii.

Lomax, D. F. (1987) *London Markets after the Financial Services Act*. London: Butterworth.

Macey J. R. (2013) *The Death of Corporate Reputation: How Integrity Has Been Destroyed on Wall Street*. Upper Saddle River, NJ: FT Press.

Macher, J. T. and Richman, B. D. (2008) Transaction cost economics: an assessment of empirical research in the social sciences. *Business and Politics* 10(1): 1–63.

Mahoney, P. (1997) The exchange as regulator. *Virginia Law Review* 83: 1453–500.

Mandel, R. (2002) *Armies without States: The Privatization of Security*. Lynne Rienner.

Masten, S. E. (1995) Transaction cost economics. In *Transaction Cost Economics*, vol. 2: *Policy and Applications* (ed. O. E. Williamson and S. E. Masten). Edward Elgar.

McManus, J. (1975) The costs of alternative economic organisations. *Canadian Journal of Economics* 8: 334–50.

Medema, S. G. (2014) The Coase Theorem down under: revisiting the economic record controversy. *History of Economics Review* 59: 1–19.

Menard, C. and Shirley, M. M. (eds) (2005) *Handbook of New Institutional Economics*. Springer.

Nelson, R. H. (2005) *Private Neighborhoods and the Transformation of Local Government*. Urban Institute Press.

Newhouse, J. (1970) Toward a theory of non-profit institutions: an economic model of a hospital. *American Economic Review*, 60(1): 64–74.

North, D. C. (1990) *Institution, Institutional Changes, and Economic Performance*. Cambridge University Press.

Olson, M. (2000) *Power and Prosperity*. New York: Basic Books.

Ostrom, E. (1990) *Governing the Commons*. Cambridge University Press.

Pawson, E. (1977) *Transport and Economy: The Turnpike Roads of Eighteenth Century England*. Academic Press.

Pennington, M. (2013) Elinor Ostrom and the robust political economy of common pool resources. *Journal of Institutional Economics* 9(4): 449–68.

Pienaar, G. J. and van der Schyff, E. (2007) The reform of water rights in South Africa. *Law, Environment and Development Journal* 3(2): 179–93.

Pigou, A. C. (1920) *The Economics of Welfare*, 4th edn. London: Macmillan.

Posner, R. A. (1972) A theory of negligence. *Journal of Legal Studies* 1: 28–96.

Posner, R. A. (1973) *Economic Analysis of Law*. Little, Brown.

Posner, R. A. (1974) Theories of economic regulation. *Bell Journal of Economics and Management Science* 2: 22–50.

Posner, R. A. (1993a) Law and economics meets the New Institutional Economics. *Journal of Institutional and Theoretical Economics* 149: 73–87.

Posner, R. A. (1993b) Ronald Coase and methodology. *Journal of Economic Perspectives* 7(4): 195–210.

Posner, R. A. (1995) *Overcoming Law*, ch. 20 Harvard University Press.

Posner, R. A. (2011) Keynes and Coase. *Journal of Law and Economics* 54: S31.

Ricketts, M. (1999) The many ways of governance: perspectives on the control of the firm. Research Report 31, Social Affairs Unit.

Robson, A. (2014) The legacy of Ronald Coase: commercial implications and policy consequences. *Policy* 30(1): 23–30.

Rose, J. (2010) *The Intellectual Life of the British Working Classes*. Yale University Press.

Sadoff, C. W., Whittington, D. and Grey, D. (2003) *Africa's International Rivers: An Economic Perspective*. Washington, DC: World Bank.

Samuelson, P. A. (1954) The pure theory of public expenditure. *Review of Economics and Statistics* 36: 387–89.

Samuelson, P. A. (1955) Diagrammatic exposition of a theory of public expenditure. *Review of Economics and Statistics* 37: 350–56.

Schumpeter, J. A. (1934) *The Theory of Economic Development*. Harvard University Press.

Shapiro, F. R. (1996) The most-cited law review articles revisited. *Chicago Kent Law Review* 71: 751–79.

Silver, M. (1984) *Enterprise and the Scope of the Firm*. Oxford: Martin Robertson.

Simpson A. W. B. (1996) Coase v Pigou reexamined. *Journal of Legal Studies* 25(1): 53–97.

Singer, P. W. (2003) *Corporate Warriors: The Rise of the Privatized Military Industry*. Cornell University Press.

Smythe, D. (1952) Facing facts about the broadcasting business. *University of Chicago Law Review* 20: 96.

Spiller, P. T. and Cardilli, C. (1999) Toward a property right approach to communications spectrum. *Yale Journal of Regulation* 16: 75–81.

Spulber, D. F. (ed.) (2002) *Famous Fables of Economics – Myths of Market Failure*. Blackwells.

Stigler, G. J. (1966) *The Intellectual and the Marketplace*. Harvard University Press.

Stigler, G. J. (1988a) *Memoirs of an Unregulated Economist*. Basic Books.

Stigler, G. J. (ed.) (1988b) *Chicago Studies in Political Economy*. University of Chicago Press.

Stiglitz, J. E. (1989) *The Economic Role of the State*. Blackwell.

Stringham, E. P. (2002) The emergence of the London Stock Exchange as a self-policing club. *Journal of Private Enterprise* 17(2): 1–19.

Stringham, E. P. (2003) The extra-legal development of securities trading in seventeenth century Amsterdam. *Quarterly Review of Economics and Finance* 43(2): 321–44.

Stringham, E. P. (2015) *Private Regulation: Creating Order in Economic and Social Life*. Oxford University Press.

Stringham, E. P. and Boettke, P. J. (2004) Brokers, bureaucrats and the emergence of financial markets. *Managerial Finance* 30(5): 57–71.

Van Zandt, D. E. (1993) The lessons of the lighthouse: 'government' or 'private' provision of goods. *Journal of Legal Studies* 22(1): 47–72.

Veljanovski, C. G. (1977) The Coase Theorem: the Say's Law of welfare economics? *Economic Record* 53: 535–41.

Veljanovski, C. G. (1982) The Coase Theorems and the economic theory of markets and law. *Kyklos* 35: 53–74.

Veljanovski, C. G. (2006) *The Economics of Law*, 2nd edn. London: Institute of Economic Affairs. www.iea.org.uk/files/upld-pub lication335pdf

Veljanovski, C. G. (2007) *Economic Principles of Law*. Cambridge University Press.

Veljanovski, C. G. (2010) Economic approaches to regulation. In *The Oxford Handbook of Regulation* (ed. R. Baldwin, M. Cave and M. Lodge). Oxford University Press.

Walker, D. L. (1995) The sliding scale revisited. Oxera Perspective, Energy Utilities, May, pp. 23–25.

Water Governance Facility (2013) Groundwater governance in India: stumbling blocks for law and compliance. WGF Report 3. Stockholm: SIWI.

Wedgwood, A. J., Pell, G. A., Leigh, L. H. and Ryan, C. L. (1986) *A Guide to the Financial Services Act 1986*. London: Financial Training Publications.

Williamson, O. E. (1975) *Markets and Hierarchies: Analysis and Antitrust Implications. A Study in the Economics of Internal*

Organization. London and New York: The Free Press, Collier Macmillan.

Williamson, O. E. (1985) *The Economic Institutions of Capitalism: Firms, Markets, Relational Contracting*. London: Collier Macmillan.

Williamson, O. E. (2000) The New Institutional Economics: taking stock, looking forward. *Journal of Economic Literature* 38: 595–613.

Williamson, O. E. (2002) Empirical microeconomics: another perspective. In *The Economics of Choice, Change and Organization* (ed. M. Augier and J. March). Edward Elgar.

Williamson, O. E. (2009a) Pragmatic methodology: a sketch, with applications to transaction cost economics. *Journal of Economic Methodology* 16: 5–157.

Williamson, O. E. (2009b) Transaction cost economics: the natural progression. Nobel Prize Lecture, 8 December.

World Bank (2010) Deep wells and prudence: towards pragmatic action for addressing groundwater overexploitation in India. http://siteresources.worldbank.org/INDIAEXTN/Resources/295583-1268190137195/DeepWellsGroundWaterMarch2010.pdf

World Governance Facility (2013) Groundwater governance in India: stumbling blocks for law and compliance. WGF Report 3. Stockholm: SIWI.

Wright, G. N. (1992) *Turnpike Roads*. Princes Risborough: Shire Publications.

ABOUT THE IEA

The Institute is a research and educational charity (No. CC 235 351), limited by guarantee. Its mission is to improve understanding of the fundamental institutions of a free society by analysing and expounding the role of markets in solving economic and social problems.

The IEA achieves its mission by:

- a high-quality publishing programme
- conferences, seminars, lectures and other events
- outreach to school and college students
- brokering media introductions and appearances

The IEA, which was established in 1955 by the late Sir Antony Fisher, is an educational charity, not a political organisation. It is independent of any political party or group and does not carry on activities intended to affect support for any political party or candidate in any election or referendum, or at any other time. It is financed by sales of publications, conference fees and voluntary donations.

In addition to its main series of publications the IEA also publishes a quarterly journal, *Economic Affairs*.

The IEA is aided in its work by a distinguished international Academic Advisory Council and an eminent panel of Honorary Fellows. Together with other academics, they review prospective IEA publications, their comments being passed on anonymously to authors. All IEA papers are therefore subject to the same rigorous independent refereeing process as used by leading academic journals.

IEA publications enjoy widespread classroom use and course adoptions in schools and universities. They are also sold throughout the world and often translated/reprinted.

Since 1974 the IEA has helped to create a worldwide network of 100 similar institutions in over 70 countries. They are all independent but share the IEA's mission.

Views expressed in the IEA's publications are those of the authors, not those of the Institute (which has no corporate view), its Managing Trustees, Academic Advisory Council members or senior staff.

Members of the Institute's Academic Advisory Council, Honorary Fellows, Trustees and Staff are listed on the following page.

The Institute gratefully acknowledges financial support for its publications programme and other work from a generous benefaction by the late Professor Ronald Coase. This volume has been published as a tribute to Ronald Coase and so that his contributions to the understanding of the role that markets play in solving economic and social problems will be more widely known.

Other papers recently published by the IEA include:

Sharper Axes, Lower Taxes – Big Steps to a Smaller State
Edited by Philip Booth
Hobart Paperback 38; ISBN 978-0-255-36648-9; £12.50

Self-employment, Small Firms and Enterprise
Peter Urwin
Research Monograph 66; ISBN 978-0-255-36610-6; £12.50

Crises of Governments – The Ongoing Global Financial Crisis and Recession
Robert Barro
Occasional Paper 146; ISBN 978-0-255-36657-1; £7.50

… and the Pursuit of Happiness – Wellbeing and the Role of Government
Edited by Philip Booth
Readings 64; ISBN 978-0-255-36656-4; £12.50

Public Choice – A Primer
Eamonn Butler
Occasional Paper 147; ISBN 978-0-255-36650-2; £10.00

The Profit Motive in Education – Continuing the Revolution
Edited by James B. Stanfield
Readings 65; ISBN 978-0-255-36646-5; £12.50

Which Road Ahead – Government or Market?
Oliver Knipping & Richard Wellings
Hobart Paper 171; ISBN 978-0-255-36619-9; £10.00

The Future of the Commons – Beyond Market Failure and Government Regulation
Elinor Ostrom et al.
Occasional Paper 148; ISBN 978-0-255-36653-3; £10.00

Redefining the Poverty Debate – Why a War on Markets Is No Substitute for a War on Poverty
Kristian Niemietz
Research Monograph 67; ISBN 978-0-255-36652-6; £12.50

The Euro – the Beginning, the Middle … and the End?
Edited by Philip Booth
Hobart Paperback 39; ISBN 978-0-255-36680-9; £12.50

The Shadow Economy
Friedrich Schneider & Colin C. Williams
Hobart Paper 172; ISBN 978-0-255-36674-8; £12.50

Quack Policy – Abusing Science in the Cause of Paternalism
Jamie Whyte
Hobart Paper 173; ISBN 978-0-255-36673-1; £10.00

Foundations of a Free Society
Eamonn Butler
Occasional Paper 149; ISBN 978-0-255-36687-8; £12.50

The Government Debt Iceberg
Jagadeesh Gokhale
Research Monograph 68; ISBN 978-0-255-36666-3; £10.00

A U-Turn on the Road to Serfdom
Grover Norquist
Occasional Paper 150; ISBN 978-0-255-36686-1; £10.00

New Private Monies – A Bit-Part Player?
Kevin Dowd
Hobart Paper 174; ISBN 978-0-255-36694-6; £10.00

From Crisis to Confidence – Macroeconomics after the Crash
Roger Koppl
Hobart Paper 175; ISBN 978-0-255-36693-9; £12.50

Advertising in a Free Society
Ralph Harris and Arthur Seldon
With an introduction by Christopher Snowdon
Hobart Paper 176; ISBN 978-0-255-36696-0; £12.50

Selfishness, Greed and Capitalism: Debunking Myths about the Free Market
Christopher Snowdon
Hobart Paper 177; ISBN 978-0-255-36677-9; £12.50

Waging the War of Ideas
John Blundell
Occasional Paper 131; ISBN 978-0-255-36684-7; £12.50

Brexit: Directions for Britain Outside the EU
Ralph Buckle, Tim Hewish, John C. Hulsman, Iain Mansfield and Robert Oulds
Hobart Paperback 178; ISBN 978-0-255-36681-6; £12.50

Flaws and Ceilings – Price Controls and the Damage They Cause
Edited by Christopher Coyne and Rachel Coyne
Hobart Paperback 179; ISBN 978-0-255-36701-1; £12.50

*Scandinavian Unexceptionalism: Culture, Markets and the Failure of
Third-Way Socialism*
Nima Sanandaji
Readings in Political Economy 1; ISBN 978-0-255-36704-2; £10.00

Classical Liberalism – A Primer
Eamonn Butler
Readings in Political Economy 2; ISBN 978-0-255-36707-3; £10.00

Other IEA publications

Comprehensive information on other publications and the wider work of the IEA can be found at www.iea.org.uk. To order any publication please see below.

Personal customers

Orders from personal customers should be directed to the IEA:

Clare Rusbridge
IEA
2 Lord North Street
FREEPOST LON10168
London SW1P 3YZ
Tel: 020 7799 8907. Fax: 020 7799 2137
Email: sales@iea.org.uk

Trade customers

All orders from the book trade should be directed to the IEA's distributor:

NBN International (IEA Orders)
Orders Dept.
NBN International
10 Thornbury Road
Plymouth PL6 7PP
Tel: 01752 202301, Fax: 01752 202333
Email: orders@nbninternational.com

IEA subscriptions

The IEA also offers a subscription service to its publications. For a single annual payment (currently £42.00 in the UK), subscribers receive every monograph the IEA publishes. For more information please contact:

Clare Rusbridge
Subscriptions
IEA
2 Lord North Street
FREEPOST LON10168
London SW1P 3YZ
Tel: 020 7799 8907, Fax: 020 7799 2137
Email: crusbridge@iea.org.uk